TRANSLATED
Translated Language Learning

The Adventures of Pinocchio

مغامرات بينوكيو

Carlo Collodi

كارلو كولودي

English / العربية

Copyright © 2024 Tranzlaty
All rights reserved
Published by Tranzlaty
ISBN: 978-1-83566-711-8
Le Avventure di Pinocchio. Storia di un Burattino
Original text by Carlo Callodi
First published in Italianin 1883
Illustrated By Alice Carsey
www.tranzlaty.com

The Piece of Wood that Laughed and Cried like a Child
قطعة الخشب التي ضحكت وبكت كطفل

Centuries ago there lived...

منذ قرون عاش هناك...

"A king!" my little readers will say immediately

"ملك" !سيقول قرائي الصغار على الفور

No, children, you are mistaken

لا يا أولادي انتم مخطئون

Once upon a time there was a piece of wood

ذات مرة كان هناك قطعة من الخشب

the wood was in the shop of an old carpenter

كان الخشب في محل نجار عجوز

this old carpenter was named Master Antonio

تم تسمية هذا النجار القديم السيد أنطونيو

Everybody, however, called him Master. Cherry

ومع ذلك ، دعاه الجميع سيدا .كرز

they called him Master. Cherry on account of his nose

دعوه سيد .الكرز على حساب أنفه

his nose was always as red and polished as a ripe cherry

كان أنفه دائما أحمر ومصقول مثل الكرز الناضج

Master Cherry set eyes upon the piece of wood

سيد الكرز وضع العيون على قطعة من الخشب

his face beamed with delight when he saw the log

كان وجهه يشع بالبهجة عندما رأى السجل

he rubbed his hands together with satisfaction

فرك يديه معا بارتياح

and the kind master softly spoke to himself

وتحدث السيد اللطيف بهدوء إلى نفسه

"This wood has come to me at the right moment"

"لقد جاءني هذا الخشب في اللحظة المناسبة"

"I have been planning to make a new table"

"لقد كنت أخطط لعمل طاولة جديدة"

"it is perfect for the leg of a little table"

"إنه مثالي لساق طاولة صغيرة"

He immediately went out to find a sharp axe
خرج على الفور ليجد فأسا حادا

he was going to remove the bark of the wood first
كان سيزيل لحاء الخشب أولا

and then he was going to remove any rough surface
ثم كان سيزيل أي سطح خشن

and he was just about to strike the wood with his axe
وكان على وشك ضرب الخشب بفأسه

but just before he struck the wood he heard something
ولكن قبل أن يضرب الخشب سمع شيئا

"Do not strike me so hard!" a small voice implored
"لا تضربني بشدة "إناشد صوت صغير

He turned his terrified eyes all around the room
أدار عينيه المرعوبتين في جميع أنحاء الغرفة

where could the little voice possibly have come from?
من أين يمكن أن يكون الصوت الصغير قد أتى؟

he looked everywhere, but he saw nobody!
نظر في كل مكان ، لكنه لم ير أحدا!

He looked under the bench, but there was nobody
نظر تحت المقعد ، لكن لم يكن هناك أحد

he looked into a cupboard that was always shut
نظر إلى خزانة كانت مغلقة دائما

but there was nobody inside the cupboard either
ولكن لم يكن هناك أحد داخل الخزانة أيضا

he looked into a basket where he kept sawdust
نظر إلى سلة حيث احتفظ بنشارة الخشب

there was nobody in the basket of sawdust either
لم يكن هناك أحد في سلة نشارة الخشب أيضا

at last he even opened the door of the shop
في النهاية فتح باب المحل

and he glanced up and down the empty street
ونظر صعودا وهبوطا في الشارع الفارغ

But there was no one to be seen in the street either
ولكن لم يكن هناك أحد يمكن رؤيته في الشارع أيضا

"Who, then, could it be?" he asked himself
"من ، إذن ، يمكن أن يكون؟" سأل نفسه

at last he laughed and scratched his wig
أخيرا ضحك وخدش شعره المستعار

"I see how it is," he said to himself, amused
"أرى كيف هو "، قال لنفسه ، مسليا

"evidently the little voice was all my imagination"
"من الواضح أن الصوت الصغير كان كل خيالي"

"Let us set to work again," he concluded
واختتم قائلا" :دعونا نبدأ العمل مرة أخرى."

he picked up his axe again and set to work
التقط فأسه مرة أخرى وبدأ العمل

he struck a tremendous blow to the piece of wood
ضرب ضربة هائلة لقطعة الخشب

"Oh! oh! you have hurt me!" cried the little voice
"أوه !وا !لقد آذيتني "إصرخ الصوت الصغير

it was exactly the same voice as it was before
كان بالضبط نفس الصوت كما كان من قبل

This time Master. Cherry was petrified
هذه المرة سيد .كان الكرز متحجرا

His eyes popped out of his head with fright
خرجت عيناه من رأسه من الخوف

his mouth remained open and his tongue hung out
ظل فمه مفتوحا ولسانه معلقا

his tongue almost came to the end of his chin
كاد لسانه يصل إلى نهاية ذقنه

and he looked just like a face on a fountain
وبدا تماما مثل وجه على نافورة

Master. Cherry first had to recover from his fright
أحسن .كان على الكرز أولا أن يتعافى من خوفه

the use of his speech returned to him
عاد استخدام كلامه إليه

and he began to talk in a stutter;
وبدأ يتكلم في تلعثم.

"where on earth could that little voice have come from?"
"من أين يمكن أن يأتي هذا الصوت الصغير على وجه الأرض؟"

"could it be that this piece of wood has learned to cry?"

"هل يمكن أن تكون هذه القطعة من الخشب قد تعلمت البكاء؟"
"I cannot believe it," he said to himself
"لا أستطيع أن أصدق ذلك "، قال لنفسه
"This piece of wood is nothing but a log for fuel"
"هذه القطعة الخشبية ليست سوى جذوع للوقود"
"it is just like all the logs of wood I have"
"إنه تماما مثل كل جذوع الخشب التي لدي"
"it would only just suffice to boil a saucepan of beans"
"يكفي فقط غلي قدر من الفاصوليا"
"Can anyone be hidden inside this piece of wood?"
"هل يمكن إخفاء أي شخص داخل قطعة الخشب هذه؟"
"If anyone is inside, so much the worse for him"
"إذا كان أي شخص في الداخل ، فهذا أسوأ بكثير بالنسبة له"
"I will finish him at once," he threatened the wood
"سأنهيه في الحال "، هدد الخشب
he seized the poor piece of wood and beat it
استولى على قطعة الخشب المسكينة وضربها
he mercilessly hit it against the walls of the room
ضربها بلا رحمة على جدران الغرفة
Then he stopped to see if he could hear the little voice
ثم توقف ليرى ما إذا كان بإمكانه سماع الصوت الصغير
He waited two minutes, nothing. Five minutes, nothing
انتظر دقيقتين ، لا شيء .خمس دقائق، لا شيء
he waited another ten minutes, still nothing!
انتظر عشر دقائق أخرى ، لا يزال لا شيء!
"I see how it is," he then said to himself
"أرى كيف هو "، ثم قال لنفسه
he forced himself to laugh and pushed up his wig
أجبر نفسه على الضحك ورفع شعره المستعار
"evidently the little voice was all my imagination!"
"من الواضح أن الصوت الصغير كان كل خيالي"!
"Let us set to work again," he decided, nervously
"دعونا نبدأ العمل مرة أخرى "، قرر بعصبية
next he started to polish the bit of wood

بعد ذلك بدأ في تلميع قطعة الخشب
but while polishing he heard the same little voice
ولكن أثناء التلميع سمع نفس الصوت الصغير
this time the little voice was laughing uncontrollably
هذه المرة كان الصوت الصغير يضحك دون حسيب ولا رقيب
"Stop! you are tickling me all over!" it said
"توقف !أنت تدغدغني في كل مكان!
poor Master. Cherry fell down as if struck by lightning
سيد الفقراء .سقط الكرز كما لو ضربه البرق
sometime later he opened his eyes again
في وقت لاحق فتح عينيه مرة أخرى
he found himself seated on the floor of his workshop
وجد نفسه جالسا على أرضية ورشته
His face was very changed from before
تغير وجهه كثيرا عن ذي قبل
and even the end of his nose had changed
وحتى نهاية أنفه قد تغيرت
his nose was not its usual bright crimson colour
لم يكن أنفه لونه القرمزي اللامع المعتاد
his nose had become icy blue from the fright
أصبح أنفه أزرق جليدي من الخوف

Master. Cherry Gives the Wood Away
أحسن .الكرز يعطي الخشب بعيدا

At that moment someone knocked at the door
في تلك اللحظة طرق أحدهم الباب
"Come in," said the carpenter to the visitor
"تعال "، قال النجار للزائر
he didn't have the strength to rise to his feet
لم يكن لديه القوة للنهوض على قدميه
A lively little old man walked into the shop
دخل رجل عجوز صغير مفعم بالحيوية إلى المتجر
this lively little man was called Geppetto

كان هذا الرجل الصغير المفعم بالحيوية يدعى Geppetto
although there was another name he was known by
على الرغم من وجود اسم آخر كان معروفا به
there was a group of naughty neighbourhood boys
كان هناك مجموعة من أولاد الحي المشاغب
when they wished to anger him they called him pudding
عندما أرادوا إغضابه أطلقوا عليه الحلوى
there is a famous yellow pudding made from Indian corn
هناك بودنغ أصفر شهير مصنوع من الذرة الهندية
and Geppetto's wig looks just like this famous pudding
وشعر Geppetto مستعار يشبه تماما هذا البودينغ الشهير
Geppetto was a very fiery little old man
كان جيبيتو رجلا عجوزا صغيرا ناريا جدا
Woe to him who called him pudding!
ويل لمن دعاه بودنغ!
when furious there was no holding him back
عندما كان غاضبا لم يكن هناك ما يعيقه
"Good-day, Master. Antonio," said Geppetto
"يوم جيد يا معلمة. أنطونيو»، قال جيبيتو
"what are you doing there on the floor?"
"ماذا تفعل هناك على الأرض؟"
"I am teaching the alphabet to the ants"
"أنا أعلم الأبجدية للنمل"
"I can't imagine what good it does to you"
"لا أستطيع أن أتخيل ما هو جيد لك"
"What has brought you to me, neighbour Geppetto?"
"ما الذي أتى بك إلي ، الجار جيبيتو؟"
"My legs have brought me here to you"
"ساقي جلبتني إلى هنا إليك"
"But let me tell you the truth, Master. Antonio"
"لكن دعني أقول لك الحقيقة يا معلم. أنطونيو"
"the real reason I came is to ask a favour of you"
"السبب الحقيقي لمجيئي هو أن أطلب منك معروفا"
"Here I am, ready to serve you," replied the carpenter

"ها أنا مستعد لخدمتك "، أجاب النجار

and he got off the floor and onto his knees

ونزل عن الأرض وعلى ركبتيه

"This morning an idea came into my head"

"هذا الصباح خطرت ببالي فكرة"

"Let us hear the idea that you had"

"دعنا نسمع الفكرة التي كانت لديك"

"I thought I would make a beautiful wooden puppet"

"اعتقدت أنني سأصنع دمية خشبية جميلة"

"a puppet that could dance and fence"

"دمية يمكن أن ترقص والسياج"

"a puppet that can leap like an acrobat"

"دمية يمكنها القفز مثل البهلوان"

"With this puppet I could travel about the world!"

"مع هذه الدمية يمكنني السفر حول العالم"!

"the puppet would let me earn a piece of bread"

"الدمية ستسمح لي بكسب قطعة خبز"

"and the puppet would let me earn a glass of wine"

"وتسمح لي الدمية بكسب كأس من النبيذ"

"What do you think of my idea, Antonio?"

"ما رأيك في فكرتي يا أنطونيو؟"

"Bravo, pudding!" exclaimed the little voice

"برافو ، بودنغ "!إهتف الصوت الصغير

it was impossible to know where the voice had came from

كان من المستحيل معرفة من أين جاء الصوت

Geppetto didn't like hearing himself called pudding

لم يحب Geppetto سماع نفسه يسمى الحلوى

you can imagine he became as red as a turkey

يمكنك أن تتخيل أنه أصبح أحمر مثل الديك الرومي

"Why do you insult me?" he asked his friend

"لماذا تهينني؟" سأل صديقه

"Who insults you?" his friend replied

"من يهينك؟" أجاب صديقه

"You called me pudding!" Geppetto accused him

"It was not I!" Antonio honestly said
"لقد اتصلت بي بودنغ "!اتهمه جيبيتو

"Do you think I called myself pudding?"
"لم أكن أنا "!أنطونيو قال بصراحة

"It was you, I say!", "No!", "Yes!", "No!"
"هل تعتقد أنني أطلقت على اسم الحلوى؟"

becoming more and more angry, they came to blows
"لقد كنت أنت ، أقول "!،" لا "!،" نعم "!،" لا"!

they flew at each other and bit and fought and scratched
أصبحوا غاضبين أكثر فأكثر ، جاءوا إلى الضربات

as quickly as it had started the fight was over again
طاروا على بعضهم البعض وعضوا وقاتلوا وخدشوا

Geppetto had the carpenter's grey wig between his teeth
بالسرعة التي بدأت بها ، انتهى القتال مرة أخرى

and Master. Antonio had Geppetto's yellow wig
أسنانه بين للنجار رمادي مستعار شعر Geppetto لدى كان

"Give me back my wig" screamed Master. Antonio
Geppetto من أصفر مستعار شعر أنطونيو لدى كان. والماجستير

"and you give me back my wig" screamed Master. Cherry
"أعيدوا لي شعر مستعار "صرخ سيد .انطونيو

"let us be friends again" they agreed
"وأنت تعيد لي شعر مستعار "صرخ سيد .كرز

The two old men gave each other their wigs back
"دعونا نكون أصدقاء مرة أخرى "وافقوا

and the old men shook each other's hands
أعطى الرجلان العجوزان بعضهما البعض الشعر المستعار

they swore that all had been forgiven
وصافح كبار السن أيدي بعضهم البعض

they would remain friends to the end of their lives
أقسموا أن الجميع قد غفر لهم

"Well, then, neighbour Geppetto" said the carpenter
سيظلون أصدقاء حتى نهاية حياتهم

he asked "what is the favour that you wish of me?"
"حسنا ، إذن ، الجار جيبيتو "قال النجار

سألني :ما هي النعمة التي تتمناها مني؟

this would prove that peace was made

هذا من شأنه أن يثبت أن السلام قد تم صنعه

"I want a little wood to make my puppet"

"أريد القليل من الخشب لأصنع دميتي"

"will you give me some wood?"

"هل ستعطيني بعض الخشب؟"

Master. Antonio was delighted to get rid of the wood

أحسن. كان أنطونيو سعيدا بالتخلص من الخشب

he immediately went to his work bench

ذهب على الفور إلى مقعد عمله

and he brought back the piece of wood

وأعاد قطعة الخشب

the piece of wood that had caused him so much fear

قطعة الخشب التي سببت له الكثير من الخوف

he was bringing the piece of wood to his friend

كان يجلب قطعة الخشب إلى صديقه

but then the piece of wood started to shake!

ولكن بعد ذلك بدأت قطعة الخشب تهتز!

the piece of wood wriggled violently out of his hands

قطعة الخشب تتلوى بعنف من يديه

this piece of wood knew how to make trouble!

عرفت هذه القطعة الخشبية كيف تثير المتاعب!

with all its might it struck against poor Geppetto

بكل قوتها ضربت ضد جيبيتو المسكين

and it hit him right on his poor dried-up shins

وضربه مباشرة على ساقيه الجافة المسكينة

you can imagine the cry that Geppetto gave

Geppetto قدمها الصرخة تتخيل أن يمكنك

"is that the courteous way you make your presents?"

"هل هذه هي الطريقة المهذبة التي تصنع بها هداياك؟"

"You have almost lamed me, Master. Antonio!"

"لقد كدت تعرجني يا معلم. أنطونيو"!

"I swear to you that it was not I!"

"أقسم لك أنه لم أكن أنا"!

"Do you think I did this to myself?"

"هل تعتقد أنني فعلت هذا؟"

"The wood is entirely to blame!"

"الخشب هو المسؤول بالكامل"!

"I know that it was the wood"

"أعلم أنه كان الخشب"

"but it was you that hit my legs with it!"

"لكنك أنت الذي ضربت ساقي بها"!

"I did not hit you with it!"

"لم أضربك به"!

"Liar!" exclaimed Geppetto

"كاذب"! هتف جيبيتو

"Geppetto, don't insult me or I will call you Pudding!"

"جيبيتو، لا تهينني وإلا سأطلق عليك اسم بودنغ"!

"Knave!", "Pudding!", "Donkey!"

"كناف "!، "بودنغ "!، "حمار"!

"Pudding!", "Baboon!", "Pudding!"

"بودنغ "!، "بابون "!، "بودنغ"!

Geppetto was mad with rage all over again

كان جيبيتو غاضبا من الغضب مرة أخرى

he had been called been called pudding three times!

كان قد دعا دعا الحلوى ثلاث مرات!

he fell upon the carpenter and they fought desperately

سقط على النجار وقاتلوا بشدة

this battle lasted just as long as the first

استمرت هذه المعركة طالما استمرت المعركة الأولى

Master. Antonio had two more scratches on his nose

أحسن. أصيب أنطونيو بخدشين آخرين على أنفه

his adversary had lost two buttons off his waistcoat

فقد خصمه زرين من صدريته

Their accounts being thus squared, they shook hands

وهكذا تربيع حساباتهم ، تصافحوا

and they swore to remain good friends for the rest of their lives

وأقسموا أن يظلوا أصدقاء حميمين لبقية حياتهم

Geppetto carried off his fine piece of wood

حمل جيبيتو قطعته الخشبية الجميلة
he thanked Master. Antonio and limped back to his house
شكر السيد. أنطونيو وعاد إلى منزله

Geppetto Names his Puppet Pinocchio
جيبيتو يسمي دميته بينوكيو

Geppetto lived in a small ground-floor room
عاش جيبيتو في غرفة صغيرة في الطابق الأرضي
his room was only lighted from the staircase
كانت غرفته مضاءة فقط من الدرج
The furniture could not have been simpler
لا يمكن أن يكون الأثاث أبسط
a rickety chair, a poor bed, and a broken table
كرسي متهالك وسرير فقير وطاولة مكسورة
At the end of the room there was a fireplace
في نهاية الغرفة كان هناك مدفأة
but the fire was painted, and gave no fire
لكن النار رسمت ولم تنبعث منها نار
and by the painted fire was a painted saucepan
وبالنار المطلية كان قدر مطلي

and the painted saucepan was boiling cheerfully

وكان القدر المطلي يغلي بمرح

a cloud of smoke rose exactly like real smoke

ارتفعت سحابة من الدخان تماما مثل الدخان الحقيقي

Geppetto reached home and took out his tools

وصل جيبيتو إلى المنزل وأخرج أدواته

and he immediately set to work on the piece of wood

وشرع على الفور في العمل على قطعة الخشب

he was going to cut out and model his puppet

كان سيقطع ويصمم دميته

"What name shall I give him?" he said to himself

"ما الاسم الذي سأعطيه؟" قال لنفسه

"I think I will call him Pinocchio"

"أعتقد أنني سأدعوه بينوكيو"

"It is a name that will bring him luck"

"إنه اسم سيجلب له الحظ"

"I once knew a whole family called Pinocchio"

"كنت أعرف ذات مرة عائلة بأكملها تدعى بينوكيو"

"There was Pinocchio the father and Pinocchio the mother"

"كان هناك بينوكيو الأب وبينوكيو الأم"

"and there were Pinocchio the children"

"وكان هناك بينوكيو الأطفال"

"and all of them did well in life"

"وكلهم أبلوا بلاء حسنا في الحياة"

"The richest of them was a beggar"

"أغنى منهم كان متسولا"

he had found a good name for his puppet

لقد وجد اسما جيدا لدميته

so he began to work in good earnest

لذلك بدأ العمل بجدية جيدة

he first made his hair, and then his forehead

صنع شعره أولا ، ثم جبهته

and then he worked carefully on his eyes

ثم عمل بعناية على عينيه

Geppetto thought he noticed the strangest thing

اعتقد جيبيتو أنه لاحظ أغرب شيء

he was sure he saw the eyes move!

كان متأكدا من أنه رأى العيون تتحرك!

the eyes seemed to look fixedly at him

بدت العيون تنظر إليه بثبات

Geppetto got angry from being stared at

غضب جيبيتو من التحديق فيه

the wooden eyes wouldn't let him out of their sight

العيون الخشبية لن تسمح له بالابتعاد عن أنظارهم

"Wicked wooden eyes, why do you look at me?"

"عيون خشبية شريرة ، لماذا تنظر إلي؟"

but the piece of wood made no answer

لكن قطعة الخشب لم تقدم إجابة

He then proceeded to carve the nose

ثم شرع في نحت الأنف

but as soon as he had made the nose it began to grow

ولكن بمجرد أن صنع الأنف بدأ ينمو

And the nose grew, and grew, and grew

ونما الأنف ونما ونما

in a few minutes it had become an immense nose

في بضع دقائق أصبح أنفا هائلا

it seemed as if it would never stop growing

بدا كما لو أنه لن يتوقف عن النمو

Poor Geppetto tired himself out with cutting it off

لقد أرهق جيبيتو المسكين نفسه بقطعه

but the more he cut, the longer the nose grew!

ولكن كلما قطع أكثر ، كلما نما الأنف!

The mouth was not even completed yet

لم يكتمل الفم بعد

but it already began to laugh and deride him

لكنها بدأت بالفعل تضحك وتسخر منه

"Stop laughing!" said Geppetto, provoked

"توقف عن الضحك "إقال جيبيتو ، مستفزا

but he might as well have spoken to the wall

لكنه ربما تحدث إلى الحائط

"Stop laughing, I say!" he roared in a threatening tone

"توقف عن الضحك ، أقول "إزأر بنبرة تهديد

The mouth then ceased laughing

ثم توقف الفم عن الضحك

but the face put out its tongue as far as it would go

لكن الوجه أخرج لسانه بقدر ما يذهب

Geppetto did not want to spoil his handiwork

لم يرغب جيبيتو في إفساد عمله اليدوي

so he pretended not to see, and continued his labours

فتظاهر بأنه لا يرى ، واستمر في أعماله

After the mouth he fashioned the chin

بعد الفم قام بتصميم الذقن

then the throat and then the shoulders

ثم الحلق ثم الكتفين

then he carved the stomach and made the arms hands

ثم نحت المعدة وصنع اليدين

now Geppetto worked on making hands for his puppet

الآن عمل جيبيتو على صنع الأيدي لدميته

and in a moment he felt his wig snatched from his head

وفي لحظة شعر بشعره المستعار ينتزع من رأسه

He turned round, and what did he see?

استدار ، وماذا رأى؟

He saw his yellow wig in the puppet's hand

رأى شعره المستعار الأصفر في يد الدمية

"Pinocchio! Give me back my wig instantly!"

"بينوكيو !أعيدوا لي شعري المستعار على الفور"!

But Pinocchio did anything but return him his wig

لكن بينوكيو فعل أي شيء سوى إعادة شعره المستعار

Pinocchio put the wig on his own head instead!

وضع بينوكيو الباروكة على رأسه بدلا من ذلك!

Geppetto didn't like this insolent and derisive behaviour

لم يعجب جيبيتو بهذا السلوك الوقح والساخر

he felt sadder and more melancholy than he had ever felt

شعر بالحزن والكآبة أكثر مما شعر به في أي وقت مضى

turning to Pinocchio, he said "You young rascal!"

التفت إلى بينوكيو ، وقال" أيها الوغد الشاب"!

"I have not even completed you yet"

"لم أكتملك بعد"

"and you are already failing to respect to your father!"

"وأنت بالفعل تفشل في احترام والدك"!

"That is bad, my boy, very bad!"

"هذا سيء يا ولدي ، سيء للغاية"!

And he dried a tear from his cheek

وجف دمعة من خده

The legs and the feet remained to be done

بقيت الساقين والقدمين ليتم القيام به

but he soon regretted giving Pinocchio feet

لكنه سرعان ما ندم على إعطاء أقدام بينوكيو

as thanks he received a kick on the point of his nose

كشكر تلقى ركلة على نقطة أنفه

"I deserve it!" he said to himself

"أنا أستحق ذلك "!قال لنفسه

"I should have thought of it sooner!"

"كان يجب أن أفكر في الأمر عاجلا"!

"Now it is too late to do anything about it!"

"الآن فات الأوان لفعل أي شيء حيال ذلك"!

He then took the puppet under the arms

ثم أخذ الدمية تحت ذراعيه

and he placed him on the floor to teach him to walk

ووضعه على الأرض ليعلمه المشي

Pinocchio's legs were stiff and he could not move

كانت ساقي بينوكيو متيبسة ولم يستطع الحركة

but Geppetto led him by the hand

لكن جيبيتو قاده بيده

and he showed him how to put one foot before the other

وبينه كيف يضع قدما قبل الأخرى

eventually Pinocchio's legs became limber

في النهاية أصبحت ساقي بينوكيو رشيقة

and soon he began to walk by himself

وسرعان ما بدأ يمشي بنفسه

and he began to run about the room

وبدأ يركض حول الغرفة

then he got out of the house door

ثم خرج من باب المنزل

and he jumped into the street and escaped

وقفز إلى الشارع وهرب

poor Geppetto rushed after him

هرع جيبيتو المسكين وراءه

of course he was not able to overtake him

بالطبع لم يكن قادرا على تجاوزه

because Pinocchio leaped in front of him like a hare

لأن بينوكيو قفز أمامه مثل الأرنب

and he knocked his wooden feet against the pavement

وضرب قدميه الخشبية على الرصيف

it made as much clatter as twenty pairs of peasants' clogs

لقد صنعت قعقعة تصل إلى عشرين زوجا من قباقيب الفلاحين

"Stop him! stop him!" shouted Geppetto

"أوقفوه !أوقفوه" !صاح جيبيتو

but the people in the street stood still in astonishment

لكن الناس في الشارع وقفوا ساكنين في دهشة.

they had never seen a wooden puppet running like a horse

لم يروا قط دمية خشبية تركض مثل الحصان

and they laughed and laughed at Geppetto's misfortune
وضحكوا وضحكوا على مصيبة جيبيتو

At last, as good luck would have it, a soldier arrived
أخيرا ، لحسن الحظ ، وصل جندي

the soldier had heard the uproar
كان الجندي قد سمع الضجة

he imagined that a colt had escaped from his master
تخيل أن قد هرب من سيده

he planted himself in the middle of the road
زرع نفسه في منتصف الطريق

he waited with the determined purpose of stopping him
انتظر بهدف حازم لإيقافه

thus he would prevent the chance of worse disasters
وبالتالي سيمنع فرصة حدوث كوارث أسوأ

Pinocchio saw the soldier barricading the whole street
رأى بينوكيو الجندي يتحصن في الشارع بأكمله

so he endeavoured to take him by surprise
لذلك سعى ليفاجئه

he planned to run between his legs
خطط للركض بين ساقيه

but the soldier was too clever for Pinocchio
لكن الجندي كان ذكيا جدا بالنسبة لبينوكيو

The soldier caught him cleverly by the nose
أمسك به الجندي بذكاء من أنفه

and he gave Pinocchio back to Geppetto
وأعاد بينوكيو إلى جيبيتو

Wishing to punish him, Geppetto intended to pull his ears
رغبة في معاقبته ، كان جيبيتو ينوي سحب أذنيه

But he could not find Pinocchio's ears!
لكنه لم يستطع العثور على آذان بينوكيو!

And do you know the reason why?
وهل تعرف السبب؟

he had forgotten to make him any ears
لقد نسي أن يجعله آذانا صاغية

so then he took him by the collar
ثم أخذه من ذوي الياقات البيضاء

"We will go home at once," he threatened him

»سنعود إلى المنزل في الحال«، هدده

"as soon as we arrive we will settle our accounts"

"بمجرد وصولنا سنقوم بتسوية حساباتنا"

At this information Pinocchio threw himself on the ground

بناء على هذه المعلومات ، ألقى بينوكيو بنفسه على الأرض

he refused to go another step

رفض أن يخطو خطوة أخرى

a crowd of inquisitive people began to assemble

بدأ حشد من الناس الفضوليين في التجمع

they made a ring around them

صنعوا حلقة حولهم

Some of them said one thing, some another

بعضهم قال شيئا والبعض الآخر

"Poor puppet!" said several of the onlookers

"دمية مسكينة "إقال العديد من المتفرجين

"he is right not to wish to return home!"

"إنه محق في عدم رغبته في العودة إلى المنزل"!

"Who knows how Geppetto will beat him!"

"من يدري كيف سيضربه جيبيتو"!

"Geppetto seems a good man!"

"يبدو جيبيتو رجلا جيدا"!

"but with boys he is a regular tyrant!"

"لكن مع الأولاد هو طاغية عادي"!

"don't leave that poor puppet in his hands"

"لا تترك تلك الدمية المسكينة بين يديه"

"he is quite capable of tearing him to pieces!"

"إنه قادر تماما على تمزيقه إلى أشلاء"!

from what was said the soldier had to step in again

مما قيل كان على الجندي أن يتدخل مرة أخرى

the soldier gave Pinocchio his freedom

أعطى الجندي بينوكيو حريته

and the soldier led Geppetto to prison

وقاد الجندي جيبيتو إلى السجن

The poor man was not ready to defend himself with words

لم يكن الرجل الفقير مستعدا للدفاع عن نفسه بالكلمات
he cried like a calf "Wretched boy!"
بكى مثل العجل" صبي بائس"!
"to think how I laboured to make him a good puppet!"
"للتفكير كيف عملت لجعله دمية جيدة"!
"But all I have done serves me right!"
"لكن كل ما فعلته يخدمني بشكل صحيح"!
"I should have thought of it sooner!"
"كان يجب أن أفكر في الأمر عاجلا"!

The Talking Little Cricket Scolds Pinocchio
الكريكيت الصغير المتكلم يوبخ بينوكيو

poor Geppetto was being taken to prison
تم نقل جيبيتو المسكين إلى السجن
all of this was not his fault, of course
كل هذا لم يكن خطأه بالطبع
he had not done anything wrong at all
لم يرتكب أي خطأ على الإطلاق
and that little imp Pinocchio found himself free
وأن العفريت الصغير بينوكيو وجد نفسه حرا
he had escaped from the clutches of the soldier
كان قد هرب من براثن الجندي
and he ran off as fast as his legs could carry him
وهرب بأسرع ما يمكن أن تحمله ساقاه
he wanted to reach home as quickly as possible
أراد الوصول إلى المنزل في أسرع وقت ممكن
therefore he rushed across the fields
لذلك هرع عبر الحقول
in his mad hurry he jumped over thorny hedges
في عجلته المجنونة قفز فوق التحوطات الشائكة
and he jumped across ditches full of water
وقفز عبر خنادق مليئة بالماء
Arriving at the house, he found the door ajar

عند وصوله إلى المنزل ، وجد الباب مواربا
He pushed it open, went in, and fastened the latch
دفعه مفتوحا ودخل وربط المزلاج
he threw himself on the floor of his house
ألقى بنفسه على أرضية منزله
and he gave a great sigh of satisfaction
وتنفس الصعداء
But soon he heard someone in the room
ولكن سرعان ما سمع شخصا في الغرفة
something was making a sound like "Cri-cri-cri!"
كان هناك شيء ما يصدر صوتا مثل!"Cri-cri-cri"
"Who calls me?" said Pinocchio in a fright
"من يتصل بي؟ "قال بينوكيو في خوف
"It is I!" answered a voice
"إنه أنا!" أجاب بصوت
Pinocchio turned round and saw a little cricket
استدار بينوكيو ورأى القليل من لعبة الكريكيت
the cricket was crawling slowly up the wall
كان الكريكيت يزحف ببطء على الحائط
"Tell me, little cricket, who may you be?"
"قل لي ، الكريكيت الصغير ، من قد تكون؟"
"who I am is the talking cricket"
"من أنا هو الكريكيت الحديث"
"and I have lived in this room a hundred years or more"
"وقد عشت في هذه الغرفة مائة عام أو أكثر"
"Now, however, this room is mine," said the puppet
"الآن ، ومع ذلك ، هذه الغرفة هي لي "، قالت الدمية
"if you would do me the pleasure, go away at once"
"إذا كنت ستفعل لي المتعة ، اذهب بعيدا في الحال"
"and when you're gone, please never come back"
"وعندما تذهب ، من فضلك لا تعود أبدا"
"I will not go until I have told you a great truth"
"لن أذهب حتى أخبرك بحقيقة عظيمة"
"Tell it me, then, and be quick about it"
"أخبرني بذلك ، إذن ، وكن سريعا في ذلك"

"Woe to those boys who rebel against their parents"
"ويل لأولئك الأولاد الذين يتمردون على والديهم"
"and woe to boys who run away from home"
"والويل للأولاد الذين يهربون من المنزل"
"They will never come to any good in the world"
"لن يأتوا أبدا إلى أي خير في العالم"
"and sooner or later they will repent bitterly"
"وعاجلا أم آجلا سوف يتوبون بمرارة"
"Sing all you want you little cricket"
"غني كل ما تريده أيها الكريكيت الصغير"
"and feel free to sing as long as you please"
"ولا تتردد في الغناء طالما كنت يحلو لك"
"For me, I have made up my mind to run away"
"بالنسبة لي ، لقد اتخذت قراري بالهروب"
"tomorrow at daybreak I will run away for good"
"غدا عند الفجر سأهرب إلى الأبد"
"if I remain I shall not escape my fate"
"إذا بقيت فلن أفلت من مصيري"
"it is the same fate as all other boys"
"إنه نفس مصير جميع الأولاد الآخرين"
"if I stay I shall be sent to school"
"إذا بقيت سأرسل إلى المدرسة"
"and I shall be made to study by love or by force"
"وسأدرس بالحب أو بالقوة"
"I tell you in confidence, I have no wish to learn"
"أقول لك بثقة ، ليس لدي رغبة في التعلم"
"it is much more amusing to run after butterflies"
"من الممتع أكثر الركض وراء الفراشات"
"I prefer climbing trees with my time"
"أفضل تسلق الأشجار مع وقتي"
"and I like taking young birds out of their nests"
"وأنا أحب إخراج الطيور الصغيرة من أعشاشها"
"Poor little goose" interjected the talking cricket
"أوزة صغيرة فقيرة "تدخلت لعبة الكريكيت الحديث

"don't you know you will grow up a perfect donkey?"
"ألا تعلم أنك ستنمو حمارا مثاليا؟"
"and every one will make fun of you"
"وكل واحد سيسخر منك"
Pinocchio was not pleased with what he heard
لم يكن بينوكيو سعيدا بما سمعه
"Hold your tongue, you wicked, ill-omened croaker!"
"أمسك لسانك ، أيها الشرير المشؤوم"!
But the little cricket was patient and philosophical
لكن الكريكيت الصغير كان صبورا وفلسفيا
he didn't become angry at this impertinence
لم يغضب من هذه الوقاحة
he continued in the same tone as he had before
استمر بنفس النبرة كما كان من قبل
"perhaps you really do not wish to go to school"
"ربما لا ترغب حقا في الذهاب إلى المدرسة"
"so why not at least learn a trade?"
"فلماذا لا تتعلم على الأقل التجارة؟"
"a job will enable you to earn a piece of bread!"
"الوظيفة ستمكنك من كسب قطعة خبز"!
"What do you want me to tell you?" replied Pinocchio
"ماذا تريد مني أن أقول لك؟ "أجاب بينوكيو
he was beginning to lose patience with the little cricket
بدأ يفقد صبره مع لعبة الكريكيت الصغيرة
"there are many trades in the world I could do"
"هناك العديد من الصفقات في العالم التي يمكنني القيام بها"
"but only one calling really takes my fancy"
"لكن مكالمة واحدة فقط تأخذ خيالي حقا"
"And what calling is it that takes your fancy?"
"وما هي الدعوة التي تأخذ خيالك؟"
"to eat, and to drink, and to sleep"
"أن يأكل ويشرب وينام"
"I am called to amuse myself all day"
"أنا مدعو لتسلية طوال اليوم"

"to lead a vagabond life from morning to night"
"لقيادة حياة متشرد من الصباح إلى الليل"

the talking little cricket had a reply for this
كان للكريكيت الصغير المتكلم رد على هذا

"most who follow that trade end in hospital or prison"
"معظم الذين يتابعون هذه التجارة ينتهي بهم المطاف في المستشفى أو السجن"

"Take care, you wicked, ill-omened croaker"
"اعتن بنفسك ، أيها الشرير المشؤوم"

"Woe to you if I fly into a passion!"
"ويل لك إذا طارت إلى شغف"!

"Poor Pinocchio I really pity you!"
"مسكين بينوكيو أنا أشفق عليك حقا"!

"Why do you pity me?"
"لماذا تشفق علي؟"

"I pity you because you are a puppet"
"أشفق عليك لأنك دمية"

"and I pity you because you have a wooden head"
"وأنا أشفق عليك لأن لديك رأسا خشبيا"

At these last words Pinocchio jumped up in a rage
في هذه الكلمات الأخيرة قفز بينوكيو في غضب

he snatched a wooden hammer from the bench
انتزع مطرقة خشبية من المقعد

and he threw the hammer at the talking cricket
وألقى المطرقة على لعبة الكريكيت الناطقة
Perhaps he never meant to hit him

ربما لم يقصد أبدا ضربه
but unfortunately it struck him exactly on the head
لكن لسوء الحظ ضربه بالضبط على رأسه
the poor Cricket had scarcely breath to cry "Cri-cri-cri!"
كان الكريكيت المسكين بالكاد يتنفس ليصرخ!"Cri-cri-cri"
he remained dried up and flattened against the wall
ظل جافا ومسطحا على الحائط

The Flying Egg
الببيضة الطائرة

The night was quickly catching up with Pinocchio
كانت الليلة تلحق بسرعة ببينوكيو

he remembered that he had eaten nothing all day
تذكر أنه لم يأكل شيئا طوال اليوم

he began to feel a gnawing in his stomach
بدأ يشعر بقضم في معدته

the gnawing very much resembled appetite
القضم يشبه إلى حد كبير الشهية

After a few minutes his appetite had become hunger
بعد بضع دقائق أصبحت شهيته جائعة

and in little time his hunger became ravenous
وفي وقت قصير أصبح جوعه مفترسا

Poor Pinocchio ran quickly to the fireplace
ركض بينوكيو المسكين بسرعة إلى المدفأة

the fireplace where a saucepan was boiling
الموقد حيث كان القدر يغلي

he was going to take off the lid
كان على وشك خلع الغطاء

then he could see what was in it
ثم استطاع أن يرى ما كان فيه

but the saucepan was only painted on the wall
لكن القدر كان مطليا فقط على الحائط

You can imagine his feelings when he discovered this
يمكنك أن تتخيل مشاعره عندما اكتشف هذا

His nose, which was already long, became even longer
أصبح أنفه ، الذي كان طويلا بالفعل ، أطول

it must have grown by at least three inches
يجب أن يكون قد نما بمقدار ثلاث بوصات على الأقل

He then began to run about the room
ثم بدأ يركض حول الغرفة

he searched in the drawers and every imaginable place
بحث في الأدراج وكل مكان يمكن تخيله

he hoped to find a bit of bread or crust

كان يأمل أن يجد القليل من الخبز أو القشرة

perhaps he could find a bone left by a dog

ربما يمكنه العثور على عظم تركه

a little moldy pudding of Indian corn

بودنغ متعفن قليلا من الذرة الهندية

somewhere someone might have left a fish bone

في مكان ما قد يكون شخص ما قد ترك عظم سمكة

even a cherry stone would be enough

حتى حجر الكرز سيكون كافيا

if only there was something that he could gnaw

إذا كان هناك شيء يمكن أن يقضم

But he could find nothing to get his teeth into

لكنه لم يجد شيئا يدخل أسنانه فيه

And in the meanwhile his hunger grew and grew

وفي هذه الأثناء نما جوعه ونما

Poor Pinocchio had no other relief than yawning

لم يكن لدى بينوكيو المسكين أي راحة أخرى سوى التثاؤب

his yawns were so big his mouth almost reached his ears

كان تثاؤبه كبيرا لدرجة أن فمه كاد يصل إلى أذنيه

and felt as if he were going to faint

وشعر كما لو كان على وشك الإغماء

Then he began to cry desperately

ثم بدأ يبكي بشدة

"The talking little cricket was right"

"الكريكيت الصغير الحديث كان على حق"

"I did wrong to rebel against my papa"

"لقد أخطأت في التمرد على أبي"

"I should not have ran away from home"

"ما كان يجب أن أهرب من المنزل"

"If my papa were here I wouldn't be dying of yawning!"

"لو كان أبي هنا لما مت من التثاؤب"!

"Oh! what a dreadful illness hunger is!"

"أوه إيا له من مرض مروع جوع!"

Just then he thought he saw something in the dust-heap

عندها فقط اعتقد أنه رأى شيئا في كومة الغبار

something round and white that looked like a hen's egg

شيء مستدير وأبيض يشبه بيضة الدجاجة

he sprung up to his feet and seized hold of the egg

نهض على قدميه وأمسك بالبيضة

It was indeed a hen's egg, as he thought

لقد كانت بالفعل بيضة دجاجة ، كما كان يعتقد

Pinocchio's joy was beyond description

كانت فرحة بينوكيو تفوق الوصف

he had to make sure that he wasn't just dreaming

كان عليه أن يتأكد من أنه لم يكن يحلم فقط

so he kept turning the egg over in his hands

لذلك ظل يقلب البيضة في يديه

he felt and kissed the egg

شعر وقبل البيضة

"And now, how shall I cook it?"

"والآن ، كيف يمكنني طهيها؟"

"Shall I make an omelet?"

"هل أصنع عجة؟"

"it would be better to cook it in a saucer!"

"سيكون من الأفضل طهيها في صحن"!

"Or would it not be more savory to fry it?"

"أم أنه لن يكون أكثر لذيذا أن تقلى؟"

"Or shall I simply boil the egg?"

"أم يجب أن أغلي البيض ببساطة؟"

"No, the quickest way is to cook it in a saucer"

"لا ، أسرع طريقة هي طهيها في صحن"

"I am in such a hurry to eat it!"

"أنا في عجلة من أمري لأكله"!

Without loss of time he got an earthenware saucer

دون ضياع الوقت حصل على صحن خزفي

he placed the saucer on a brazier full of red-hot embers

وضع الصحن على موقد ملئ بالجمر الأحمر الحار

he didn't have any oil or butter to use

لم يكن لديه أي زيت أو زبدة ليستخدمها

so he poured a little water into the saucer

لذلك سكب القليل من الماء في الصحن

and when the water began to smoke, crack!

وعندما بدأ الماء في التدخين ، الكراك!

he broke the egg-shell over the saucer

كسر قشرة البيضة فوق الصحن

and he let the contents of the egg drop into the saucer

وترك محتويات البيضة تسقط في الصحن

but the egg was not full of white and yolk

لكن البيضة لم تكن مليئة بالبيض وصفار البيض

instead, a little chicken popped out the egg

بدلا من ذلك ، برزت دجاجة صغيرة من البيضة

it was a very gay and polite little chicken

كان دجاجة صغيرة مثلي الجنس ومهذبة جدا

the little chicken made a beautiful courtesy

صنع الدجاج الصغير مجاملة جميلة

"A thousand thanks, Master. Pinocchio"

"ألف شكر يا معلمة .بينوكيو"

"you have saved me the trouble of breaking the shell"
"لقد أنقذتني من عناء كسر القشرة"
"Adieu, until we meet again" the chicken said
الدجاج قال "أخرى مرة نلتقي حتى ، Adieu"
"Keep well, and my best compliments to all at home!"
"حافظ على صحتك ، وأفضل تحياتي للجميع في المنزل"!
the little chicken spread its little wings
الدجاجة الصغيرة تنشر أجنحتها الصغيرة
and the little chicken darted through the open window
وانطلقت الدجاجة الصغيرة من خلال النافذة المفتوحة
and then the little chicken flew out of sight
ثم طارت الدجاجة الصغيرة بعيدا عن الأنظار
The poor puppet stood as if he had been bewitched
وقفت الدمية المسكينة كما لو كان مسحورا
his eyes were fixed, and his mouth was open
كانت عيناه ثابتتين ، وكان فمه مفتوحا
and he still had the egg-shell in his hand
وكان لا يزال يحمل قشرة البيضة في يده
slowly he Recovered from his stupefaction
ببطء تعافى من ذهوله
and then he began to cry and scream
ثم بدأ يبكي ويصرخ
he stamped his feet on the floor in desperation
داس قدميه على الأرض في يأس
amidst his sobs he gathered his thoughts
وسط تنهداته جمع أفكاره
"Ah, indeed, the talking little cricket was right"
"آه ، في الواقع ، كان الكريكيت الصغير الحديث على حق"
"I should not have run away from home"
"ما كان يجب أن أهرب من المنزل"
"then I would not now be dying of hunger!"
"إذن لن أموت الآن من الجوع"!
"and if my papa were here he would feed me"
"ولو كان أبي هنا لكان يطعمني"
"Oh! what a dreadful illness hunger is!"

"أوه إيا له من مرض مروع جوع!

his stomach cried out more than ever

صرخت معدته أكثر من أي وقت مضى

and he did not know how to quiet his hunger

ولم يعرف كيف يهدئ جوعه

he thought about leaving the house

فكر في مغادرة المنزل

perhaps he could make an excursion in the neighborhood

ربما يمكنه القيام برحلة في الحي

he hoped to find some charitable person

كان يأمل في العثور على شخص خيري

maybe they would give him a piece of bread

ربما يعطونه قطعة خبز

Pinocchio's Feet Burn to Cinders
أقدام بينوكيو تحترق إلى رماد

It was an especially wild and stormy night

كانت ليلة برية وعاصفة بشكل خاص

The thunder was tremendously loud and fearful

كان الرعد عاليا وخائفا للغاية

the lightning was so vivid that the sky seemed on fire

كان البرق نابضا بالحياة لدرجة أن السماء بدت مشتعلة

Pinocchio had a great fear of thunder

كان لدى بينوكيو خوف كبير من الرعد

but hunger can be stronger than fear

لكن الجوع يمكن أن يكون أقوى من الخوف

so he closed the door of the house

فأغلق باب المنزل

and he made a desperate rush for the village

وقام باندفاع يائس للقرية

he reached the village in a hundred bounds

وصل إلى القرية في مائة حدود

his tongue was hanging out of his mouth

كان لسانه يتدلى من فمه

and he was panting for breath like a dog
وكان يلهث لالتقاط الأنفاس مثل
But he found the village all dark and deserted
لكنه وجد القرية مظلمة ومهجورة
The shops were closed and the windows were shut
كانت المحلات مغلقة والنوافذ مغلقة
and there was not so much as a dog in the street
ولم يكن هناك الكثير مثل في الشارع
It seemed like he had arrived in the land of the dead
يبدو أنه وصل إلى أرض الموتى
Pinocchio was urged on by desperation and hunger
تم حث بينوكيو بسبب اليأس والجوع
he took hold of the bell of a house
أمسك بجرس منزل
and he began to ring the bell with all his might
وبدأ يقرع الجرس بكل قوته
"That will bring somebody," he said to himself
"هذا سيجلب شخصا ما"، قال لنفسه
And it did bring somebody!
وقد جلبت شخصا ما!
A little old man appeared at a window
ظهر رجل عجوز صغير عند النافذة
the little old man still had a night-cap on his head
الرجل العجوز الصغير لا يزال لديه قبعة ليلية على رأسه
he called to him angrily
ناداه بغضب
"What do you want at such an hour?"
"ماذا تريد في مثل هذه الساعة؟"
"Would you be kind enough to give me a little bread?"
"هل ستكون لطيفا بما يكفي لإعطائي القليل من الخبز؟"
the little old man was very obliging
كان الرجل العجوز الصغير ملزما للغاية
"Wait there, I will be back directly"
"انتظر هناك، سأعود مباشرة"
he thought it was one of the local rascals
كان يعتقد أنه كان أحد الأوغاد المحليين

they amuse themselves by ringing the house-bells at night
يسلون أنفسهم بقرع أجراس المنزل في الليل

After half a minute the window opened again
بعد نصف دقيقة فتحت النافذة مرة أخرى

the voice of the same little old man shouted to Pinocchio
صرخ صوت نفس الرجل العجوز الصغير إلى بينوكيو

"Come underneath and hold out your cap"
"تعال إلى الأسفل وامسك قبعتك"

Pinocchio pulled off his cap and held it out
خلع بينوكيو قبعته وأمسكها

but Pinocchio's cap was not filled with bread or food
لكن قبعة بينوكيو لم تكن مليئة بالخبز أو الطعام

an enormous basin of water was poured down on him
تم سكب حوض هائل من الماء عليه

the water soaked him from head to foot
غمره الماء من الرأس إلى القدم

as if he had been a pot of dried-up geraniums
كما لو كان قدرا من إبرة الراعي المجففة

He returned home like a wet chicken
عاد إلى المنزل مثل دجاجة مبللة

he was quite exhausted with fatigue and hunger
كان مرهقا جدا من التعب والجوع

he no longer had the strength to stand
لم يعد لديه القوة للوقوف

so he sat down and rested his damp and muddy feet
فجلس وأراح قدميه الرطبتين والموحلتتين

he put his feet on a brazier full of burning embers
وضع قدميه على موقد مليء بالجمر المحترق

and then he fell asleep, exhausted from the day
ثم نام ، مرهقا من اليوم

we all know that Pinocchio has wooden feet
نعلم جميعا أن بينوكيو له أقدام خشبية

and we know what happens to wood on burning embers
ونحن نعرف ما يحدث للخشب على الجمر المحترق

little by little his feet burnt away and became cinders
شيئا فشيئا احترقت قدميه وأصبحت رماد

Pinocchio continued to sleep and snore
استمر بينوكيو في النوم والشخير

his feet might as well have belonged to someone else
ربما كانت قدميه تنتمي إلى شخص آخر

At last he awoke because someone was knocking at the door
أخيرا استيقظ لأن شخصا ما كان يطرق الباب

"Who is there?" he asked, yawning and rubbing his eyes
"من هناك؟" سأل وهو يتثاءب ويفرك عينيه

"It is I!" answered a voice
"إنه أنا "أجاب بصوت

And Pinocchio recognized Geppetto's voice
وتعرف بينوكيو على صوت جيبيتو

Geppetto Gives his own Breakfast to Pinocchio
جيبيتو يقدم وجبة الإفطار الخاصة به إلى بينوكيو

Poor Pinocchio's eyes were still half shut from sleep
كانت عيون بينوكيو المسكينة لا تزال نصف مغلقة من النوم

he had not yet discovered what had happened
لم يكتشف بعد ما حدث

his feet had were completely burnt off
كانت قدماه قد احترقتا تماما

he heard the voice of his father at the door
سمع صوت والده عند الباب

and he jumped off the chair he had slept on
وقفز من الكرسي الذي نام عليه

he wanted to run to the door and open it
أراد أن يركض إلى الباب ويفتحه

but he stumbled around and fell on the floor
لكنه تعثر وسقط على الأرض

imagine having a sack of wooden ladles
تخيل وجود كيس من المغارف الخشبية

imagine throwing the sack off the balcony
تخيل رمي الكيس من الشرفة

that is was the sound of Pinocchio falling to the floor

كان هذا هو صوت سقوط بينوكيو على الأرض

"Open the door!" shouted Geppetto from the street

"افتح الباب "!صاح جيبيتو من الشارع

"Dear papa, I cannot," answered the puppet

"عزيزي بابا ، لا أستطيع "، أجابت الدمية

and he cried and rolled about on the ground

وبكى وتدحرج على الأرض

"Why can't you open the door?"

"لماذا لا يمكنك فتح الباب؟"

"Because my feet have been eaten"

"لأن قدمي قد أكلت"

"And who has eaten your feet?"

"ومن أكل قدميك؟"

Pinocchio looked around for something to blame

نظر بينوكيو حوله بحثا عن شيء يلومه

eventually he answered "the cat ate my feet"

في النهاية أجاب" القطة أكلت قدمي"

"Open the door, I tell you!" repeated Geppetto

"افتح الباب ، أقول لك "!كرر جيبيتو

"If you don't open it, you shall have the cat from me!"

"إذا لم تفتحه ، فستحصل على القطة مني"!

"I cannot stand up, believe me"

"لا أستطيع الوقوف ، صدقني"

"Oh, poor me!" lamented Pinocchio

"أوه ، أنا مسكين "!إرثى بينوكيو

"I shall have to walk on my knees for the rest of my life!"

"يجب أن أمشي على ركبتي لبقية حياتي"!

Geppetto thought this was another one of the puppet's tricks

اعتقد جيبيتو أن هذه كانت إحدى حيل الدمية الأخرى

he thought of a means of putting an end to his tricks

فكر في وسيلة لوضع حد لحيله

he climbed up the wall and got in through the window

تسلق الجدار ودخل من النافذة

He was very angry when he first saw Pinocchio

كان غاضبا جدا عندما رأى بينوكيو لأول مرة

and he did nothing but scold the poor puppet
ولم يفعل شيئا سوى توبيخ الدمية المسكينة

but then he saw Pinocchio really was without feet
ولكن بعد ذلك رأى بينوكيو حقا بدون أقدام
and he was quite overcome with sympathy again
وقد تغلب عليه التعاطف مرة أخرى
Geppetto took his puppet in his arms
أخذ جييبتو دميته بين ذراعيه
and he began to kiss and caress him
وبدأ يقبله ويداعبه
he said a thousand endearing things to him
قال له الف شيء محبب
big tears ran down his rosy cheeks
انهمرت دموع كبيرة على خديه الوردية
"My little Pinocchio!" he comforted him
"بينوكيو الصغير!" إعزاه
"how did you manage to burn your feet?"
"كيف تمكنت من حرق قدميك؟"

"I don't know how I did it, papa"

"لا أعرف كيف فعلت ذلك يا بابا"

"but it has been such a dreadful night"

"لكنها كانت ليلة مروعة"

"I shall remember it as long as I live"

"سأتذكرها ما دمت على قيد الحياة"

"there was thunder and lightning all night"

"كان هناك رعد وبرق طوال الليل"

"and I was very hungry all night"

"وكنت جائعا جدا طوال الليل"

"and then the talking cricket scolded me"

"ثم وبخني الكريكيت الحديث"

"the talking cricket said 'it serves you right'"

"قال الكريكيت الناطق "إنه يخدمك بشكل صحيح""

"he said; 'you have been wicked and deserve it'"

"قال. لقد كنتم أشرارا وتستحقون ذلك."

"and I said to him: 'Take care, little Cricket!'"

"وقلت له' :اعتن بنفسك ، أيها الكريكيت الصغير"!"

"and he said; 'You are a puppet'"

"فقال. أنت دمية"

"and he said; 'you have a wooden head'"

"فقال. لديك رأس خشبي."

"and I threw the handle of a hammer at him"

"وألقيت عليه مقبض مطرقة"

"and then the talking little cricket died"

"ثم مات الكريكيت الصغير الحديث"

"but it was his fault that he died"

"لكن خطأه أنه مات"

"because I didn't wish to kill him"

"لأنني لم أرغب في قتله"

"and I have proof that I didn't mean to"

"ولدي دليل على أنني لم أقصد ذلك"

"I had put an earthenware saucer on burning embers"

"كنت قد وضعت صحنا خزفيا على الجمر المحترق"

"but a chicken flew out of the egg"
"لكن دجاجة طارت من البيضة"
"the chicken said; 'Adieu, until we meet again'"
"قالت الدجاجة وداعا حتى نلتقي مرة أخرى"
'send my compliments to all at home'
"أرسل تحياتي للجميع في المنزل"
"and then I got even more hungry"
"ثم شعرت بجوع أكثر"
"then there was that little old man in a night-cap"
"ثم كان هناك ذلك الرجل العجوز الصغير في قبعة ليلية"
"he opened the window up above me"
"فتح النافذة فوقي"
"and he told me to hold out my hat"
"وقال لي أن أرفع قبعتي"
"and he poured a basinful of water on me"
"وسكب علي حوضا من الماء"
"asking for a little bread isn't a disgrace, is it?"
"طلب القليل من الخبز ليس وصمة عار ، أليس كذلك؟"
"and then I returned home at once"
"ثم عدت إلى المنزل على الفور"
"I was hungry and cold and tired"
"كنت جائعا وباردا ومتعبا"
"and I put my feet on the brazier to dry them"
"وأضع قدمي على الموقد لتجفيفها"
"and then you returned in the morning"
"ثم عدت في الصباح"
"and I found my feet were burnt off"
"ووجدت قدمي محترقة"
"and I am still hungry"
"وما زلت جائعا"
"but I no longer have any feet!"
"لكن لم يعد لدي أي قدم"!

And poor Pinocchio began to cry and roar
وبدأ بينوكيو المسكين في البكاء والزئير

he cried so loudly that he was heard five miles off

بكى بصوت عالٍ لدرجة أنه سمع على بعد خمسة أميال

Geppetto, only understood one thing from all this

لم يفهم جيبيتو سوى شيء واحد من كل هذا

he understood that the puppet was dying of hunger

لقد فهم أن الدمية كانت تموت من الجوع

so he drew from his pocket three pears

فأخرج من جيبه ثلاثة كمثرى

and he gave the pears to Pinocchio

وأعطى الكمثرى لبينوكيو

"These three pears were intended for my breakfast"

"هذه الكمثرى الثلاثة كانت مخصصة لتناول الإفطار"

"but I will give you my pears willingly"

"لكنني سأعطيك الكمثرى عن طيب خاطر"

"Eat them, and I hope they will do you good"

"أكلهم ، وآمل أن يفيدوك"

Pinocchio looked at the pears distrustfully

نظر بينوكيو إلى الكمثرى بعدم ثقة

"but you can't expect me to eat them like that"

"لكن لا يمكنك أن تتوقع مني أن آكلها هكذا"

"be kind enough to peel them for me"

"كن لطيفا بما يكفي لتقشيرها من أجلي"

"Peel them?" said Geppetto, astonished

"قشرهم؟" قال جيبيتو مندهشا

"I didn't know you were so dainty and fastidious"

"لم أكن أعرف أنك كنت لذيذا وحساسا"

"These are bad habits to have, my boy!"

"هذه عادات سيئة ، يا ولدي"!

"we must accustom ourselves to like and to eat everything"

"يجب أن نعتاد على حب وأكل كل شيء"

"there is no knowing to what we may be brought"

"لا معرفة لما قد يتم إحضاره"

"There are so many chances!"

"هناك الكثير من الفرص"!

"You are no doubt right," interrupted Pinocchio

"أنت بلا شك على حق "، قاطع بينوكيو
"but I will never eat fruit that has not been peeled"
"لكنني لن آكل الفاكهة التي لم يتم تقشيرها"
"I cannot bear the taste of rind"
"لا أستطيع تحمل طعم القشرة"
So good Geppetto peeled the three pears
لقد قام جيبيتو بشكل جيد بتقشير الكمثرى الثلاث
and he put the pear's rinds on a corner of the table
ووضع قشور الكمثرى على زاوية من الطاولة
Pinocchio had eaten the first pear
كان بينوكيو قد أكل الكمثرى الأولى
he was about to throw away the pear's core
كان على وشك التخلص من لب الكمثرى
but Geppetto caught hold of his arm
لكن جيبيتو أمسك بذراعه
"Do not throw the core of the pear away"
"لا ترمي جوهر الكمثرى بعيدا"
"in this world everything may be of use"
"في هذا العالم قد يكون كل شيء مفيدا"
But Pinocchio refused to see the sense in it
لكن بينوكيو رفض رؤية المعنى فيه
"I am determined I will not eat the core of the pear"
"أنا مصمم على أنني لن آكل لب الكمثرى"
and Pinocchio turned upon him like a viper
وانقلب بينوكيو عليه مثل الأفعى
"Who knows!" repeated Geppetto
"من يدري"! كرر جيبيتو
"there are so many chances," he said
"هناك الكثير من الفرص، "قال.
and Geppetto never lost his temper even once
ولم يفقد جيبيتو أعصابه ولو مرة واحدة
And so the three pear cores were not thrown out
وهكذا لم يتم التخلص من نوى الكمثرى الثلاثة
they were placed on the corner of the table with the rinds
تم وضعها على زاوية الطاولة مع القشور

after his small feast Pinocchio yawned tremendously

بعد وليمة صغيرة تثاءب بينوكيو بشكل هائل

and he spoke again in a fretful tone

وتحدث مرة أخرى بنبرة غاضبة

"I am as hungry as ever!"

"أنا جائع أكثر من أي وقت مضى"!

"But, my boy, I have nothing more to give you!"

"لكن يا ولدي ، ليس لدي ما أعطيك إياه"!

"You have nothing? Really? Nothing?"

"ليس لديك شيء؟ حقا؟ لا شيء؟"

"I have only the rind and the cores of the pears"

"ليس لدي سوى القشرة ونوى الكمثرى"

"One must have patience!" said Pinocchio

"يجب على المرء أن يتحلى بالصبر"! قال بينوكيو

"if there is nothing else I will eat the pear's rind"

"إذا لم يكن هناك شيء آخر فسوف آكل قشرة الكمثرى"

And he began to chew the rind of the pear

وبدأ يمضغ قشرة الكمثرى

At first he made a wry face

في البداية صنع وجها ساخرا

but then, one after the other, he quickly ate them

ولكن بعد ذلك ، واحدا تلو الآخر ، أكلها بسرعة.

and after the pear's rinds he even ate the cores

وبعد قشور الكمثرى أكل النوى

when he had eaten everything he rubbed his belly

عندما أكل كل شيء فرك بطنه

"Ah! now I feel comfortable again"

"آه !الآن أشعر بالراحة مرة أخرى"

"Now you see I was right," smiled Gepetto

ابتسم جيبيتو قائلاً: "الآن ترى أنني كنت على حق."

"it's not good to accustom ourselves to our tastes"

"ليس من الجيد أن نعتاد على أذواقنا"

"We can never know, my dear boy, what may happen to us"

"لا يمكننا أبدا أن نعرف ، يا ولدي العزيز ، ما قد يحدث لنا"

"There are so many chances!"

"هناك الكثير من الفرص"!

Geppetto Makes Pinocchio New Feet
جيبيتو يجعل بينوكيو أقدام جديدة

the puppet had satisfied his hunger

كانت الدمية قد أشبعت جوعه

but he began to cry and grumble again

لكنه بدأ في البكاء والتذمر مرة أخرى

he remembered he wanted a pair of new feet

تذكر أنه يريد زوجا من الأقدام الجديدة

But Geppetto punished him for his naughtiness

لكن جيبيتو عاقبه على شقاوته

he allowed him to cry and to despair a little

سمح له بالبكاء واليأس قليلا

Pinocchio had to accept his fate for half the day

كان على بينوكيو قبول مصيره لمدة نصف يوم

at the end of the day he said to him:

في نهاية اليوم قال له:

"Why should I make you new feet?"

"لماذا يجب أن أصنع لك أقداما جديدة؟"

"To enable you to escape again from home?"

"لتمكينك من الهروب مرة أخرى من المنزل؟"

Pinocchio sobbed at his situation

بكى بينوكيو على وضعه

"I promise you that for the future I will be good"

"أعدك أنني سأكون جيدا في المستقبل"

but Geppetto knew Pinocchio's tricks by now

لكن جيبيتو كان يعرف حيل بينوكيو الآن

"All boys who want something say the same thing"

"كل الأولاد الذين يريدون شيئا يقولون نفس الشيء"

"I promise you that I will go to school"

"أعدك بأنني سأذهب إلى المدرسة"

"and I will study and bring home a good report"

"وسأدرس وأحضر تقريرا جيدا إلى المنزل"

"All boys who want something repeat the same story"

"جميع الأولاد الذين يريدون شيئا يكررون نفس القصة"

"But I am not like other boys!" Pinocchio objected

"لكنني لست مثل الأولاد الآخرين"! إعترض بينوكيو

"I am better than all of them," he added

وأضاف "أنا أفضل منهم جميعا."

"and I always speak the truth," he lied

"وأنا دائما أقول الحقيقة "، كذب

"I promise you, papa, that I will learn a trade"

"أعدك يا بابا بأنني سأتعلم التجارة"

"I promise that I will be the consolation of your old age"

"أعدك بأنني سأكون عزاء شيخوختك"

Geppetto's eyes filled with tears on hearing this

امتلأت عيون جيبيتو بالدموع عند سماع هذا

his heart was sad at seeing his son like this

كان قلبه حزينا لرؤية ابنه هكذا

Pinocchio was in such a pitiable state

كان بينوكيو في مثل هذه الحالة المثيرة للشفقة

He did not say another word to Pinocchio

لم يقل كلمة أخرى لبينوكيو

he got his tools and two small pieces of seasoned wood

حصل على أدواته وقطعتين صغيرتين من الخشب المحنك

he set to work with great diligence

شرع في العمل باجتهاد كبير

In less than an hour the feet were finished

في أقل من ساعة تم الانتهاء من القدمين

They might have been modelled by an artist of genius

ربما تم تصميمها من قبل فنان عبقري

Geppetto then spoke to the puppet

ثم تحدث جيبيتو إلى الدمية

"Shut your eyes and go to sleep!"

"أغمض عينيك واذهب للنوم"!

And Pinocchio shut his eyes and pretended to sleep

وأغلق بينوكيو عينيه وتظاهر بالنوم

Geppetto got an egg-shell and melted some glue in it
حصل جيبيتو على قشرة بيضة وأذاب فيها بعض الغراء

and he fastened Pinocchio's feet in their place
وثبت قدمي بينوكيو في مكانهما

it was masterfully done by Geppetto
تم القيام به ببراعة من قبل جيبيتو

not a trace could be seen of where the feet were joined
لا يمكن رؤية أي أثر لمكان ربط القدمين

Pinocchio soon realized that he had feet again
سرعان ما أدرك بينوكيو أن لديه أقدام مرة أخرى

and then he jumped down from the table
ثم قفز من على الطاولة

he jumped around the room with energy and joy
قفز في جميع أنحاء الغرفة بالطاقة والفرح

he danced as if he had gone mad with his delight
رقص كما لو أنه أصيب بالجنون من فرحته

"thank you for all you have done for me"
"شكرا لك على كل ما فعلته من أجلي"

"I will go to school at once," Pinocchio promised
"سأذهب إلى المدرسة في الحال "، وعد بينوكيو

"but to go to school I shall need some clothes"
"ولكن للذهاب إلى المدرسة سأحتاج إلى بعض الملابس"

by now you know that Geppetto was a poor man
الآن أنت تعرف أن جيبيتو كان رجلا فقيرا

he had not so much as a penny in his pocket
لم يكن لديه الكثير من بنس واحد في جيبه

so he made him a little dress of flowered paper
فصنع له ثوبا صغيرا من الورق المزهر

a pair of shoes from the bark of a tree
زوج من الأحذية من لحاء شجرة

and he made a hat out of the bread
وصنع قبعة من الخبز

Pinocchio ran to look at himself in a crock of water
ركض بينوكيو لينظر إلى نفسه في فخار من الماء
he was ever so pleased with his appearance
كان سعيدا جدا بمظهره
and he strutted about the room like a peacock
وتبختر حول الغرفة مثل الطاووس
"I look quite like a gentleman!"
"أنا أبدو تماما مثل رجل نبيل"!
"Yes, indeed," answered Geppetto
"نعم ، بالفعل "، أجاب جيبيتو
"it is not fine clothes that make the gentleman"
"ليست الملابس الجميلة هي التي تصنع الرجل"
"rather, it is clean clothes that make a gentleman"
"بدلا من ذلك ، فإن الملابس النظيفة هي التي تصنع الرجل النبيل"
"By the way," added the puppet
"بالمناسبة "، أضافت الدمية
"to go to school there's still something I need"
"للذهاب إلى المدرسة لا يزال هناك شيء أحتاجه"

"I am still without the best thing"
"ما زلت بدون أفضل شيء"

"it is the most important thing for a school boy"
"إنه أهم شيء بالنسبة لصبي المدرسة"

"And what is it?" asked Geppetto
"وما هذا؟ "سأل جيبيتو

"I have no spelling-book"
"ليس لدي كتاب إملائي"

"You are right" realized Geppetto
"أنت على حق "أدرك جيبيتو

"but what shall we do to get one?"
"ولكن ماذا سنفعل للحصول على واحدة؟"

Pinocchio comforted Geppetto, "It is quite easy"
أراح بينوكيو جيبيتو ،" إنه سهل للغاية"

"all we have to do is go to the bookseller's"
"كل ما علينا فعله هو الذهاب إلى بائع الكتب"

"all I have to do is buy from them"
"كل ما علي فعله هو الشراء منهم"

"but how do we buy it without money?"
"ولكن كيف نشتريه بدون مال؟"

"I have got no money," said Pinocchio
"ليس لدي مال"، قال بينوكيو

"Neither have I," added the good old man, very sadly
"ولا أنا "، أضاف الرجل العجوز الطيب ، للأسف الشديد

although he was a very merry boy, Pinocchio became sad
على الرغم من أنه كان فتى مرحا للغاية ، إلا أن بينوكيو أصبح حزينا

poverty, when it is real, is understood by everybody
الفقر، عندما يكون حقيقيا، يفهمه الجميع

"Well, patience!" exclaimed Geppetto, rising to his feet
"حسنا ، الصبر "!هتف جيبيتو ، ونهض على قدميه

and he put on his old corduroy jacket
وارتدى سترته القديمة سروال قصير

and he ran out of the house into the snow
وركض من المنزل إلى الثلج

- 45 -

He returned back to the house soon after
عاد إلى المنزل بعد فترة وجيزة
in his hand he held a spelling-book for Pinocchio
في يده كان يحمل كتاب تهجئة لبينوكيو
but the old jacket he had left with was gone
لكن السترة القديمة التي تركها قد اختفت
The poor man was in his shirt-sleeves
كان الرجل الفقير في أكمام قميصه
and outdoors it was cold and snowing
وفي الهواء الطلق كان الجو باردا وثلجا
"And your jacket, papa?" asked Pinocchio
"وسترتك يا بابا؟" سأل بينوكيو
"I have sold it," confirmed old Geppetto
"لقد بعتها "، أكد جيبيتو القديم
"Why did you sell it?" asked Pinocchio
"لماذا قمت ببيعها؟" سأل بينوكيو
"Because I found my jacket was too hot"
"لأنني وجدت سترتي ساخنة جدا"
Pinocchio understood this answer in an instant
فهم بينوكيو هذه الإجابة في لحظة
Pinocchio was unable to restrain the impulse of his heart
لم يكن بينوكيو قادرا على كبح جماح نبض قلبه
Because Pinocchio did have a good heart after all
لأن بينوكيو كان لديه قلب طيب بعد كل شيء
he sprang up and threw his arms around Geppetto's neck
نهض وألقى ذراعيه حول رقبة جيبيتو
and he kissed him again and again a thousand times
وقبله مرارا وتكرارا ألف مرة

Pinocchio Goes to See a Puppet Show
بينوكيو يذهب لمشاهدة عرض الدمى

eventually it stopped snowing outside
في النهاية توقف الثلج في الخارج
and Pinocchio set out to go to school
وانطلق بينوكيو للذهاب إلى المدرسة
and he had his fine spelling-book under his arm
وكان لديه كتاب التهجئة الجيد تحت ذراعه
he walked along with a thousand ideas in his head
مشى مع ألف فكرة في رأسه
his little brain thought of all the possibilities
فكر دماغه الصغير في كل الاحتمالات
and he built a thousand castles in the air
وبنى ألف قلعة في الهواء
each castle was more beautiful than the other
كانت كل قلعة أجمل من الأخرى
And, talking to himself, he said;
وتحدث إلى نفسه ، قال.
"Today at school I will learn to read at once"
"اليوم في المدرسة سأتعلم القراءة في الحال"
"then tomorrow I will begin to write"
"ثم غدا سأبدأ في الكتابة"
"and the day after tomorrow I will learn the numbers"
"وبعد غد سأتعلم الأرقام"
"all of these things will prove very useful"
"كل هذه الأشياء ستثبت أنها مفيدة للغاية"
"and then I will earn a great deal of money"
"وبعد ذلك سأكسب قدرا كبيرا من المال"
"I already know what I will do with the first money"
"أنا أعرف بالفعل ما سأفعله بالمال الأول"
"I will immediately buy a beautiful new cloth coat"
"سأشتري على الفور معطفا جديدا جميلا من القماش"
"my papa will not have to be cold anymore"
"لن يكون بابا باردا بعد الآن"

"But what am I saying?" he realized

"ولكن ماذا أقول؟" أدرك

"It shall be all made of gold and silver"

"يكون كله من ذهب وفضة"

"and it shall have diamond buttons"

"ويجب أن يكون لها أزرار الماس"

"That poor man really deserves it"

"هذا الرجل الفقير يستحق ذلك حقا"

"he bought me books and is having me taught"

"لقد اشترى لي كتبا وعلمني"

"and to do so he has remained in a shirt"

"وللقيام بذلك بقي في قميص"

"he has done all this for me in such cold weather"

"لقد فعل كل هذا من أجلي في مثل هذا الطقس البارد"

"only papas are capable of such sacrifices!"

"فقط باباس قادرون على مثل هذه التضحيات"!

he said all this to himself with great emotion

قال كل هذا لنفسه بعاطفة كبيرة

but in the distance he thought he heard music

ولكن في المسافة اعتقد أنه سمع الموسيقى

it sounded like pipes and the beating of a big drum

بدا الأمر مثل الأنابيب وضرب طبلة كبيرة

He stopped and listened to hear what it could be

توقف واستمع لسماع ما يمكن أن يكون

The sounds came from the end of a street

جاءت الأصوات من نهاية الشارع

and the street led to a little village on the seashore

وأدى الشارع إلى قرية صغيرة على شاطئ البحر

"What can that music be?" he wondered

"ماذا يمكن أن تكون تلك الموسيقى؟" "تساءل

"What a pity that I have to go to school"

"يا للأسف أن أذهب إلى المدرسة"

"if only I didn't have to go to school..."

"لو لم يكن علي الذهاب إلى المدرسة"...

And he remained irresolute

وظل غير حازم

It was, however, necessary to come to a decision

غير أنه كان من الضروري التوصل إلى قرار.

"Should I go to school?" he asked himself

"هل يجب أن أذهب إلى المدرسة؟" سأل نفسه

"or should I go after the music?"

"أم يجب أن أذهب بعد الموسيقى؟"

"Today I will go and hear the music" he decided

"اليوم سأذهب وأسمع الموسيقى" قرر

"and tomorrow I will go to school"

"وغدا سأذهب إلى المدرسة"

the young scapegrace of a boy had decided

كان كبش الفداء الصغير لصبي قد قرر

and he shrugged his shoulders at his choice

وهز كتفيه حسب اختياره

The more he ran the nearer came the sounds of the music

كلما ركض أكثر كلما اقتربت أصوات الموسيقى

and the beating of the big drum became louder and louder

وأصبح قرع الطبل الكبير أعلى وأعلى

At last he found himself in the middle of a town square

أخيرا وجد نفسه في وسط ساحة البلدة

the square was quite full of people

كانت الساحة مليئة بالناس

all the people were all crowded round a building

كان جميع الناس مزدحمين حول مبنى

and the building was made of wood and canvas

وكان المبنى مصنوعا من الخشب والقماش

and the building was painted a thousand colours

وتم طلاء المبنى بألف لون

"What is that building?" asked Pinocchio

"ما هو هذا المبنى؟" سأل بينوكيو

and he turned to a little boy

والتفت إلى صبي صغير

"Read the placard," the boy told him

"اقرأ اللافتة"، قال له الصبي

"it is all written there," he added

وأضاف: "كل شيء مكتوب هناك."

"read it and and then you will know"

"اقرأها وبعد ذلك ستعرف"

"I would read it willingly," said Pinocchio

قال بينوكيو: "سأقرأها عن طيب خاطر"

"but it so happens that today I don't know how to read"

"لكن يحدث اليوم أنني لا أعرف كيف أقرأ"

"Bravo, blockhead! Then I will read it to you"

"برافو ، بلوكهيد !ثم سأقرأها لك"

"you see those words as red as fire?"

"هل ترى هذه الكلمات حمراء مثل النار؟"

"The Great Puppet Theatre," he read to him

"مسرح العرائس العظيم "، قرأ له

"Has the play already begun?"

"هل بدأت المسرحية بالفعل؟"

"It is beginning now," confirmed the boy

"لقد بدأت الآن "، أكد الصبي

"How much does it cost to go in?"

"كم يكلف الدخول؟"

"A dime is what it costs you"

"عشرة سنتات هو ما يكلفك"

Pinocchio was in a fever of curiosity

كان بينوكيو في حمى الفضول

full of excitement he lost all control of himself

مليء بالإثارة فقد كل السيطرة على نفسه

and Pinocchio lost all sense of shame

وفقد بينوكيو كل شعور بالعار

"Would you lend me a dime until tomorrow?"

"هل ستقرضني سنتا حتى الغد؟"

"I would lend it to you willingly," said the boy

"أود أن أقرضها لك عن طيب خاطر "، قال الصبي

"but unfortunately today I cannot give it to you"

"لكن للأسف اليوم لا أستطيع أن أعطيها لك"

Pinocchio had another idea to get the money
كان لدى بينوكيو فكرة أخرى للحصول على المال
"I will sell you my jacket for a dime"
"سأبيع لك سترتي مقابل عشرة سنتات"
"but your jacket is made of flowered paper"
"لكن سترتك مصنوعة من ورق مزهر"
"what use could I have for such a jacket?"
"ما الفائدة التي يمكنني الحصول عليها لمثل هذه السترة؟"
"imagine it rained and the jacket got wet"
"تخيل أنها أمطرت وتبللت السترة"
"it would be impossible to get it off my back"
"سيكون من المستحيل إزالته من ظهري"
"Will you buy my shoes?" tried Pinocchio
"هل ستشتري حذائي؟" حاول بينوكيو
"They would only be of use to light the fire"
"ستكون مفيدة فقط لإشعال النار"
"How much will you give me for my cap?"
"كم ستعطيني مقابل قبعتي؟"
"That would be a wonderful acquisition indeed!"
"سيكون هذا استحواذا رائعا حقا"!
"A cap made of bread crumb!" joked the boy
"قبعة مصنوعة من فتات الخبز" !مازح الصبي
"There would be a risk of the mice coming to eat it"
"سيكون هناك خطر من أن تأتي الفئران لتناوله"
"they might eat it whilst it was still on my head!"
"قد يأكلونه بينما كان لا يزال على رأسي"!
Pinocchio was on thorns about his predicament
كان بينوكيو على الأشواك بشأن مأزقه
He was on the point of making another offer
كان على وشك تقديم عرض آخر
but he had not the courage to ask him
لكنه لم يكن لديه الشجاعة لسؤاله
He hesitated, felt irresolute and remorseful
تردد ، وشعر بعدم الحزم والندم

At last he raised the courage to ask
في النهاية رفع الشجاعة ليسأل
"Will you give me a dime for this new spelling-book?"
"هل ستعطيني سنتا لهذا الكتاب الإملائي الجديد؟"
but the boy declined this offer too
لكن الصبي رفض هذا العرض أيضا
"I am a boy and I don't buy from boys"
"أنا صبي ولا أشتري من الأولاد"
a hawker of old clothes had overheard them
سمعهم بائع متجول من الملابس القديمة
"I will buy the spelling-book for a dime"
"سأشتري كتاب التهجئة مقابل عشرة سنتات"
And the book was sold there and then
وبيع الكتاب هناك ثم
poor Geppetto had remained at home trembling with cold
بقي جيبيتو المسكين في المنزل يرتجف من البرد
in order that his son could have a spelling-book
من أجل أن يتمكن ابنه من الحصول على كتاب تهجئة

The Puppets Recognize their Brother Pinocchio
الدمى تتعرف على شقيقها بينوكيو

Pinocchio was in the little puppet theatre
كان بينوكيو في مسرح العرائس الصغير
an incident occurred that almost produced a revolution
وقعت حادثة كادت أن تنتج ثورة
The curtain had gone up and the play had already begun
كان الستار قد رفع وبدأت المسرحية بالفعل
Harlequin and Punch were quarrelling with each other
كان المهرج واللكمة يتشاجران مع بعضهما البعض
every moment they were threatening to come to blows
في كل لحظة كانوا يهددون بالضرب
All at once Harlequin stopped and turned to the public
توقف المهرج دفعة واحدة وتحول إلى الجمهور

he pointed with his hand to someone far down in the pit
أشار بيده إلى شخص بعيد في الحفرة

and he exclaimed in a dramatic tone
وهتف بنبرة درامية

"Gods of the firmament!"
"آلهة السماء"!

"Do I dream or am I awake?"
"هل أحلم أم أنا مستيقظ؟"

"But, surely that is Pinocchio!"
"لكن ، بالتأكيد هذا هو بينوكيو"!

"It is indeed Pinocchio!" cried Punch
"إنه بالفعل بينوكيو "إصرخ لكمة

And Rose peeped out from behind the scenes
وروز اختلس النظر من وراء الكواليس

"It is indeed himself!" screamed Rose
"إنه بالفعل نفسه "إصرخت روز

and all the puppets shouted in chorus
وصرخت جميع الدمى في جوقة

"It is Pinocchio! it is Pinocchio!"
"إنه بينوكيو! إنه بينوكيو"!

and they leapt from all sides onto the stage
وقفزوا من جميع الجهات إلى المسرح

"It is Pinocchio!" all the puppets exclaimed
"إنه بينوكيو "إهتفت جميع الدمى

"It is our brother Pinocchio!"
"إنه أخونا بينوكيو"!

"Long live Pinocchio!" they cheered together
"يعيش بينوكيو "إهتفوا معا

"Pinocchio, come up here to me," cried Harlequin
"بينوكيو ، تعال إلى هنا لي "، صرخ هارليكوين

"throw yourself into the arms of your wooden brothers!"
"ارم نفسك في أحضان إخوانك الخشبيين"!

Pinocchio couldn't decline this affectionate invitation
لم يستطع بينوكيو رفض هذه الدعوة الحنونة

he leaped from the end of the pit into the reserved seats

قفز من نهاية الحفرة إلى المقاعد المحجوزة

another leap landed him on the head of the drummer

قفزة أخرى هبطت به على رأس عازف الدرامز

and he then sprang upon the stage

ثم صعد على المسرح

The embraces and the friendly pinches

العناق والقرصات الودية

and the demonstrations of warm brotherly affection

ومظاهر المودة الأخوية الدافئة

Pinocchio reception from the puppets was beyond description

كان استقبال بينوكيو من الدمى يفوق الوصف

The sight was doubtless a moving one

كان المشهد بلا شك مشهدا مؤثرا

but the public in the pit had become impatient

لكن الجمهور في الحفرة نفد صبره

they began to shout, "we came to watch a play"

بدأوا في الصراخ ،" جئنا لمشاهدة مسرحية"

"go on with the play!" they demanded

"استمر في المسرحية "!طالبوا

but the puppets didn't continue the recital

لكن الدمى لم تستمر في الحيثية

the puppets doubled their noise and outcries

ضاعفت الدمى ضجيجها وصراخها

they put Pinocchio on their shoulders

وضعوا بينوكيو على أكتافهم

and they carried him in triumph before the footlights

وحملوه منتصرا أمام أضواء القدم

At that moment the ringmaster came out

في تلك اللحظة خرج مدير الحلقة

He was a big and ugly man

كان رجلا كبيرا وقبيحا

the sight of him was enough to frighten anyone

كان منظره كافيا لتخويف أي شخص

His beard was as black as ink and long

كانت لحيته سوداء مثل الحبر وطويلة

and his beard reached from his chin to the ground
ووصلت لحيته من ذقنه إلى الأرض
and he trod upon his beard when he walked
وداس على لحيته عندما مشى
His mouth was as big as an oven
كان فمه كبيرا مثل الفرن
and his eyes were like two lanterns of burning red glass
وكانت عيناه مثل فانوسين من الزجاج الأحمر المحترق
He carried a large whip of twisted snakes and foxes' tails
كان يحمل سوطا كبيرا من الثعابين الملتوية وذيول الثعالب
and he cracked his whip constantly
وكان يكسر سوطه باستمرار
At his unexpected appearance there was a profound silence
في ظهوره غير المتوقع كان هناك صمت عميق
no one dared to even breathe
لم يجرؤ أحد حتى على التنفس
A fly could have been heard in the stillness
كان من الممكن سماع ذبابة في السكون
The poor puppets of both sexes trembled like leaves
ارتجفت الدمى المسكينة من كلا الجنسين مثل أوراق الشجر
"have you come to raise a disturbance in my theatre?"
"هل جئت لإثارة اضطراب في مسرحي؟"
he had the gruff voice of a goblin
كان لديه صوت عفريت خشن
a goblin suffering from a severe cold
عفريت يعاني من نزلة برد شديدة
"Believe me, honoured sir, it it not my fault!"
"صدقني يا سيدي المحترم ، هذا ليس خطأي"!
"That is enough from you!" he blared
"هذا يكفي منك"!
"Tonight we will settle our accounts"
"الليلة سنقوم بتسوية حساباتنا"
soon the play was over and the guests left
سرعان ما انتهت المسرحية وغادر الضيوف
the ringmaster went into the kitchen
ذهب مدير الحلقة إلى المطبخ

a fine sheep was being prepared for his supper

كان يتم تحضير خروف جيد لعشائه

it was turning slowly on the fire

كان يتحول ببطء على النار

there was not enough wood to finish roasting the lamb

لم يكن هناك ما يكفي من الخشب لإنهاء تحميص الخروف

so he called for Harlequin and Punch

لذلك دعا إلى المهرج واللكمة

"Bring that puppet here," he ordered them

"أحضروا تلك الدمية إلى هنا "، أمرهم

"you will find him hanging on a nail"

"ستجده معلقا على مسمار"

"It seems to me that he is made of very dry wood"

"يبدو لي أنه مصنوع من خشب جاف جدا"

"I am sure he would make a beautiful blaze"

"أنا متأكد من أنه سيصنع حريقا جميلا"

At first Harlequin and Punch hesitated

في البداية تردد المهرج ولكمة

but they were appalled by a severe glance from their master

لكنهم فزعوا من نظرة شديدة من سيدهم

and they had no choice but to obey his wishes

ولم يكن لديهم خيار سوى طاعة رغباته

In a short time they returned to the kitchen

في وقت قصير عادوا إلى المطبخ

this time they were carrying poor Pinocchio

هذه المرة كانوا يحملون بينوكيو المسكين

he was wriggling like an eel out of water

كان يتلوى مثل ثعبان البحر من الماء

and he was screaming desperately

وكان يصرخ بيأس

"Papa! papa! save me! I will not die!"

"بابا !بابا !أنقذني !لن أموت"!

The Fire-Eater Sneezes and Pardons Pinocchio
آكل النار يعطس ويعفو عن بينوكيو

The ringmaster looked like a wicked man
بدا مدير الحلقة وكأنه رجل شرير
and he was known by all as Fire-eater
وكان معروفا من قبل الجميع باسم آكل النار
his black beard covered his chest and legs
غطت لحيته السوداء صدره وساقيه
it was like he was wearing an apron
كان الأمر كما لو كان يرتدي مئزرا
and this made him look especially wicked
وهذا جعله يبدو شريرا بشكل خاص
On the whole, however, he did not have a bad heart
على العموم ، ومع ذلك ، لم يكن لديه قلب سيئ
he saw poor Pinocchio brought before him
رأى بينوكيو المسكين يحضر أمامه
he saw the puppet struggling and screaming
رأى الدمية تكافح وتصرخ
"I will not die, I will not die!"
"لن أموت ، لن أموت"!
and he was quite moved by what he saw
وقد تأثر كثيرا بما رآه
he felt very sorry for the helpless puppet
شعر بالأسف الشديد على الدمية العاجزة
he tried to hold his sympathies within himself
حاول أن يتعاطف مع نفسه
but after a little they all came out
ولكن بعد قليل خرجوا جميعا
he could contain his sympathy no longer
لم يعد بإمكانه احتواء تعاطفه
and he let out an enormous violent sneeze
وأطلق عطسا عنيفا هائلا
up until that moment Harlequin had been worried
حتى تلك اللحظة كان المهرج قلقا
he had been bowing down like a weeping willow

كان ينحني مثل صفصاف يبكي
but when he heard the sneeze he became cheerful
ولكن عندما سمع العطس أصبح مبتهجا
he leaned towards Pinocchio and whispered;
انحنى نحو بينوكيو وهمس.
"Good news, brother, the ringmaster has sneezed"
"أخبار سارة ، أخي ، لقد عطس مدير الحلبة"
"that is a sign that he pities you"
"هذه علامة على أنه يشفق عليك"
"and if he pities you, then you are saved"
"وإذا أشفق عليك ، فأنت مخلص"
most men weep when they feel compassion
يبكي معظم الرجال عندما يشعرون بالتعاطف
or at least they pretend to dry their eyes
أو على الأقل يتظاهرون بتجفيف عيونهم
Fire-Eater, however, had a different habit
ومع ذلك ، كان لدى آكل النار عادة مختلفة
when moved by emotion his nose would tickle him
عندما تحركه العاطفة ، كان أنفه يدغدغه
the ringmaster didn't stop acting the ruffian
لم يتوقف مدير الحلقة عن تمثيل الرافيان
"are you quite done with all your crying?"
"هل انتهيت تماما من كل بكائك؟"
"my stomach hurts from your lamentations"
"معدتي تؤلمني من رثائك"
"I feel a spasm that almost..."
"أشعر بتشنج يكاد يكون"...
and the ringmaster let out another loud sneeze
وأطلق مدير الحلقة عطسا عاليا آخر
"Bless you!" said Pinocchio, quite cheerfully
"بارك الله فيك "إقال بينوكيو بمرح شديد
"Thank you! And your papa and your mamma?"
"شكرا لك إووالدك وأمك؟"
"are they still alive?" asked Fire-Eater
"هل ما زالوا على قيد الحياة؟ "سأل آكل النار

"My papa is still alive and well," said Pinocchio
"أبي لا يزال على قيد الحياة وبصحة جيدة "، قال بينوكيو

"but my mamma I have never known," he added
وأضاف» :لكن أمي لم أعرفها من قبل.«

"good thing I did not have you thrown on the fire"
"شيء جيد لم ألقي بك على النار"

"your father would have lost all who he still had"
"كان والدك سيفقد كل من كان لا يزال لديه"

"Poor old man! I pity him!"
"رجل عجوز مسكين !أنا أشفق عليه"!

"Etchoo! etchoo! etchoo!" Fire-eater sneezed
"إتشو !إتشو !إتشو "!عطس آكل النار

and he sneezed again three times
وعطس مرة أخرى ثلاث مرات

"Bless you," said Pinocchio each time
"بارك الله فيك "، قال بينوكيو في كل مرة

"Thank you! Some compassion is due to me"
"شكرا لك !بعض التعاطف مستحق لي"

"as you can see I have no more wood"
"كما ترون ليس لدي المزيد من الخشب"

"so I will struggle to finish roasting my mutton"
"لذلك سأكافح لإنهاء تحميص لحم الضأن"

"you would have been of great use to me!"
"كنت ستعود بفائدة كبيرة بالنسبة لي"!

"However, I have had pity on you"
"ومع ذلك ، فقد أشفقت عليك"

"so I must have patience with you"
"لذلك يجب أن أتحلى بالصبر معك"

"Instead of you I will burn another puppet"
"بدلا منك سأحرق دمية أخرى"

At this call two wooden gendarmes immediately appeared
في هذه الدعوة ظهر اثنان من رجال الدرك الخشبي على الفور

They were very long and very thin puppets
كانت دمى طويلة جدا ورقيقة جدا

and they had wonky hats on their heads
وكان لديهم قبعات متزعزعة على رؤوسهم
and they held unsheathed swords in their hands
وحملوا سيوفا غير مغلفة في أيديهم
The ringmaster said to them in a hoarse voice:
قال لهم رئيس الحلقة بصوت أجش:
"Take Harlequin and bind him securely"
"خذ المهرج واربطه بأمان"
"and then throw him on the fire to burn"
"ثم رميه على النار ليحترق"
"I am determined that my mutton shall be well roasted"
"أنا مصمم على أن يتم تحميص لحم الضأن جيدا"
imagine how poor Harlequin must have felt!
تخيل كيف شعر المهرج الفقير!
His terror was so great that his legs bent under him
كان رعبه كبيرا لدرجة أن ساقيه انحنت تحته
and he fell with his face on the ground
وسقط ووجهه على الأرض
Pinocchio was agonized by what he was seeing
كان بينوكيو متألما مما كان يراه
he threw himself at the ringmaster's feet
ألقى بنفسه عند قدمي مدير الحلقة
he bathed his long beard with his tears
اغتسل لحيته الطويلة بدموعه
and he tried to beg for Harlequin's life
وحاول التسول من أجل حياة المهرج
"Have pity, Sir Fire-Eater!" Pinocchio begged
"أشفق يا سيدي آكل النار "إتوسل بينوكيو
"Here there are no sirs," the ringmaster answered severely
"هنا لا يوجد سادة "، أجاب مدير العصابة بشدة
"Have pity, Sir Knight!" Pinocchio tried
"أشفق يا سيدي نايت "إحاول بينوكيو
"Here there are no knights!" the ringmaster answered
"هنا لا يوجد فرسان "!أجاب مدير الحلبة
"Have pity, Commander!" Pinocchio tried

"أشفق أيها القائد "إحاول بينوكيو
"Here there are no commanders!"
"هنا لا يوجد قادة"!
"Have pity, Excellence!" Pinocchio pleaded
"أشفق ، التميز "إناشد بينوكيو
Fire-eater quite liked what he had just heard
آكل النار أحب تماما ما سمعه للتو
Excellence was something he did aspire to
كان التميز شيئا يطمح إليه
and the ringmaster began to smile again
وبدأ مدير الحلقة يبتسم مرة أخرى
and he became at once kinder and more tractable
وأصبح في الحال أكثر لطفا وأكثر قابلية للسير
Turning to Pinocchio, he asked:
التفت إلى بينوكيو ، سأل:
"Well, what do you want from me?"
"حسنا ، ماذا تريد مني؟"
"I implore you to pardon poor Harlequin"
"أناشدك أن تعفو عن المهرج المسكين"
"For him there can be no pardon"
"بالنسبة له لا يمكن أن يكون هناك عفو"
"I have spared you, if you remember"
"لقد أنقذتك ، إذا كنت تتذكر"
"so he must be put on the fire"
"لذلك يجب وضعه على النار"
"I am determined that my mutton shall be well roasted"
"أنا مصمم على أن يتم تحميص لحم الضأن جيدا"
Pinocchio stood up proudly to the ringmaster
وقف بينوكيو بفخر أمام مدير الحلبة
and he threw away his cap of bread crumb
وألقى غطاء فتات الخبز
"In that case I know my duty"
"في هذه الحالة أعرف واجبي"
"Come on, gendarmes!" he called the soldiers

"هيا أيها الدرك" إدعا الجنود
"Bind me and throw me amongst the flames"
"اربطني وارميني بين النيران"
"it would not be just for Harlequin to die for me!"
"لن يكون من العدل أن يموت المهرج من أجلي"!
"he has been a true friend to me"
"لقد كان صديقا حقيقيا لي"
Pinocchio had spoken in a loud, heroic voice
تحدث بينوكيو بصوت عال وبطولي
and his heroic actions made all the puppets cry
وأفعاله البطولية جعلت كل الدمى تبكي
Even though the gendarmes were made of wood
على الرغم من أن رجال الدرك كانوا مصنوعين من الخشب
they wept like two newly born lambs
بكوا مثل اثنين من الحملان حديثي الولادة
Fire-eater at first remained as hard and unmoved as ice
ظل آكل النار في البداية صلبا وغير متحرك مثل الجليد
but little by little he began to melt and sneeze
ولكن شيئا فشيئا بدأ يذوب ويعطس
he sneezed again four or five times
عطس مرة أخرى أربع أو خمس مرات
and he opened his arms affectionately
وفتح ذراعيه بمودة
"You are a good and brave boy!" he praised Pinocchio
"أنت فتى جيد وشجاع"! أشاد بينوكيو
"Come here and give me a kiss"
"تعال إلى هنا وأعطني قبلة"
Pinocchio ran to the ringmaster at once
ركض بينوكيو إلى مدير الحلبة في الحال
he climbed up the ringmaster's beard like a squirrel
تسلق لحية مدير الحلبة مثل السنجاب
and he deposited a hearty kiss on the point of his nose
وأودع قبلة قلبية على نقطة أنفه
"Then the pardon is granted?" asked poor Harlequin
"ثم يتم منح العفو؟" سأل المهرج المسكين

in a faint voice that was scarcely audible
بصوت خافت بالكاد كان مسموعا

"The pardon is granted!" answered Fire-Eater
"العفو ممنوح "!أجاب آكل النار

he then added, sighing and shaking his head:
ثم أضاف وهو يتنهد ويهز رأسه:

"I must have patience with my puppets!"
"يجب أن أتحلى بالصبر مع الدمى الخاصة بي"!

"Tonight I shall have to eat the mutton half raw;"
"الليلة يجب أن آكل لحم الضأن نصف نيئا ؛"

"but another time, woe to him who displeases me!"
"ولكن مرة أخرى ، ويل لمن لا يرضيني"!

At the news of the pardon the puppets all ran to the stage
في خبر العفو ، ركضت جميع الدمى إلى المسرح

they lit all the lamps and chandeliers of the show
أضاءوا جميع المصابيح والثريات في العرض

it was as if there was a full-dress performance
كان الأمر كما لو كان هناك أداء كامل

they began to leap and to dance merrily
بدأوا في القفز والرقص بمرح

when dawn had come they were still dancing
عندما طلع الفجر كانوا لا يزالون يرقصون

Pinocchio Receives Five Gold Pieces
بينوكيو يحصل على خمس قطع ذهبية

The following day Fire-eater called Pinocchio over
في اليوم التالي دعا آكل النار بينوكيو أكثر

"What is your father's name?" he asked Pinocchio
"ما هو اسم والدك؟ "سأل بينوكيو

"My father is called Geppetto," Pinocchio answered
"والدي يدعى جييبتو "، أجاب بينوكيو

"And what trade does he follow?" asked Fire-eater
"وما هي التجارة التي يتبعها؟ "سأل آكل النار

"He has no trade, he is a beggar"
"ليس لديه تجارة، إنه متسول"

"Does he earn much?" asked Fire-eater
"هل يكسب الكثير؟ "سأل آكل النار

"No, he has never a penny in his pocket"
"لا ، ليس لديه فلس واحد في جيبه"

"once he bought me a spelling-book"
"ذات مرة اشترى لي كتابا إملائيا"

"but he had to sell the only jacket he had"
"لكنه اضطر إلى بيع السترة الوحيدة التي كان لديه"

"Poor devil! I feel almost sorry for him!"
"الشيطان المسكين !أشعر بالأسف تقريبا تجاهه!"

"Here are five gold pieces for him"
"هنا خمس قطع ذهبية له"

"Go at once and take the gold to him"
"اذهب في الحال وخذ الذهب إليه"

Pinocchio was overjoyed by the present
شعر بينوكيو بسعادة غامرة بالحاضر

he thanked the ringmaster a thousand times
شكر مدير الحلبة ألف مرة

He embraced all the puppets of the company
احتضن جميع دمى الشركة

he even embraced the troop of gendarmes

حتى أنه احتضن قوات الدرك

and then he set out to return straight home

ثم انطلق للعودة مباشرة إلى المنزل

But Pinocchio didn't get very far

لكن بينوكيو لم يذهب بعيدا

on the road he met a Fox with a lame foot

على الطريق التقى ثعلب بقدم عرجاء

and he met a Cat blind in both eyes

والتقى قطة عمياء في كلتا عينيه

they were going along helping each other

كانوا يسيرون لمساعدة بعضهم البعض

they were good companions in their misfortune

كانوا رفقاء جيدين في مصيبتهم

The Fox, who was lame, walked leaning on the Cat

مشى الثعلب ، الذي كان أعرج ، متكئا على القط

and the Cat, who was blind, was guided by the Fox

والقط ، الذي كان أعمى ، كان يقوده الثعلب

the Fox greeted Pinocchio very politely

استقبل الثعلب بينوكيو بأدب شديد

"Good-day, Pinocchio," said the Fox

"يوم جيد ، بينوكيو "، قال الثعلب

"How do you come to know my name?" asked the puppet

"كيف تعرفين اسمي؟ "سألت الدمية

"I know your father well," said the fox

"أنا أعرف والدك جيدا "، قال الثعلب

"Where did you see him?" asked Pinocchio

"أين رأيته؟ "سأل بينوكيو

"I saw him yesterday, at the door of his house"

"رأيته أمس، عند باب منزله"

"And what was he doing?" asked Pinocchio

"وماذا كان يفعل؟ "سأل بينوكيو

"He was in his shirt and shivering with cold"

"كان يرتدي قميصه ويرتجف من البرد"

"Poor papa! But his suffering is over now"

"بابا المسكين !لكن معاناته انتهت الآن"

"in the future he shall shiver no more!"

"في المستقبل لن يرتجف بعد الآن"!

"Why will he shiver no more?" asked the fox

"لماذا لن يرتجف أكثر؟ "سأل الثعلب

"Because I have become a gentleman" replied Pinocchio

"لأنني أصبحت رجلا نبيلا "أجاب بينوكيو

"A gentleman—you!" said the Fox

"رجل نبيل ـ أنت "!قال الثعلب

and he began to laugh rudely and scornfully

وبدأ يضحك بوقاحة وسخرية

The Cat also began to laugh with the fox

بدأت القطة أيضا تضحك مع الثعلب

but she did better at concealing her laughter

لكنها فعلت أفضل في إخفاء ضحكتها

and she combed her whiskers with her forepaws

ومشطت شعيراتها بأقدامها الأمامية

"There is little to laugh at," cried Pinocchio angrily

"هناك القليل لتضحك عليه "، صرخ بينوكيو بغضب

"I am really sorry to make your mouth water"

"أنا آسف حقا لجعل فمك يسيل"

"if you know anything then you know what these are"

"إذا كنت تعرف أي شيء فأنت تعرف ما هي"

"you can see that they are five pieces of gold"

"يمكنك أن ترى أنها خمس قطع من الذهب"

And he pulled out the money that Fire-eater had given him

وأخرج المال الذي أعطاه له آكل النار

for a moment the fox and the cat did a strange thing

للحظة فعل الثعلب والقط شيئا غريبا

the jingling of the money really got their attention

جلجلة المال جذبت انتباههم حقا

the Fox stretched out the paw that seemed crippled

مد الثعلب المخلب الذي بدا مشلولا

and the Cat opened wide her two eyes

وفتحت القطة عينيها على مصراعيها

her eyes looked like two green lanterns

بدت عيناها مثل فانوسين أخضرين

it is true that she shut her eyes again
صحيح أنها أغمضت عينيها مرة أخرى
she was so quick that Pinocchio didn't notice
كانت سريعة جدا لدرجة أن بينوكيو لم يلاحظ
the Fox was very curious about what he had seen
كان الثعلب فضوليا جدا بشأن ما رآه
"what are you going to do with all that money?"
"ماذا ستفعل بكل هذه الأموال؟"
Pinocchio was all too proud to tell them his plans
كان بينوكيو فخورا جدا بإخبارهم بخططه
"First of all, I intend to buy a new jacket for my papa"
"بادئ ذي بدء ، أنوي شراء سترة جديدة لأبي"
"the jacket will be made of gold and silver"
"السترة ستكون مصنوعة من الذهب والفضة"
"and the coat will come with diamond buttons"
"وسيأتي المعطف بأزرار ماسية"
"and then I will buy a spelling-book for myself"

"وبعد ذلك سأشتري كتابا إملائيا لنفسي"

"You will buy a spelling book for yourself?"

"سوف تشتري كتاب تهجئة لنفسك؟"

"Yes indeed, for I wish to study in earnest"

"نعم بالفعل ، لأنني أرغب في الدراسة بجدية"

"Look at me!" said the Fox

"انظر إلي "إقال الثعلب

"Through my foolish passion for study I have lost a leg"

"من خلال شغفي الأحمق بالدراسة فقدت ساقي"

"Look at me!" said the Cat

"انظر إلي "إقال القط

"Through my foolish passion for study I have lost my eyes"

"من خلال شغفي الأحمق بالدراسة فقدت عيني"

At that moment a white Blackbird began his usual song

في تلك اللحظة بدأ الشحرور الأبيض أغنيته المعتادة

"Pinocchio, don't listen to the advice of bad companions"

"بينوكيو ، لا تستمع إلى نصيحة الصحابة السيئين"

"if you listen to their advice you will repent it!"

"إذا استمعت إلى نصائحهم فسوف تتوب عنها"!

Poor Blackbird! If only he had not spoken!

الشحرور المسكين !لو لم يتكلم!

The Cat, with a great leap, sprang upon him

القط ، مع قفزة كبيرة ، نشأت عليه

she didn't even give him time to say "Oh!"

لم تمنحه حتى الوقت ليقول" أوه"!

she ate him in one mouthful, feathers and all

أكلته في فم واحد ، ريش وكل شيء

Having eaten him, she cleaned her mouth

بعد أن أكلته ، نظفت فمها

and then she shut her eyes again

ثم أغمضت عينيها مرة أخرى

and she feigned blindness just as before

وتظاهرت بالعمى تماما كما كان من قبل

"Poor Blackbird!" said Pinocchio to the Cat

"The poor Chirper!" Pinocchio said to the cat
"الشحرور المسكين "إقال بينوكيو للقط
"why did you treat him so badly?"
"لماذا عاملته بشكل سيء للغاية؟"
"I did it to give him a lesson"
"لقد فعلت ذلك لإعطائه درسا"
"He will learn not to meddle in other people's affairs"
"سيتعلم عدم التدخل في شؤون الآخرين"
by now they had gone almost half-way home
حتى الآن كانوا قد ذهبوا إلى منتصف الطريق تقريبا إلى المنزل
the Fox, halted suddenly, and spoke to the puppet
توقف الثعلب فجأة وتحدث إلى الدمية
"Would you like to double your money?"
"هل ترغب في مضاعفة أموالك؟"
"In what way could I double my money?"
"بأي طريقة يمكنني مضاعفة أموالي؟"
"Would you like to multiply your five miserable coins?"
"هل ترغب في مضاعفة عملاتك الخمس البائسة؟"
"I would like that very much! but how?"
"أود ذلك كثيرا !لكن كيف؟"
"The way to do it is easy enough"
"طريقة القيام بذلك سهلة بما فيه الكفاية"
"Instead of returning home you must go with us"
"بدلا من العودة إلى المنزل يجب أن تذهب معنا"
"And where do you wish to take me?"
"وإلى أين تريد أن تأخذني؟"
"We will take you to the land of the Owls"
"سنأخذك إلى أرض البوم"
Pinocchio reflected a moment to think
فكر بينوكيو لحظة للتفكير
and then he said resolutely "No, I will not go"
ثم قال بحزم" لا ، لن أذهب"
"I am already close to the house"
"أنا بالفعل قريب من المنزل"
"and I will return home to my papa"

"وسأعود إلى المنزل إلى أبي"
"he has been waiting for me in the cold"
"لقد كان ينتظرني في البرد"
"all day yesterday I did not come back to him"
"طوال يوم أمس لم أعود إليه"
"Who can tell how many times he sighed!"
"من يستطيع أن يقول كم مرة تنهد"!
"I have indeed been a bad son"
"لقد كنت بالفعل ابنا سيئا"
"and the talking little cricket was right"
"وكان الكريكيت الصغير الحديث على حق"
"Disobedient boys never come to any good"
"الأولاد العصاة لا يأتون أبدا إلى أي خير."
"what the talking little cricket said is true"
"ما قاله الكريكيت الصغير الحديث صحيح"
"many misfortunes have happened to me"
"لقد حدثت لي العديد من المصائب"
"Even yesterday in fire-eater's house I took a risk"
"حتى بالأمس في منزل آكل النار خاطرت"
"Oh! it makes me shudder to think of it!"
"أوه !إيجعلني أرتجف للتفكير في الأمر!"
"Well, then," said the Fox, "you've decided to go home?"
"حسنا ، إذن ، "قال الثعلب ،" هل قررت العودة إلى المنزل؟"
"Go, then, and so much the worse for you"
"اذهب ، إذن ، والأسوأ بكثير بالنسبة لك"
"So much the worse for you!" repeated the Cat
"أسوأ بكثير بالنسبة لك "إكرر القط
"Think well of it, Pinocchio," they advised him
"فكر جيدا في الأمر ، بينوكيو "، نصحوه
"because you are giving a kick to fortune"
"لأنك تعطي ركلة للثروة"
"a kick to fortune!" repeated the Cat
"ركلة للثروة "إكرر القط
"all it would have taken would have been a day"

"كل ما كان سيتطلبه الأمر كان يوما واحدا"
"by tomorrow your five coins could have multiplied"
"بحلول الغد يمكن أن تتضاعف عملاتك الخمس عملات"
"your five coins could have become two thousand"
"كان من الممكن أن تصبح عملاتك الخمس ألفي عملة"
"Two thousand sovereigns!" repeated the Cat
"ألفي ملك "!كرر القط
"But how is it possible?" asked Pinocchio
"ولكن كيف يكون ذلك ممكنا؟" سأل بينوكيو
and he remained with his mouth open from astonishment
وبقي وفمه مفتوح من الدهشة
"I will explain it to you at once," said the Fox
"سأشرح لك ذلك على الفور "، قال الثعلب
"in the land of the Owls there is a sacred field"
"في أرض البوم يوجد حقل مقدس"
"everybody calls it the field of miracles"
"الجميع يسميه مجال المعجزات"
"In this field you must dig a little hole"
"في هذا المجال يجب عليك حفر حفرة صغيرة"
"and you must put a gold coin into the hole"
"ويجب أن تضع عملة ذهبية في الحفرة"
"then you cover up the hole with a little earth"
"ثم تغطي الحفرة بقليل من الأرض"
"you must get water from the fountain nearby"
"يجب أن تحصل على الماء من النافورة القريبة"
"you must water they hole with two pails of water"
"يجب أن تسقي ثقبا بدلاء من الماء"
"then sprinkle the hole with two pinches of salt"
"ثم يرش الحفرة بقرصتين من الملح"
"and when night comes you can go quietly to bed"
"وعندما يأتي الليل يمكنك الذهاب بهدوء إلى السرير"
"during the night the miracle will happen"
"خلال الليل ستتحدث المعجزة"
"the gold pieces you planted will grow and flower"

"القطع الذهبية التي زرعتها ستنمو وتزهر"

"and what do you think you will find in the morning?"

"وماذا تعتقد أنك ستجد في الصباح؟"

"You will find a beautiful tree where you planted it"

"ستجد شجرة جميلة حيث زرعتها"

"they tree will be laden with gold coins"

"ستكون الشجرة محملة بالعملات الذهبية"

Pinocchio grew more and more bewildered

نما بينوكيو أكثر فأكثر في حيرة

"let's suppose I bury my five coins in that field"

"لنفترض أنني دفنت عملاتي الخمس في هذا المجال"

"how many coins might I find the following morning?"

"كم عدد العملات المعدنية التي قد أجدها في صباح اليوم التالي؟"

"That is an exceedingly easy calculation," replied the Fox

"هذا حساب سهل للغاية "، أجاب الثعلب

"a calculation you can make with your hands"

"عملية حسابية يمكنك إجراؤها بيديك"

"Every coin will give you an increase of five-hundred"

"كل عملة ستمنحك زيادة قدرها خمسمائة"

"multiply five hundred by five and you have your answer"

"اضرب خمسمائة في خمسة ولديك إجابتك"

"you will find two-thousand-five-hundred shining gold pieces"

"ستجد ألفين وخمسمائة قطعة ذهبية لامعة"

"Oh! how delightful!" cried Pinocchio, dancing for joy

"أوه !كم هو ممتع "!بكى بينوكيو وهو يرقص من الفرح

"I will keep two thousand for myself"

"سأحتفظ بألفي لنفسي"

"and the other five hundred I will give you two"

"والخمسمائة الأخرى سأعطيك اثنين"

"A present to us?" cried the Fox with indignation

"هدية لنا؟ "صرخ الثعلب بسخط

and he almost appeared offended at the offer

وكاد يبدو مستاء من العرض

"What are you dreaming of?" asked the Fox

"ما الذي تحلم به؟ "سأل الثعلب

"What are you dreaming of?" repeated the Cat

"ما الذي تحلم به؟ "كرر القط

"We do not work to accumulate interest"

"نحن لا نعمل على تجميع الفائدة"

"we work solely to enrich others"

"نحن نعمل فقط لإثراء الآخرين"

"to enrich others!" repeated the Cat

"لإثراء الآخرين! "كرر القط

"What good people!" thought Pinocchio to himself

"يا له من أناس طيبين "إفكر بينوكيو في نفسه

and he forgot all about his papa and the new jacket

ونسي كل شيء عن والده والسترة الجديدة

and he forgot about the spelling-book

ونسي كتاب الإملاء

and he forgot all of his good resolutions

ونسي كل قراراته الجيدة

"Let us be off at once" he suggested

"دعونا نغادر في الحال "اقترح

"I will go with you two to the field of Owls"

"سأذهب معكما إلى حقل البوم"

The Inn of the Red Craw-Fish
ذا إن أوف ذا ريد جراد فيش

They walked, and walked, and walked

مشوا ، ومشوا ، ومشوا

all tired out, they finally arrived at an inn

كلهم متعبون ، وصلوا أخيرا إلى نزل

The Inn of The Red Craw-Fish

ذا إن أوف ذا ريد جراد فيش

"Let us stop here a little," said the Fox

"دعونا نتوقف هنا قليلا "، قال الثعلب
"we should have something to eat," he added
وأضاف» :يجب أن يكون لدينا شيء نأكله.«
"we need to rest ourselves for an hour or two"
"نحن بحاجة إلى إراحة أنفسنا لمدة ساعة أو ساعتين"
"and then we will start again at midnight"
"وبعد ذلك سنبدأ مرة أخرى في منتصف الليل"
"we'll arrive at the Field of Miracles in the morning"
"سنصل إلى ميدان المعجزات في الصباح"
Pinocchio was also tired from all the walking
كان بينوكيو متعبا أيضا من كل المشي
so he was easily convinced to go into the inn
لذلك كان مقتنعا بسهولة بالذهاب إلى النزل
all three of them sat down at a table
جلس الثلاثة على طاولة
but none of them really had any appetite
لكن لم يكن لدى أي منهم أي شهية حقا.

The Cat was suffering from indigestion
كانت القطة تعاني من عسر الهضم
and she was feeling seriously indisposed
وكانت تشعر بعدم الاستعداد بشكل خطير
she could only eat thirty-five fish with tomato sauce
يمكنها فقط أن تأكل خمسة وثلاثين سمكة مع صلصة الطماطم
and she had just four portions of noodles with Parmesan
وكان لديها أربعة حصص فقط من المعكرونة مع جبن البارميزان
but she thought the noodles weres not seasoned enough
لكنها اعتقدت أن المعكرونة لم تكن محنكة بما فيه الكفاية
so she asked three times for the butter and grated cheese!
لذلك طلبت ثلاث مرات الزبدة والجبن المبشور!
The Fox could also have gone without eating
كان من الممكن أيضا أن يذهب الثعلب دون تناول الطعام
but his doctor had ordered him a strict diet
لكن طبيبه أمره بنظام غذائي صارم
so he was forced to content himself simply with a hare
لذلك اضطر إلى الاكتفاء ببساطة بالأرنب
the hare was dressed with a sweet and sour sauce
كان الأرنب يرتدي صلصة حلوة وحامضة
it was garnished lightly with fat chickens
تم تزيينه بخفة بالدجاج السمين
then he ordered a dish of partridges and rabbits
ثم أمر طبق من الحجل والأرانب
and he also ate some frogs, lizards and other delicacies
كما أكل بعض الضفادع والسحالي وغيرها من الأطباق الشهية
he really could not eat anything else
لم يستطع حقا تناول أي شيء آخر
He cared very little for food, he said
قال إنه لم يهتم كثيرا بالطعام
and he said he struggled to put it to his lips
وقال إنه كافح لوضعها على شفتيه
The one who ate the least was Pinocchio
الشخص الذي أكل أقل كان بينوكيو
He asked for some walnuts and a hunch of bread
طلب بعض الجوز وحدس الخبز

and he left everything on his plate

وترك كل شيء على طبقه

The poor boy's thoughts were not with the food

لم تكن أفكار الصبي المسكين مع الطعام

he continually fixed his thoughts on the Field of Miracles

لقد ثبت أفكاره باستمرار في مجال المعجزات

When they had supped, the Fox spoke to the host

عندما تناولوا العشاء ، تحدث الثعلب إلى المضيف

"Give us two good rooms, dear inn-keeper"

"أعطنا غرفتين جيدتين ، عزيزي حارس النزل"

"please provide us one room for Mr. Pinocchio"

"يرجى تزويدنا بغرفة واحدة للسيد بينوكيو"

"and I will share the other room with my companion"

"وسأشارك الغرفة الأخرى مع رفيقي"

"We will snatch a little sleep before we leave"

"سنخطف القليل من النوم قبل أن نغادر"

"Remember, however, that we wish to leave at midnight"

"تذكر ، مع ذلك ، أننا نرغب في المغادرة في منتصف الليل"

"so please call us, to continue our journey"

"لذا يرجى الاتصال بنا لمواصلة رحلتنا"

"Yes, gentlemen," answered the host

"نعم أيها السادة "، أجاب المضيف

and he winked at the Fox and the Cat

وغمز في الثعلب والقط

it was as if he said "I know what you are up to"

كان الأمر كما لو أنه قال" أعرف ما الذي تنوي القيام به"

the wink seemed to say, "we understand one another!"

بدا أن الغمزة تقول ،" نحن نفهم بعضنا البعض"!

Pinocchio was very tired from the day

كان بينوكيو متعبا جدا من اليوم

he fell asleep as soon as he got into his bed

نام بمجرد دخوله سريره

and as soon as he started sleeping he started to dream

وبمجرد أن بدأ ينام بدأ يحلم

he dreamed that he was in the middle of a field

حلم أنه كان في وسط حقل

the field was full of shrubs as far as the eye could see

كان الحقل مليئا بالشجيرات بقدر ما يمكن أن تراه العين

the shrubs were covered with clusters of gold coins

كانت الشجيرات مغطاة بمجموعات من العملات الذهبية

the gold coins swung in the wind and rattled

تأرجحت العملات الذهبية في مهب الريح وهزت

and they made a sound like, "tzinn, tzinn, tzinn"

وجعلوا صوتا مثل ،" تزين ، تزين ، تزين"

they sounded as if they were speaking to Pinocchio

بدوا كما لو كانوا يتحدثون إلى بينوكيو

"Let who whoever wants to come and take us"

"من يريد أن يأتي ويأخذنا"

Pinocchio was just about to stretch out his hand

كان بينوكيو على وشك مد يده

he was going to pick handfuls of those beautiful gold pieces

كان سيختار حفنة من تلك القطع الذهبية الجميلة

and he almost was able to put them in his pocket

وكاد أن يضعها في جيبه

but he was suddenly awakened by three knocks on the door

لكنه استيقظ فجأة على ثلاث طرق على الباب

It was the host who had come to wake him up

كان المضيف هو الذي جاء لإيقاظه

"I have come to let you know it's midnight"

"لقد جئت لأخبرك أنه منتصف الليل"

"Are my companions ready?" asked the puppet

"هل رفاقي مستعدون؟" سألت الدمية

"Ready! Why, they left two hours ago"

"جاهز !لماذا، غادروا قبل ساعتين"

"Why were they in such a hurry?"

"لماذا كانوا في عجلة من أمرهم؟"

"Because the Cat had received a message"

"لأن القطة تلقت رسالة"

"she got news that her eldest kitten was ill"

"تلقت أخبارا تفيد بأن قطتها الكبرى مريضة"

"Did they pay for the supper?"

"هل دفعوا ثمن العشاء؟"

"What are you thinking of?"

"ما الذي تفكر فيه؟"

"They are too well educated to dream of insulting you"

"إنهم متعلمون جيدا لدرجة أنهم لا يحلمون بإهانتك"

"a gentleman like you would not let his friends pay"

"رجل نبيل مثلك لن يسمح لأصدقائه بالدفع"

"What a pity!" thought Pinocchio

"يا للأسف" إفكر بينوكيو

"such an insult would have given me much pleasure!"

"مثل هذه الإهانة كانت ستمنحني الكثير من المتعة"!

"And where did my friends say they would wait for me?"

"وأين قال أصدقائي إنهم سينتظرونني؟"

"At the Field of Miracles, tomorrow morning at daybreak"

"في ميدان المعجزات ، صباح الغد عند الفجر"

Pinocchio paid a coin for the supper of his companions

دفع بينوكيو عملة معدنية لعشاء رفاقه

and then he left for the field of Miracles

ثم غادر إلى مجال المعجزات

Outside the inn it was almost pitch black

خارج النزل كان الظلام تقريبا

Pinocchio could only make progress by groping his way

لم يستطع بينوكيو إحراز تقدم إلا من خلال تلمس طريقه

it was impossible to see his hand's in front of him

كان من المستحيل رؤية يده أمامه

Some night-birds flew across the road

طارت بعض الطيور الليلية عبر الطريق

they brushed Pinocchio's nose with their wings

قاموا بتنظيف أنف بينوكيو بأجنحتهم

it caused him a terrible fright

تسبب له خوفا رهيبا

springing back, he shouted: "who goes there?"

عاد إلى الوراء ، صرخ" :من يذهب إلى هناك؟"

and the echo in the hills repeated in the distance

ويتكرر الصدى في التلال في المسافة
"Who goes there?" - "Who goes there?" - "Who goes there?"
"من يذهب إلى هناك؟" - "من يذهب إلى هناك؟" - "من يذهب إلى هناك؟"
on the trunk of the tree he saw a little light
على جذع الشجرة رأى القليل من الضوء
it was a little insect he saw shining dimly
كانت حشرة صغيرة رآها مشرقة بشكل خافت
like a night-light in a lamp of transparent china
مثل ضوء الليل في مصباح من الصين الشفافة
"Who are you?" asked Pinocchio
"من أنت؟ "سأل بينوكيو
the insect answered in a low voice;
أجابت الحشرة بصوت منخفض.
"I am the ghost of the talking little cricket"
"أنا شبح الكريكيت الصغير الناطق"
the voice was fainter than can be described
كان الصوت خافتا مما يمكن وصفه
the voice seemed to come from the other world
بدا أن الصوت يأتي من العالم الآخر
"What do you want with me?" said the puppet
"ماذا تريد معي؟ "قالت الدمية
"I want to give you some advice"
"أريد أن أقدم لك بعض النصائح"
"Go back and take the four coins that you have left"
"عد وخذ العملات المعدنية الأربعة التي تركتها"
"take your coins to your poor father"
"خذ عملاتك المعدنية إلى والدك المسكين"
"he is weeping and in despair at home"
"إنه يبكي ويأس في المنزل"
"because you have not returned to him"
"لأنك لم تعد إليه"
but Pinocchio had already thought of this
لكن بينوكيو كان قد فكر بالفعل في هذا
"By tomorrow my papa will be a gentleman"
"بحلول الغد سيكون بابا رجلا نبيلا"

"these four coins will become two thousand"

"هذه العملات الأربع ستصبح ألفي عملة"

"Don't trust those who promise to make you rich in a day"

"لا تثق في أولئك الذين يعدونك بجعلك ثريا في يوم واحد"

"Usually they are either mad or rogues!"

"عادة ما يكونون إما مجانين أو مارقين"!

"Give ear to me, and go back, my boy"

"أعطني أذنا ، وارجع يا ولدي"

"On the contrary, I am determined to go on"

"على العكس من ذلك ، أنا مصمم على الاستمرار"

"The hour is late!" said the cricket

"الساعة متأخرة "إقال الكريكيت

"I am determined to go on"

"أنا مصمم على الاستمرار"

"The night is dark!" said the cricket

"الليل مظلم "إقال الكريكيت

"I am determined to go on"

"أنا مصمم على الاستمرار"

"The road is dangerous!" said the cricket

"الطريق خطير "إقال الكريكيت

"I am determined to go on"

"أنا مصمم على الاستمرار"

"boys are bent on following their wishes"

"الأولاد عازمون على اتباع رغباتهم"

"but remember, sooner or later they repent it"

"لكن تذكر ، عاجلا أم آجلا يتوبون عنها"

"Always the same stories. Good-night, little cricket"

"دائما نفس القصص. تصبح على خير ، لعبة الكريكيت الصغيرة"

The Cricket wished Pinocchio a good night too

تمنى الكريكيت لبينوكيو ليلة سعيدة أيضا

"may Heaven preserve you from dangers and assassins"

"الله يحفظكم من الأخطار والقتلة"

then the talking little cricket vanished suddenly

ثم اختفى الكريكيت الصغير المتكلم فجأة

like a light that has been blown out
مثل الضوء الذي تم تفجيره
and the road became darker than ever
وأصبح الطريق أكثر قتامة من أي وقت مضى

Pinocchio Falls into the Hands of the Assassins
بينوكيو يقع في أيدي القتلة

Pinocchio resumed his journey and spoke to himself
استأنف بينوكيو رحلته وتحدث إلى نفسه
"how unfortunate we poor boys are"
"كم نحن الأولاد الفقراء مؤسفون"
"Everybody scolds us and gives us good advice"
"الجميع يوبخنا ويعطينا نصيحة جيدة"
"but I don't choose to listen to that tiresome little cricket"
"لكنني لا أختار الاستماع إلى لعبة الكريكيت الصغيرة المملة"
"who knows how many misfortunes are to happen to me!"
"من يدري كم من المصائب ستحدث لي"!
"I haven't even met any assassins yet!"
"لم أقابل حتى أي قتلة حتى الآن"!
"That is, however, of little consequence"
"هذا ، مع ذلك ، ليس له عواقب تذكر"
"for I don't believe in assassins"
"لأني لا أؤمن بالقتلة"
"I have never believed in assassins"
"لم أؤمن أبدا بالقتلة"
"I think that assassins have been invented purposely"
"أعتقد أن القتلة قد اخترعوا عمدا"
"papas use them to frighten little boys"
"باباس يستخدمونها لتخويف الأولاد الصغار"
"and then little boys are scared of going out at night"
"ثم يخاف الأولاد الصغار من الخروج ليلا".
"Anyway, let's suppose I was to come across assassins"

"على أي حال ، لنفترض أنني صادفت قتلة"
"do you imagine they would frighten me?"
"هل تتخيل أنهم سيخيفونني؟"
"they would not frighten me in the least"
"لن يخيفونني على الأقل"
"I will go to meet them and call to them"
"سأذهب لمقابلتهم وأتصل بهم"
'Gentlemen assassins, what do you want with me?'
"أيها السادة القتلة ، ماذا تريد معي؟"
'Remember that with me there is no joking'
"تذكر أنه معي لا يوجد مزاح"
'Therefore, go about your business and be quiet!'
"لذلك ، اذهب إلى عملك وكن هادئا"!
"At this speech they would run away like the wind"
"في هذا الخطاب كانوا يهربون مثل الريح"
"it could be that they are badly educated assassins"
"يمكن أن يكونوا قتلة متعلمين تعليما سيئا"
"then the assassins might not run away"
"ثم قد لا يهرب القتلة"
"but even that isn't a great problem"
"لكن حتى هذه ليست مشكلة كبيرة"
"then I would just run away myself"
"ثم سأهرب"
"and that would be the end of that"
"وستكون هذه نهاية ذلك"
But Pinocchio had no time to finish his reasoning
لكن بينوكيو لم يكن لديه الوقت لإنهاء تفكيره
he thought that he heard a slight rustle of leaves
اعتقد أنه سمع حفيفا طفيفا من الأوراق
He turned to look where the noise had come from
التفت لينظر من أين أتى الضجيج
and he saw in the gloom two evil-looking black figures
ورأى في الكآبة شخصيتين سوداوين شريرة المظهر
they were completely enveloped in charcoal sacks

كانت مغلفة بالكامل بأكياس الفحم

They were running after him on their tiptoes

كانوا يركضون وراءه على أطراف أصابعهم

and they were making great leaps like two phantoms

وكانوا يحققون قفزات كبيرة مثل اثنين من الأشباح

"Here they are in reality!" he said to himself

"ها هم في الواقع "إقال لنفسه

he didn't have anywhere to hide his gold pieces

لم يكن لديه مكان لإخفاء قطعه الذهبية

so he put them in his mouth, under his tongue

فوضعهم في فمه ، تحت لسانه

Then he turned his attention to escaping

ثم حول انتباهه إلى الهروب

But he did not manage to get very far

لكنه لم يتمكن من الذهاب بعيدا

he felt himself seized by the arm

شعر بنفسه ممسكا بذراعه

- 83 -

and he heard two horrid voices threatening him
وسمع صوتين فظيعين يهددانه

"Your money or your life!" they threatened
"أموالك أو حياتك "إهددوا

Pinocchio was not able to answer in words
لم يكن بينوكيو قادرا على الإجابة بالكلمات

because he had put his money in his mouth
لأنه وضع ماله في فمه

so he made a thousand low bows
لذلك صنع ألف قوس منخفض

and he offered a thousand pantomimes
وقدم ألف بانتوميم

He tried to make the two figures understand
حاول أن يجعل الشخصين يفهمان

he was just a poor puppet without any money
لقد كان مجرد دمية فقيرة بدون أي مال

he had not as much as a nickel in his pocket
لم يكن لديه الكثير من النيكل في جيبه

but the two robbers were not convinced
لكن اللصوص لم يقتنعا

"Less nonsense and out with the money!"
"أقل هراء والخروج بالمال"!

And the puppet made a gesture with his hands
وقام الدمية بإيماءة بيديه

he pretended to turn his pockets inside out
تظاهر بقلب جيوبه من الداخل إلى الخارج

Of course Pinocchio didn't have any pockets
بالطبع لم يكن لدى بينوكيو أي جيوب

but he was trying to signify, "I have no money"
لكنه كان يحاول أن يشير ،" ليس لدي مال"

slowly the robbers were losing their patience
ببطء بدأ اللصوص يفقدون صبرهم

"Deliver up your money or you are dead," said the taller one
"سلم أموالك أو أنت ميت "، قال الأطول

"Dead!" repeated the smaller one
"ميت "!إكرر الأصغر

"And then we will also kill your father!"

"وبعد ذلك سنقتل والدك أيضا"!

"Also your father!" repeated the smaller one again

"أيضا والدك !"كرر الأصغر مرة أخرى

"No, no, no, not my poor papa!" cried Pinocchio in despair

"لا ، لا ، لا ، ليس بابا المسكين "!صرخ بينوكيو في يأس

and as he said it the coins clinked in his mouth

وكما قال ذلك ، ارتطمت العملات المعدنية في فمه

"Ah! you rascal!" realized the robbers

"آه !أيها الوغد "!أدرك اللصوص

"you have hidden your money under your tongue!"

"لقد أخفيت أموالك تحت لسانك"!

"Spit it out at once!" he ordered him

"ابصقها في الحال "!أمره

"spit it out," repeated the smaller one

"ابصقها "، كرر الأصغر

Pinocchio was obstinate to their commands

كان بينوكيو عنيدا لأوامرهم

"Ah! you pretend to be deaf, do you?"

"آه !أنت تتظاهر بالصمم ، أليس كذلك؟

"leave it to us to find a means"

"اترك الأمر لنا لإيجاد وسيلة"

"we will find a way to make you give up your money"

"سنجد طريقة لجعلك تتخلى عن أموالك"

"We will find a way," repeated the smaller one

"سنجد طريقة "، كرر الأصغر

And one of them seized the puppet by his nose

واستولى أحدهم على الدمية من أنفه

and the other took him by the chin

وأخذه الآخر من ذقنه

and they began to pull brutally

وبدأوا في الانسحاب بوحشية

one pulled up and the other pulled down

سحب واحد لأعلى والآخر سحب لأسفل

they tried to force him to open his mouth

حاولوا إجباره على فتح فمه
But it was all to no purpose
لكن كل ذلك لم يكن له أي غرض
Pinocchio's mouth seemed to be nailed together
بدا فم بينوكيو مسمرا معا
Then the shorter assassin drew out an ugly knife
ثم أخرج القاتل الأقصر سكينا قبيحا
and he tried to put it between his lips
وحاول أن يضعها بين شفتيه
But Pinocchio, as quick as lightning, caught his hand
لكن بينوكيو ، بسرعة البرق ، أمسك بيده
and he bit him with his teeth
وعضه بأسنانه
and with one bite he bit the hand clean off
وبعضة واحدة قام بتنظيف اليد
but it wasn't a hand that he spat out
لكنها لم تكن يدا بصق بها
it was hairier than a hand, and had claws
كان أكثر شعرا من اليد ، وكان له مخالب
imagine Pinocchio's astonishment when saw a cat's paw
تخيل دهشة بينوكيو عندما رأى مخلب قطة
or at least that's what he thought he saw
أو على الأقل هذا ما اعتقد أنه رآه
Pinocchio was encouraged by this first victory
شجع بينوكيو بهذا الانتصار الأول
now he used his fingernails to break free
الآن استخدم أظافره للتحرر
he succeeded in liberating himself from his assailants
نجح في تحرير نفسه من مهاجميه
he jumped over the hedge by the roadside
قفز فوق السياج على جانب الطريق
and began to run across the fields
وبدأت في الجري عبر الحقول
The assassins ran after him like two dogs chasing a hare
ركض القتلة وراءه مثل كلبين يطاردان الأرنب
and the one who had lost a paw ran on one leg

والشخص الذي فقد مخلبا ركض على ساق واحدة
and no one ever knew how he managed it
ولم يعرف أحد كيف تمكن من إدارتها
After a race of some miles Pinocchio could run no more
بعد سباق دام بضعة أميال ، لم يعد بإمكان بينوكيو الركض
he thought his situation was lost
كان يعتقد أن وضعه قد ضاع
he climbed the trunk of a very high pine tree
تسلق جذع شجرة صنوبر عالية جدا
and he seated himself in the topmost branches
وجلس في أعلى الفروع
The assassins attempted to climb after him
حاول القتلة التسلق وراءه
when they reached half-way up the tree they slid down again
عندما وصلوا إلى منتصف الطريق إلى أعلى الشجرة انزلقوا مرة أخرى
and they arrived on the ground with their skin grazed
ووصلوا إلى الأرض مع جلدهم يرعى
But they didn't give up so easily
لكنهم لم يستسلموا بسهولة
they piled up some dry wood beneath the pine
كدسوا بعض الخشب الجاف تحت الصنوبر
and then they set fire to the wood
ثم أضرموا النار في الخشب
very quickly the pine began to burn higher
بسرعة كبيرة بدأ الصنوبر يحترق أعلى
like a candle blown by the wind
مثل شمعة تهب عليها الريح
Pinocchio saw the flames rising higher and higher
رأى بينوكيو ألسنة اللهب ترتفع أعلى وأعلى
he did not wish to end his life like a roasted pigeon
لم يرغب في إنهاء حياته مثل حمامة مشوية
so he made a stupendous leap from the top of the tree
لذلك قام بقفزة هائلة من أعلى الشجرة
and he ran across the fields and vineyards
وركض عبر الحقول وكروم العنب

The assassins followed him again

تبعه القتلة مرة أخرى

and they kept behind him without giving up

وظلوا وراءه دون أن يستسلموا

The day began to break and they were still pursuing him

بدأ اليوم ينكسر وكانوا لا يزالون يلاحقونه

Suddenly Pinocchio found his way barred by a ditch

فجأة وجد بينوكيو طريقه مسدودا بخندق

it was full of stagnant water the colour of coffee

كانت مليئة بالمياه الراكدة بلون القهوة

What was our Pinocchio to do now?

ماذا كان بينوكيو لدينا أن يفعل الآن؟

"One! two! three!" cried the puppet

"واحد !اثنان !ثلاثة "إصرخت الدمية

making a rush, he sprang to the other side

اندفع ، انطلق إلى الجانب الآخر

The assassins also tried to jump over the ditch

حاول القتلة أيضا القفز فوق الخندق

but they had not measured the distance

لكنهم لم يقيسوا المسافة

splish splash! they fell into the middle of the ditch

سبلاش دفقة !سقطوا في منتصف الخندق

Pinocchio heard the plunge and the splashing
سمع بينوكيو الغطس والرش
"A fine bath to you, gentleman assassins"
"حمام جيد لك ، القتلة النبيل"
And he felt convinced that they were drowned
وشعر بالاقتناع بأنهم غرقوا
but it's good that Pinocchio did look behind him
لكن من الجيد أن بينوكيو نظر خلفه
because his two assassins had not drowned
لأن قاتليه لم يغرقا
the two assassins had got out the water again
خرج القاتلان من الماء مرة أخرى
and they were both still running after him
وكانا لا يزالان يركضان وراءه
they were still enveloped in their sacks
كانوا لا يزالون مغلفين في أكياسهم
and the water was dripping from them
وكان الماء يقطر منهم
as if they had been two hollow baskets
كما لو كانا سلتين مجوفتين

The Assassins Hang Pinocchio to the Big Oak Tree
القتلة يعلقون بينوكيو على شجرة البلوط الكبيرة

At this sight, the puppet's courage failed him
في هذا المنظر ، خذلته شجاعة الدمية
he was on the point of throwing himself on the ground
كان على وشك إلقاء نفسه على الأرض
and he wanted to give himself over for lost
وأراد أن يسلم نفسه للضياع
he turned his eyes in every direction
أدار عينيه في كل اتجاه
he saw a small house as white as snow
رأى منزلا صغيرا أبيض مثل الثلج

"If only I had breath to reach that house"
"لو كان لدي نفس للوصول إلى هذا المنزل"
"perhaps then I might be saved"
"ربما بعد ذلك قد أخلص"
without delaying an instant he recommenced running
دون تأخير لحظة استأنف الجري
poor little Pinocchio was running for his life
كان بينوكيو الصغير المسكين يركض للنجاة بحياته
he ran through the wood with the assassins after him
ركض عبر الغابة مع القتلة من بعده
there was a desperate race of nearly two hours
كان هناك سباق يائس لمدة ساعتين تقريبا
and finally he arrived quite breathless at the door
وأخيرا وصل لاهثا تماما عند الباب
he desperately knocked on the door of the house
طرق باب المنزل بيأس
but no one answered Pinocchio's knock
لكن لم يرد أحد على ضربة بينوكيو
He knocked at the door again with great violence
طرق الباب مرة أخرى بعنف شديد
because he heard the sound of steps approaching him
لأنه سمع صوت خطوات تقترب منه
and he heard the the heavy panting of his persecutors
وسمع اللهاث الثقيل لمضطهديه
there was the same silence as before
كان هناك نفس الصمت كما كان من قبل
he saw that knocking was useless
رأى أن الطرق كان عديم الفائدة
so he began in desperation to kick and pommel the door
لذلك بدأ في يأس لركل الباب وضربه
The window next to the door then opened
ثم فتحت النافذة المجاورة للباب
and a beautiful Child appeared at the window
وظهر طفل جميل عند النافذة
the beautiful child had blue hair
كان للطفل الجميل شعر أزرق

and her face was as white as a waxen image

وكان وجهها أبيض مثل صورة شمعية

her eyes were closed as if she was asleep

كانت عيناها مغمضتين كما لو كانت نائمة

and her hands were crossed on her breast

وعبرت يديها على صدرها

Without moving her lips in the least, she spoke

دون أن تحرك شفتيها على الأقل ، تحدثت

"In this house there is no one, they are all dead"

"في هذا المنزل لا يوجد أحد، كلهم ماتوا"

and her voice seemed to come from the other world

وبدا صوتها وكأنه يأتي من العالم الآخر

but Pinocchio shouted and cried and implored

لكن بينوكيو صرخ وبكى وتوسل

"Then at least open the door for me"

"ثم على الأقل افتح الباب لي"

"I am also dead," said the waxen image

"أنا أيضا ميت "، قالت الصورة الشمعية

"Then what are you doing there at the window?"

"إذن ماذا تفعل هناك عند النافذة؟"

"I am waiting to be taken away"

"أنا في انتظار أن يؤخذ بعيدا"

Having said this she immediately disappeared

بعد قولي هذا اختفت على الفور

and the window was closed again without the slightest noise

وتم إغلاق النافذة مرة أخرى دون أدنى ضوضاء

"Oh! beautiful Child with blue hair," cried Pinocchio"

"أوه! طفل جميل ذو شعر أزرق«، بكى بينوكيو«

"open the door, for pity's sake!"

"افتح الباب من أجل الشفقة"!

"Have compassion on a poor boy pursued..."

"ارحم صبيا فقيرا مطاردا"...

But he could not finish the sentence

لكنه لم يستطع إنهاء الجملة

because he felt himself seized by the collar

لأنه شعر بنفسه مأخوذا من ذوي الياقات البيضاء
the same two horrible voices said to him threateningly:
نفس الصوتين الرهيبين قالا له مهددا:
"You shall not escape from us again!"
"لن تهرب منا مرة أخرى"!
"You shall not escape," panted the little assassin
"لن تهرب "، يلهث القاتل الصغير
The puppet saw death was staring him in the face
رأت الدمية الموت يحدق به في وجهه
he was taken with a violent fit of trembling
تم أخذه بنوبة ارتعاش عنيفة
the joints of his wooden legs began to creak
بدأت مفاصل ساقيه الخشبية في الصرير
and the coins hidden under his tongue began to clink
وبدأت العملات المخبأة تحت لسانه في الخفقان
"will you open your mouth—yes or no?" demanded the assassins
"هل ستفتح فمك - نعم أم لا؟" طالب القتلة
"Ah! no answer? Leave it to us"
"آه !لا جواب؟ اتركوا الأمر لنا"
"this time we will force you to open it!"
"هذه المرة سنجبرك على فتحه"!
"we will force you," repeated the second assassin
"سنجبرك "، كرر القاتل الثاني
And they drew out two long, horrid knives
وأخرجوا سكينين طويلين فظيعين
and the knives were as sharp as razors
وكانت السكاكين حادة مثل شفرات الحلاقة
they attempted to stab him twice
حاولوا طعنه مرتين
but the puppet was lucky in one regard
لكن الدمية كانت محظوظة من ناحية واحدة
he had been made from very hard wood
كان مصنوعا من خشب صلب جدا
the knives broke into a thousand pieces

اقتحمت السكاكين ألف قطعة
and the assassins were left with just the handles
وترك القتلة مع المقابض فقط
for a moment they could only stare at each other
للحظة كان بإمكانهم فقط التحديق في بعضهم البعض
"I see what we must do," said one of them
"أرى ما يجب أن نفعله"، قال أحدهم.
"He must be hung! Let us hang him!"
"يجب أن يتم تعليقه !دعونا نشنقه"!
"Let us hang him!" repeated the other
"دعونا نشنقه "!كرر الآخر
Without loss of time they tied his arms behind him
دون ضياع الوقت ربطوا ذراعيه خلفه
and they passed a running noose round his throat
ومروا حبل المشنقة حول حلقه
and they hung him to the branch of the Big Oak
وعلقوه إلى فرع البلوط الكبير
They then sat down on the grass watching Pinocchio
ثم جلسوا على العشب يشاهدون بينوكيو
and they waited for his struggle to end
وانتظروا انتهاء كفاحه
but three hours had already passed
ولكن مرت ثلاث ساعات بالفعل
the puppet's eyes were still open
كانت عيون الدمية لا تزال مفتوحة
his mouth was closed just as before
كان فمه مغلقا تماما كما كان من قبل
and he was kicking more than ever
وكان يركل أكثر من أي وقت مضى
they had finally lost their patience with him
لقد فقدوا صبرهم معه أخيرا
they turned to Pinocchio and spoke in a bantering tone
التفتوا إلى بينوكيو وتحدثوا بنبرة مزاح
"Good-bye Pinocchio, see you again tomorrow"
"وداعا بينوكيو ، أراك مرة أخرى غدا"
"hopefully you'll be kind enough to be dead"

"آمل أن تكون لطيفا بما يكفي لتكون ميتا"
"and hopefully you will have your mouth wide open"
"ونأمل أن يكون فمك مفتوحا على مصراعيه"
And they walked off in a different direction
وساروا في اتجاه مختلف
In the meantime a northerly wind began to blow and roar
في غضون ذلك بدأت رياح شمالية تهب وتهدر
and the wind beat the poor puppet from side to side
وضربت الريح الدمية المسكينة من جانب إلى آخر

the wind made him swing about violently
جعلته الريح يتأرجح بعنف
like the clatter of a bell ringing for a wedding
مثل قعقعة جرس يرن لحضور حفل زفاف
And the swinging gave him atrocious spasms

وأعطاه التأرجح تشنجات فظيعة

and the noose became tighter and tighter around his throat

وأصبح الخناق أكثر إحكاما وإحكاما حول حلقه

and finally it took away his breath

وأخيرا أخذ أنفاسه

Little by little his eyes began to grow dim

شيئا فشيئا بدأت عيناه تصبح خافتة

he felt that death was near

شعر أن الموت كان قريبا

but Pinocchio never gave up hope

لكن بينوكيو لم يفقد الأمل أبدا

"perhaps some charitable person will come to my assistance"

"ربما يأتي شخص خيري لمساعدتي"

But he waited and waited and waited

لكنه انتظر وانتظر وانتظر

and in the end no one came, absolutely no one

وفي النهاية لم يأت أحد ، لا أحد على الإطلاق

then he remembered his poor father

ثم تذكر والده المسكين

thinking he was dying, he stammered out

معتقدا أنه كان يحتضر ، تلعثم

"Oh, papa! papa! if only you were here!"

"أوه ، بابا إبابا إلو كنت هنا فقط"!

His breath failed him and he could say no more

خذلته أنفاسه ولم يستطع أن يقول أكثر من ذلك

He shut his eyes and opened his mouth

أغمض عينيه وفتح فمه

and he stretched out his arms and legs

ومد ذراعيه وساقيه

he gave one final long shudder

أعطى قشعريرة طويلة أخيرة

and then he hung stiff and insensible

ثم قاسية وغير حساسة

The Beautiful Child Rescues the Puppet
الطفل الجميل ينقذ الدمية

poor Pinocchio was still suspended from the Big Oak tree
كان بينوكيو المسكين لا يزال معلقا من شجرة البلوط الكبيرة
but apparently Pinocchio was more dead than alive
ولكن يبدو أن بينوكيو كان ميتا أكثر من كونه حيا
the beautiful Child with blue hair came to the window again
جاء الطفل الجميل ذو الشعر الأزرق إلى النافذة مرة أخرى
she saw the unhappy puppet hanging by his throat
رأت الدمية التعيسة معلقة من حلقه
she saw him dancing up and down in the gusts of the wind
رأته يرقص صعودا وهبوطا في هبوب الريح
and she was moved by compassion for him
وقد تأثرت بالشفقة عليه
the beautiful child struck her hands together
ضربت الطفلة الجميلة يديها معا
and she gave three little claps
وأعطت ثلاث تصفيقات صغيرة
there came a sound of wings flying rapidly
جاء صوت أجنحة تحلق بسرعة
a large Falcon flew on to the window-sill
طار صقر كبير إلى عتبة النافذة

"What are your orders, gracious Fairy?" he asked
"ما هي أوامرك ، الجنية الكريمة؟" "سأل

and he inclined his beak in sign of reverence
ويميل منقاره في علامة الخشوع

"Do you see that puppet dangling from the Big Oak tree?"
"هل ترى تلك الدمية تتدلى من شجرة البلوط الكبيرة؟"

"I see him," confirmed the falcon
«أنا أراه»، أكد الصقر

"Fly over to him at once," she ordered him
"سافر إليه في الحال "، أمرته

"use your strong beak to break the knot"
"استخدم منقارك القوي لكسر العقدة"

"lay him gently on the grass at the foot of the tree"
"ضعه برفق على العشب عند سفح الشجرة"

The Falcon flew away to carry out his orders
طار الصقر بعيدا لتنفيذ أوامره

and after two minutes he returned to the child
وبعد دقيقتين عاد إلى الطفل

"I have done as you commanded"
"لقد فعلت كما أمرت"

"And how did you find him?"
"وكيف وجدته؟"

"when I first saw him he appeared dead"
"عندما رأيته لأول مرة بدا ميتا"

"but he couldn't really have been entirely dead"
"لكنه لم يكن من الممكن أن يكون ميتا تماما"

"I loosened the noose around his throat"
"لقد خففت حبل المشنقة حول حلقه"

"and then he gave soft a sigh"
"ثم تنهد ناعما"

"he muttered to me in a faint voice"
"تمتم لي بصوت خافت"

"'Now I feel better!' he said"

"الآن أشعر بتحسن "إقال"

The Fairy then struck her hands together twice

ثم ضربت الجنية يديها معا مرتين

as soon as she did this a magnificent Poodle appeared

بمجرد أن فعلت هذا ظهر رائع

the poodle walked upright on his hind legs

مشى القلطي منتصبا على رجليه الخلفيتين

it was exactly as if he had been a man

كان الأمر تماما كما لو كان رجلا

He was in the full-dress livery of a coachman

كان يرتدي كسوة كاملة لمدرب

On his head he had a three-cornered cap braided with gold

على رأسه كان لديه قبعة ثلاثية الزوايا مضفرة بالذهب

his curly white wig came down on to his shoulders

نزل شعر مستعار أبيض مجعد على كتفيه

he had a chocolate-collared waistcoat with diamond buttons

كان لديه صدرية بياقة شوكولاتة مع أزرار ماسية

and he had two large pockets to contain bones

وكان لديه جيبان كبيران لاحتواء العظام

the bones that his mistress gave him at dinner

العظام التي أعطتها له عشيقته في العشاء

he also had a pair of short crimson velvet breeches

كان لديه أيضا زوج من المؤخرات المخملية القرمزية القصيرة

and he wore some silk stockings

وكان يرتدي بعض الجوارب الحريرية

and he wore smart Italian leather shoes

وكان يرتدي أحذية جلدية إيطالية أنيقة

hanging behind him was a species of umbrella case

شنقا خلفه كان نوعا من حالة مظلة

the umbrella case was made of blue satin

كانت العلبة المظلة مصنوعة من الساتان الأزرق

he put his tail into it when the weather was rainy

وضع ذيله فيه عندما كان الطقس ممطرا

"Be quick, Medoro, like a good dog!"

"كن سريعا ، ميدورو ، مثل جيد"!

and the fairy gave her poodle the commands

وأعطت الجنية كلبها الأوامر
"get the most beautiful carriage harnessed"
"الحصول على أجمل عربة تسخير"
"and have the carriage waiting in my coach-house"
"وجعل العربة تنتظر في منزل المدرب الخاص بي"
"and go along the road to the forest"
"والذهاب على طول الطريق إلى الغابة"
"When you come to the Big Oak tree you will find a poor puppet"
"عندما تأتي إلى شجرة البلوط الكبيرة ستجد دمية فقيرة"
"he will be stretched on the grass half dead"
"سوف يتمدد على العشب نصف ميت"
"you will have to pick him up gently"
"سيكون عليك اصطحابه برفق"
"lay him flat on the cushions of the carriage"
"ضعه مسطحا على وسائد العربة"
"when you have done this bring him here to me"
"عندما تفعل هذا أحضره إلي هنا"
"Do you understand?" she asked one last time
"هل تفهم؟ "سألت مرة أخيرة
The Poodle showed that he had understood
أظهر القلطي أنه قد فهم
he shook the case of blue satin three or four times
هز علبة الساتان الأزرق ثلاث أو أربع مرات
and then he ran off like a race-horse
ثم هرب مثل حصان السباق
soon a beautiful carriage came out of the coach-house
سرعان ما خرجت عربة جميلة من بيت الحافلات
The cushions were stuffed with canary feathers
كانت الوسائد محشوة بريش الكناري
the carriage was lined on the inside with whipped cream
كانت العربة مبطنة من الداخل بالكريمة المخفوقة
and custard and vanilla wafers made the seating
وصنع الكاسترد ورقائق الفانيليا الجلوس
The little carriage was drawn by a hundred white mice

تم رسم العربة الصغيرة بواسطة مائة فأر أبيض

and the Poodle was seated on the coach-box

وكان القلطي جالسا على صندوق الحافلات

he cracked his whip from side to side

كسر سوطه من جانب إلى آخر

like a driver when he is afraid that he is behind time

مثل السائق عندما يخاف من أنه متأخر عن الزمن

less than a quarter of an hour passed

مرت أقل من ربع ساعة

and the carriage returned to the house

وعادت العربة إلى المنزل

The Fairy was waiting at the door of the house

كانت الجنية تنتظر عند باب المنزل

she took the poor puppet in her arms

أخذت الدمية المسكينة بين ذراعيها

and she carried him into a little room

وحملته إلى غرفة صغيرة

the room was wainscoted with mother-of-pearl

كانت الغرفة مزينة بعرق اللؤلؤ

she called for the most famous doctors in the neighbourhood

دعت أشهر الأطباء في الحي

They came immediately, one after the other

جاءوا على الفور ، واحدا تلو الآخر

a Crow, an Owl, and a talking little cricket

غراب وبومة وكريكيت صغير يتحدث

"I wish to know something from you, gentlemen," said the Fairy

"أتمنى أن أعرف شيئا منكم ، أيها السادة "، قالت الجنية

"is this unfortunate puppet alive or dead?"

"هل هذه الدمية المؤسفة حية أم ميتة؟"

the Crow started by feeling Pinocchio's pulse

بدأ الغراب بالشعور بنبض بينوكيو

he then felt his nose and his little toe

ثم شعر بأنفه وإصبع قدمه الصغير

he carefully made his diagnosis of the puppet

قام بعناية بتشخيصه للدمية

and then he solemnly pronounced the following words:
ثم نطق رسميا الكلمات التالية:

"To my belief the puppet is already dead"
"في اعتقادي أن الدمية قد ماتت بالفعل"

"but there is always the chance he's still alive"
"ولكن هناك دائما احتمال أنه لا يزال على قيد الحياة"

"I regret," said the Owl, "to contradict the Crow"
قالت البومة" :يؤسفني أن أتناقض مع الغراب"

"my illustrious friend and colleague"
"صديقي وزميلي اللامع"

"in my opinion the puppet is still alive"
"في رأيي الدمية لا تزال على قيد الحياة"

"but there's always a chance he's already dead"
"ولكن هناك دائما احتمال أن يكون قد مات بالفعل"

lastly the Fairy asked the talking little Cricket
أخيرا ، سألت الجنية لعبة الكريكيت الصغيرة الناطقة

"And you, have you nothing to say?"
"وأنت ، أليس لديك ما تقوله؟"

"doctors are not always called upon to speak"
"لا يطلب من الأطباء دائما التحدث"

"sometimes the wisest thing is to be silent"
"في بعض الأحيان يكون الشيء الأكثر حكمة هو الصمت"

"but let me tell you what I know"
"لكن دعني أخبرك بما أعرفه"

"that puppet has a face that is not new to me"
"تلك الدمية لها وجه ليس جديدا بالنسبة لي"

"I have known him for some time!"
"لقد عرفته لبعض الوقت"!

Pinocchio had lain immovable up to that moment
كان بينوكيو لا يزال ثابتا حتى تلك اللحظة

he was just like a real piece of wood
كان مثل قطعة خشب حقيقية

but then he was seized with a fit of convulsive trembling
ولكن بعد ذلك تم القبض عليه بنوبة من الارتعاش المتشنج

and the whole bed shook from his shaking
واهتز السرير كله من اهتزازه

the talking little Cricket continued talking
واصل الكريكيت الصغير الحديث

"That puppet there is a confirmed rogue"
"تلك الدمية هناك مارقة مؤكدة"

Pinocchio opened his eyes, but shut them again immediately
فتح بينوكيو عينيه ، لكنه أغلقهما مرة أخرى على الفور

"He is a good for nothing ragamuffin vagabond"
"إنه جيد مقابل لا شيء راجاموفين متشرد"

Pinocchio hid his face beneath the clothes
أخفى بينوكيو وجهه تحت الملابس

"That puppet there is a disobedient son"
"تلك الدمية هناك ابن غير مطيع"

"he will make his poor father die of a broken heart!"
"سيجعل والده المسكين يموت من قلب مكسور"!

At that instant everyone could hear something
في تلك اللحظة يمكن للجميع سماع شيء ما

suffocated sound of sobs and crying was heard
سمع صوت تنهدات وبكاء مختنق

the doctors raised the sheets a little
رفع الأطباء الملاءات قليلا

Imagine their astonishment when they saw Pinocchio
تخيل دهشتهم عندما رأوا بينوكيو

the crow was the first to give his medical opinion
كان الغراب أول من أعطى رأيه الطبي

"When a dead person cries he's on the road to recovery"
"عندما يبكي شخص ميت فهو في طريقه إلى الشفاء"

but the owl was of a different medical opinion
لكن البومة كانت ذات رأي طبي مختلف

"I grieve to contradict my illustrious friend"
"أنا حزين لتناقض صديقي اللامع"

"when the dead person cries it means he's is sorry to die"
"عندما يبكي الميت فهذا يعني أنه آسف للموت"

Pinocchio Refuses to Take his Medicine
بينوكيو يرفض تناول دوائه

The doctors had done all that they could
لقد فعل الأطباء كل ما في وسعهم

so they left Pinocchio with the fairy
لذلك تركوا بينوكيو مع الجنية

the Fairy touched Pinocchio's forehead
لمست الجنية جبين بينوكيو

she could tell that he had a high fever
يمكنها أن تقول أنه يعاني من ارتفاع في درجة الحرارة

the Fairy knew exactly what to give Pinocchio
عرفت الجنية بالضبط ما يجب أن تعطيه بينوكيو

she dissolved a white powder in some water
قامت بإذابة مسحوق أبيض في بعض الماء

and she offered Pinocchio the tumbler of water
وقدمت لبينوكيو بهلوان الماء

and she reassured him that everything would fine
وطمأنته أن كل شيء على ما يرام

"Drink it and in a few days you will be cured"
"اشربه وفي غضون أيام قليلة سيتم شفاؤك"

Pinocchio looked at the tumbler of medicine
نظر بينوكيو إلى بهلوان الطب

and he made a wry face at the medicine
وجعل وجها ساخرا في الدواء

"Is it sweet or bitter?" he asked plaintively
"هل هو حلو أم مر؟ "سأل بحزن

"It is bitter, but it will do you good"
"إنه مر ، لكنه سيفيدك جيدا"

"If it is bitter, I will not drink it"
"إذا كان مرا ، فلن أشربه"

"Listen to me," said the Fairy, "drink it"
"اسمعني "، قالت الجنية ،" اشربها"

"I don't like anything bitter," he objected
»أنا لا أحب أي شيء مرير«، اعترض

"I will give you a lump of sugar"

"سأعطيك قطعة من السكر"

"it will take away the bitter taste"

"سوف يسلب الطعم المر"

"but first you have to drink your medicine"

"ولكن عليك أولا أن تشرب دوائك"

"Where is the lump of sugar?" asked Pinocchio

"أين كتلة السكر؟" سأل بينوكيو

"Here is the lump of sugar," said the Fairy

"هنا كتلة السكر"، قالت الجنية

and she took out a piece from a gold sugar-basin

وأخرجت قطعة من حوض سكر ذهبي

"please give me the lump of sugar first"

"من فضلك أعطني كتلة السكر أولا"

"and then I will drink that bad bitter water"

"وبعد ذلك سأشرب هذا الماء المر السيىء"

"Do you promise me?" she asked Pinocchio

"هل تعدني؟" سألت بينوكيو

"Yes, I promise," answered Pinocchio

"نعم، أعدك"، أجاب بينوكيو

so the Fairy gave Pinocchio the piece of sugar

لذلك أعطت الجنية بينوكيو قطعة السكر

and Pinocchio crunched up the sugar and swallowed it

وقام بينوكيو بطحن السكر وابتلعه

he licked his lips and enjoyed the taste

لعق شفتيه واستمتع بالطعم

"It would be a fine thing if sugar were medicine!"

"سيكون شيئا جيدا إذا كان السكر دواء"!

"then I would take medicine every day"

"ثم كنت أتناول الدواء كل يوم"

the Fairy had not forgotten Pinocchio's promise

الجنية لم تنس وعد بينوكيو

"keep your promise and drink this medicine"

"حافظ على وعدك واشرب هذا الدواء"

"it will restore you back to health"

"سيعيدك إلى الصحة"

Pinocchio took the tumbler unwillingly

أخذ بينوكيو البهلوان عن غير قصد

he put the point of his nose to the tumbler

وضع نقطة أنفه على البهلوان

and he lowered the tumbler to his lips

وأنزل البهلوان إلى شفتيه

and then again he put his nose to it

ثم مرة أخرى وضع أنفه عليها

and at last he said, "It is too bitter!"

وأخيرا قال ،" إنه مر جدا"!

"I cannot drink anything so bitter"

"لا أستطيع أن أشرب أي شيء مر جدا"

"you don't know yet if you can't," said the Fairy

"أنت لا تعرف بعد ما إذا كنت لا تستطيع "، قالت الجنية

"you have not even tasted it yet"

"أنت لم تتذوقه بعد"

"I can imagine how it's going to taste!"

"أستطيع أن أتخيل كيف سيكون طعمه"!

"I know it from the smell," objected Pinocchio

"أنا أعرف ذلك من الرائحة "، اعترض بينوكيو

"first I want another lump of sugar please"

"أولا أريد قطعة أخرى من السكر من فضلك"

"and then I promise that will drink it!"

"ثم أعدك أن تشربه"!

The Fairy had all the patience of a good mamma

كان لدى الجنية كل صبر ماما جيدة

and she put another lump of sugar in his mouth

ووضعت كتلة أخرى من السكر في فمه

and again, she presented the tumbler to him

ومرة أخرى ، قدمت له البهلوان

"I still cannot drink it!" said the puppet

"ما زلت لا أستطيع شربه "!قالت الدمية

and Pinocchio made a thousand grimaced faces

وصنع بينوكيو ألف وجه متجهم

"Why can't you drink it?" asked the fairy

"لماذا لا يمكنك شربه؟" سألت الجنية

"Because that pillow on my feet bothers me"

"لأن تلك الوسادة على قدمي تزعجني"

The Fairy removed the pillow from his feet

أزالت الجنية الوسادة من قدميه

Pinocchio excused himself again

بينوكيو عذر نفسه مرة أخرى

"I've tried my best but it doesn't help me"

"لقد بذلت قصارى جهدي ولكن هذا لا يساعدني"

"Even without the pillow I cannot drink it"

"حتى بدون الوسادة لا أستطيع شربها"

"What is the matter now?" asked the fairy

"ما الأمر الآن؟" سألت الجنية

"The door of the room is half open"

"باب الغرفة نصف مفتوح"

"it bothers me when doors are half open"

"يزعجني عندما تكون الأبواب نصف مفتوحة"

The Fairy went and closed the door for Pinocchio

ذهبت الجنية وأغلقت الباب أمام بينوكيو

but this didn't help, and he burst into tears

لكن هذا لم يساعد ، وانفجر في البكاء

"I will not drink that bitter water—no, no, no!"

"لن أشرب هذا الماء المر - لا ، لا ، لا"!

"My boy, you will repent it if you don't"

"يا ولدي ، سوف تتوب إذا لم تفعل"

"I don't care if I will repent it," he replied

أجاب» :لا يهمني إذا كنت سأتوب عنها.«

"Your illness is serious," warned the Fairy

"مرضك خطير "، حذرت الجنية

"I don't care if my illness is serious"

"لا يهمني إذا كان مرضي خطيرا"

"The fever will carry you into the other world"

"الحمى ستنقلك إلى العالم الآخر"

"then let the fever carry me into the other world"

"ثم دع الحمى تحملني إلى العالم الآخر"

"Are you not afraid of death?"

"ألا تخاف من الموت؟"

"I am not in the least afraid of death!"

"أنا لست خائفا من الموت"!

"I would rather die than drink bitter medicine"

"أفضل الموت على شرب الدواء المر"

At that moment the door of the room flew open

في تلك اللحظة طار باب الغرفة مفتوحا

four rabbits as black as ink entered the room

دخلت الغرفة أربعة أرانب سوداء مثل الحبر

on their shoulders they carried a little bier

على أكتافهم حملوا القليل من البيرة

"What do you want with me?" cried Pinocchio

"ماذا تريد معي؟ "صرخ بينوكيو

and he sat up in bed in a great fright

وجلس في السرير في خوف عظيم

"We have come to take you," said the biggest rabbit

"لقد جئنا لنأخذك "، قال أكبر أرنب

"you cannot take me yet; I am not dead"

"لا يمكنك أن تأخذني بعد. أنا لست ميتا"

"where are you planning to take me to?"

"إلى أين تخطط لأخذي إلى؟"

"No, you are not dead yet," confirmed the rabbit

"لا ، أنت لم تمت بعد "، أكد الأرنب

"but you have only a few minutes left to live"

"لكن لم يتبق لك سوى بضع دقائق للعيش"

"because you refused the bitter medicine"

"لأنك رفضت الدواء المر"

"the bitter medicine would have cured your fever"

"الدواء المر كان سيشفي حمتك"

"Oh, Fairy, Fairy!" the puppet began to scream

"أوه ، جنية ، جنية "إبدأت الدمية في الصراخ

"give me the tumbler at once," he begged

"أعطني البهلوان في الحال "، توسل

"be quick, for pity's sake, I do not want die"

"كن سريعا ، من أجل الشفقة ، لا أريد أن أموت"

"no, I will not die today"

"لا ، لن أموت اليوم"

Pinocchio took the tumbler with both hands

أخذ بينوكيو البهلوان بكلتا يديه

and he emptied the water one one big gulp
وأفرغ الماء جرعة واحدة كبيرة
"We must have patience!" said the rabbits
"يجب أن نتحلى بالصبر" اقال الأرانب
"this time we have made our journey in vain"
"هذه المرة قمنا برحلتنا دون جدوى"
they took the little bier on their shoulders again
أخذوا البير الصغير على أكتافهم مرة أخرى
and they left the room back to where they came from
وغادروا الغرفة عائدين إلى المكان الذي أتوا منه
and they grumbled and murmured between their teeth
وتذمروا وتذمروا بين أسنانهم
Pinocchio's recovery did not take long at all
لم يستغرق تعافي بينوكيو وقتا طويلا على الإطلاق
a few minutes later he jumped down from the bed
بعد بضع دقائق قفز من السرير
wooden puppets have a special privilege
الدمى الخشبية لها امتياز خاص
they seldom get seriously ill like us
نادرا ما يصابون بمرض خطير مثلنا

and they are lucky to be cured very quickly

وهم محظوظون لشفائهم بسرعة كبيرة

"has my medicine done you good?" asked the fairy

"هل دوائي جيد لك؟" سألت الجنية

"your medicine has done me more than good"

"لقد أفادني دواؤك أكثر من جيد"

"your medicine has saved my life"

"دواؤك أنقذ حياتي"

"why didn't you take your medicine sooner?"

"لماذا لم تتناول الدواء عاجلا؟"

"Well, Fairy, we boys are all like that!"

"حسنا ، الجنية ، نحن الأولاد جميعا هكذا"!

"We are more afraid of medicine than of the illness"

"نحن خائفون من الدواء أكثر من خوفنا من المرض"

"Disgraceful!" cried the fairy in indignation

"مشين"! إصرخت الجنية في سخط

"Boys ought to know the power of medicine"

"يجب أن يعرف الأولاد قوة الطب"

"a good remedy may save them from a serious illness"

"العلاج الجيد قد ينقذهم من مرض خطير"

"and perhaps it even saves you from death"

"وربما ينقذك من الموت"

"next time I shall not require so much persuasion"

"في المرة القادمة لن أحتاج إلى الكثير من الإقناع"

"I shall remember those black rabbits"

"سأتذكر تلك الأرانب السوداء"

"and I shall remember the bier on their shoulders"

"وسأتذكر البير على أكتافهم"

"and then I shall immediately take the tumbler"

"وبعد ذلك سآخذ البهلوان على الفور"

"and I will drink all the medicine in one go!"

"وسأشرب كل الدواء دفعة واحدة"!

The Fairy was happy with Pinocchio's words

كانت الجنية سعيدة بكلمات بينوكيو

"Now, come here to me and sit on my lap"

"الآن ، تعال إلى هنا لي واجلس في حضني"

"and tell me all about the assassins"

"وأخبرني كل شيء عن القتلة"

"how did you end up hanging from the big Oak tree?"

"كيف انتهى بك الأمر معلقا من شجرة البلوط الكبيرة؟"

And Pinocchio ordered all the events that happened

وأمر بينوكيو بكل الأحداث التي حدثت

"You see, there was a ringmaster; Fire-eater"

"كما ترى ، كان هناك مدير عصابة .آكل النار"

"Fire-eater gave me some gold pieces"

"أعطاني آكل النار بعض القطع الذهبية"

"he told me to take the gold to my father"

"قال لي أن آخذ الذهب إلى والدي"

"but I didn't take the gold straight to my father"

"لكنني لم آخذ الذهب مباشرة إلى والدي"

"on the way home I met a Fox and a Cat"

"في طريقي إلى المنزل قابلت ثعلبا وقطة"

"they made me an offer I couldn't refuse"

"قدموا لي عرضا لم أستطع رفضه"

'Would you like those pieces of gold to multiply?'

"هل ترغب في أن تتكاثر قطع الذهب هذه؟"

"'Come with us and,' they said"

"قالوا :تعال معنا و"

'we will take you to the Field of Miracles'

"سنأخذك إلى ميدان المعجزات"

"and I said, 'Let's go to the Field of Miracles'"

"فقلت :دعنا نذهب إلى ميدان المعجزات"

"And they said, 'Let us stop at this inn'"

"وقالوا :دعونا نتوقف عند هذا النزل"

"and we stopped at the Red Craw-Fish in"

"وتوقفنا عند سمك الجراد الأحمر في"

"all of us went to sleep after our food"

"ذهبنا جميعا للنوم بعد طعامنا"

"when I awoke they were no longer there"
"عندما استيقظت لم يعودوا هناك"
"because they had to leave before me"
"لأنهم اضطروا إلى المغادرة قبلي"
"Then I began to travel by night"
"ثم بدأت السفر ليلا"
"you cannot imagine how dark it was"
"لا يمكنك تخيل كم كان الظلام"
"that's when I met the two assassins"
"هذا عندما قابلت القاتلين"
"and they were wearing charcoal sacks"
"وكانوا يرتدون أكياس الفحم"
"they said to me: 'Out with your money'"
"قالوا لي: اخرج بأموالك"
"and I said to them, 'I have no money'"
"وقلت لهم: ليس لدي مال"
"because I had hidden the four gold pieces"
"لأنني أخفيت القطع الذهبية الأربعة"
"I had put the money in my mouth"
"كنت قد وضعت المال في فمي"
"one tried to put his hand in my mouth"
"حاول أحدهم وضع يده في فمي"
"and I bit his hand off and spat it out"
"وعضت يده وبصقتها"
"but instead of a hand it was a cat's paw"
"ولكن بدلا من اليد كان مخلب قطة"
"and then the assassins ran after me"
"ثم ركض القتلة ورائي"
"and I ran and ran as fast as I could"
"وركضت وركضت بأسرع ما يمكن"
"but in the end they caught me anyway"
"لكن في النهاية أمسكوا بي على أي حال"
"and they tied a noose around my neck"
"وربطوا حبل المشنقة حول رقبتي"

"and they hung me from the Big Oak tree"
"وعلقوني من شجرة البلوط الكبير"
"they waited for me to stop moving"
"انتظروا مني أن أتوقف عن الحركة"
"but I never stopped moving at all"
"لكنني لم أتوقف عن الحركة على الإطلاق"
"and then they called up to me"
"ثم نادوا علي"
'Tomorrow we shall return here'
"غدا سنعود إلى هنا"
'then you will be dead with your mouth open'
"حينئذ ستكون ميتا وفمك مفتوح"
'and we will have the gold under your tongue'
"وسيكون لدينا الذهب تحت لسانك"
the Fairy was interested in the story
كانت الجنية مهتمة بالقصة
"And where have you put the pieces of gold now?"
"وأين وضعت قطع الذهب الآن؟"
"I have lost them!" said Pinocchio, dishonestly
"لقد فقدتهم "إقال بينوكيو ، بطريقة غير شريفة
he had the pieces of gold in his pocket
كان لديه قطع الذهب في جيبه
as you know Pinocchio already had a long nose
كما تعلمون بينوكيو كان لديه بالفعل أنف طويل
but lying made his nose grow even longer
لكن الكذب جعل أنفه ينمو لفترة أطول
and his nose grew another two inches
ونما أنفه بوصتين أخريين
"And where did you lose the gold?"
"وأين خسرت الذهب؟"
"I lost it in the woods," he lied again
"لقد فقدته في الغابة "، كذب مرة أخرى
and his nose also grew at his second lie
ونما أنفه أيضا في كذبته الثانية
"worry not about the gold," said the fairy

"لا تقلق بشأن الذهب"، قالت الجنية

"we will go to the woods and find your gold"

"سنذهب إلى الغابة ونجد ذهبك"

"all that is lost in those woods is always found"

"كل ما يضيع في تلك الغابة موجود دائما"

Pinocchio got quite confused about his situation

أصبح بينوكيو مرتبكا تماما بشأن وضعه

"Ah! now I remember all about it," he replied

"آه !الآن أتذكر كل شيء عن ذلك»،، أجاب

"I didn't lose the four gold pieces at all"

"لم أفقد القطع الذهبية الأربع على الإطلاق"

"I just swallowed your medicine, didn't I?"

"لقد ابتلعت دواءك للتو ، أليس كذلك؟"

"I swallowed the coins with the medicine"

"ابتلعت العملات المعدنية مع الدواء"

at this daring lie his nose grew even longer

في هذه الكذبة الجريئة نما أنفه لفترة أطول

now Pinocchio could not move in any direction

الآن بينوكيو لا يمكن أن تتحرك في أي اتجاه

he tried to turn to his left side

حاول أن يلتفت إلى جانبه الأيسر

but his nose struck the bed and window-panes

لكن أنفه ضرب السرير وزجاج النوافذ

he tried to turn to the right side

حاول أن يتحول إلى الجانب الأيمن

but now his nose struck against the walls

ولكن الآن ضرب أنفه على الجدران

and he could not raise his head either

ولم يستطع رفع رأسه أيضا

because his nose was long and pointy

لأن أنفه كان طويلا ومدببا

and his nose could have poke the Fairy in the eye

وكان من الممكن أن يكون أنفه قد كزة الجنية في العين

the Fairy looked at him and laughed

نظرت إليه الجنية وضحكت

Pinocchio was very confused about his situation
كان بينوكيو مرتبكا للغاية بشأن وضعه

he did not know why his nose had grown
لم يكن يعرف لماذا نما أنفه

"What are you laughing at?" asked the puppet
"ما الذي تضحك عليه؟" سألت الدمية

"I am laughing at the lies you've told me"
"أنا أضحك على الأكاذيب التي قلتها لي"

"how can you know that I have told lies?"
"كيف يمكنك أن تعرف أنني قلت الأكاذيب؟"

"Lies, my dear boy, are found out immediately"
"الأكاذيب ، يا ولدي العزيز ، يتم اكتشافها على الفور"

"in this world there are two sorts of lies"
"في هذا العالم هناك نوعان من الأكاذيب"

"There are lies that have short legs"
"هناك أكاذيب لها أرجل قصيرة"

"and there are lies that have long noses"
"وهناك أكاذيب لها أنوف طويلة"

"Your lie is one of those that has a long nose"
"كذبتك هي واحدة من تلك التي لها أنف طويل"

Pinocchio did not know where to hide himself
لم يعرف بينوكيو أين يختبئ

he was ashamed of his lies being discovered
كان يخجل من اكتشاف أكاذيبه

he tried to run out of the room
حاول الركض خارج الغرفة

but he did not succeed at escaping
لكنه لم ينجح في الهروب

his nose had gotten too long to escape
كان أنفه قد استغرق وقتا طويلا جدا للهروب

and he could no longer pass through the door
ولم يعد بإمكانه المرور عبر الباب

Pinocchio Meets the Fox and the Cat Again
بينوكيو يلتقي الثعلب والقط مرة أخرى

the Fairy understood the importance of the lesson
فهمت الجنية أهمية الدرس

she let the puppet to cry for a good half-hour
تركت الدمية تبكي لمدة نصف ساعة جيدة

his nose could no longer pass through the door
لم يعد أنفه قادرا على المرور عبر الباب

telling lies is the worst thing a boy can do
قول الأكاذيب هو أسوأ شيء يمكن أن يفعله الصبي

and she wanted him to learn from his mistakes
وأرادت منه أن يتعلم من أخطائه

but she could not bear to see him weeping
لكنها لم تستطع تحمل رؤيته يبكي

she felt full of compassion for the puppet
شعرت بالتعاطف الكامل مع الدمية

so she clapped her hands together again
لذلك صفقت يديها معا مرة أخرى

a thousand large Woodpeckers flew in from the window
طار ألف نقار الخشب الكبير من النافذة

The woodpeckers immediately perched on Pinocchio's nose
نقار الخشب تطفو على الفور على أنف بينوكيو

and they began to peck at his nose with great zeal
وبدأوا في النقر على أنفه بحماس كبير

you can imagine the speed of a thousand woodpeckers
يمكنك أن تتخيل سرعة ألف نقار الخشب

within no time at all Pinocchio's nose was normal
في أي وقت من الأوقات على الإطلاق كان أنف بينوكيو طبيعيا

of course you remember he always had a big nose
بالطبع تتذكر أنه كان لديه دائما أنف كبير

"What a good Fairy you are," said the puppet
"يا لها من جنية جيدة أنت "، قالت الدمية

and Pinocchio dried his tearful eyes
وجفف بينوكيو عينيه الدامعة

"and how much I love you!" he added

"وكم أحبك"!

"I love you also," answered the Fairy

"أنا أحبك أيضا "، أجابت الجنية

"if you remain with me you shall be my little brother"

"إذا بقيت معي فستكون أخي الصغير"

"and I will be your good little sister"

"وسأكون أختك الصغيرة الطيبة"

"I would like to remain very much," said Pinocchio

"أود أن أبقى كثيرا "، قال بينوكيو

"but I have to go back to my poor papa"

"لكن يجب أن أعود إلى أبي المسكين"

"I have thought of everything," said the fairy

"لقد فكرت في كل شيء "، قالت الجنية

"I have already let your father know"

"لقد أخبرت والدك بالفعل"

"and he will come here tonight"

"وسيأتي إلى هنا الليلة"

"Really?" shouted Pinocchio, jumping for joy

"حقا؟ "صاح بينوكيو ، والقفز من الفرح

"Then, little Fairy, I have a wish"

"ثم ، الجنية الصغيرة ، لدي أمنية"

"I would very much like to go and meet him"

"أود بشدة أن أذهب لمقابلته"

"I want to give a kiss to that poor old man"

"أريد أن أعطي قبلة لهذا الرجل العجوز المسكين"

"he has suffered so much on my account"

"لقد عانى كثيرا على حسابي"

"Go, but be careful not to lose your way"

"اذهب ، لكن احرص على ألا تضل طريقك"

"Take the road that goes through the woods"

"اسلك الطريق الذي يمر عبر الغابة"

"I am sure that you will meet him there"

"أنا متأكد من أنك ستقابله هناك"

Pinocchio set out to go through the woods

شرع بينوكيو في المرور عبر الغابة
once in the woods he began to run like a kid
مرة واحدة في الغابة بدأ يركض مثل طفل
But then he had reached a certain spot in the woods
ولكن بعد ذلك وصل إلى مكان معين في الغابة
he was almost in front of the Big Oak tree
كان تقريبا أمام شجرة البلوط الكبير
he thought he heard people amongst the bushes
ظن أنه سمع الناس بين الأدغال
In fact, two persons came out on to the road
في الواقع ، خرج شخصان إلى الطريق
Can you guess who they were?
هل يمكنك تخمين من هم؟
they were his two travelling companions
كانا رفيقيه في السفر
in front of him was the Fox and the Cat
أمامه كان الثعلب والقط
his companions who had taken him to the inn
أصحابه الذين أخذوه إلى النزل

"Why, here is our dear Pinocchio!" cried the Fox

"لماذا ، هنا عزيزنا بينوكيو "إصرخ الثعلب

and he kissed and embraced his old friend

وقبل واحتضن صديقه القديم

"How came you to be here?" asked the fox

"كيف جئت لتكون هنا؟ "سأل الثعلب"

"How come you to be here?" repeated the Cat

"كيف تأتي لتكون هنا؟ "كرر القط"

"It is a long story," answered the puppet

»إنها قصة طويلة»، أجابت الدمية

"I will tell you the story when I have time"

"سأخبرك القصة عندما يكون لدي الوقت"

"but I must tell you what happened to me"

"لكن يجب أن أخبرك بما حدث لي"

"do you know that the other night I met with assassins?"

"هل تعلم أنه في الليلة الماضية التقيت بالقتلة؟"

"Assassins! Oh, poor Pinocchio!" worried the Fox

"القتلة !أوه ، مسكين بينوكيو "إقلق الثعلب

"And what did they want?" he asked

"وماذا يريدون؟ "سأل"

"They wanted to rob me of my gold pieces"

"أرادوا أن يسرقوني قطعي الذهبية"

"Villains!" said the Fox

"الأشرار "إقال الثعلب"

"Infamous villains!" repeated the Cat

"الأشرار سيئة السمعة "إكرر القط"

"But I ran away from them," continued the puppet

"لكنني هربت منهم "، تابعت الدمية

"they did their best to catch me"

"لقد بذلوا قصارى جهدهم للقبض علي"

"and after a long chase they did catch me"

"وبعد مطاردة طويلة أمسكوا بي"

"they hung me from a branch of that oak tree"

"علقوني من غصن شجرة البلوط تلك"

And Pinocchio pointed to the Big Oak tree
وأشار بينوكيو إلى شجرة البلوط الكبيرة

the Fox was appalled by what he had heard
شعر الثعلب بالفزع مما سمعه

"Is it possible to hear of anything more dreadful?"
"هل من الممكن أن نسمع عن أي شيء أكثر ترويعاً؟"

"In what a world we are condemned to live!"
"في أي عالم محكوم علينا أن نعيشه"!

"Where can respectable people like us find a safe refuge?"
"أين يمكن للأشخاص المحترمين مثلنا أن يجدوا ملاذا آمناً؟"

the conversation went on this way for some time
استمرت المحادثة على هذا النحو لبعض الوقت

in this time Pinocchio observed something about the Cat
في هذا الوقت لاحظ بينوكيو شيئًا عن القط

the Cat was lame of her front right leg
كانت القطة عرجاء من ساقها اليمنى الأمامية

in fact, she had lost her paw and all its claws
في الواقع ، فقدت مخلبها وكل مخالبها

Pinocchio wanted to know what had happened
أراد بينوكيو معرفة ما حدث

"What have you done with your paw?"
"ماذا فعلت بمخلبك؟"

The Cat tried to answer, but became confused
حاولت القطة الإجابة ، لكنها أصبحت مرتبكة

the Fox jumped in to explain what had happened
قفز الثعلب لشرح ما حدث

"you must know that my friend is too modest"
"يجب أن تعرف أن صديقي متواضع للغاية"

"her modesty is why she doesn't usually speak"
"تواضعها هو السبب في أنها لا تتحدث عادة"

"so let me tell the story for her"
"لذا دعني أروي القصة لها"

"an hour ago we met an old wolf on the road"
"قبل ساعة التقينا بذئب عجوز على الطريق"

"he was almost fainting from want of food"

"كان على وشك الإغماء بسبب نقص الطعام"

"and he asked alms of us"

"وطلب منا الصدقات"

"we had not so much as a fish-bone to give him"

"لم يكن لدينا الكثير من عظم السمكة لإعطائه"

"but what did my friend do?"

"ولكن ماذا فعل صديقي؟"

"well, she really has the heart of a César"

"حسنا ، لديها حقا قلب سيزار"

"She bit off one of her fore paws"

"لقد عضت أحد كفوفها الأمامية"

"and the threw her paw to the poor beast"

"وألقت مخلبها إلى الوحش المسكين"

"so that he might appease his hunger"

"لكي يرضي جوعه"

And the Fox was brought to tears by his story

وجلب الثعلب إلى البكاء من قصته

Pinocchio was also touched by the story

تأثر بينوكيو أيضا بالقصة

approaching the Cat, he whispered into her ear

اقترب من القطة ، همس في أذنها

"If all cats resembled you, how fortunate the mice would be!"

"إذا كانت جميع القطط تشبهك ، فكم ستكون الفئران محظوظة"!

"And now, what are you doing here?" asked the Fox

"والآن ، ماذا تفعل هنا؟ "سأل الثعلب

"I am waiting for my papa," answered the puppet

"أنا في انتظار بابا "، أجابت الدمية

"I am expecting him to arrive at any moment now"

"أتوقع وصوله في أي لحظة الآن"

"And what about your pieces of gold?"

"وماذا عن قطع الذهب الخاصة بك؟"

"I have got them in my pocket," confirmed Pinocchio

"لقد حصلت عليها في جيبي "، أكد بينوكيو

although he had to explain that he had spent one coin
على الرغم من أنه كان عليه أن يشرح أنه أنفق عملة واحدة

the cost of their meal had come to one piece of gold
وصلت تكلفة وجبتهم إلى قطعة واحدة من الذهب

but he told them not to worry about that
لكنه أخبرهم ألا يقلقوا بشأن ذلك

but the Fox and the Cat did worry about it
لكن الثعلب والقط قلقان بشأن ذلك

"Why do you not listen to our advice?"
"لماذا لا تستمع إلى نصيحتنا؟"

"by tomorrow you could have one or two thousand!"
"بحلول الغد يمكن أن يكون لديك ألف أو ألفين"!

"Why don't you bury them in the Field of Miracles?"
"لماذا لا تدفنهم في حقل المعجزات؟"

"Today it is impossible," objected Pinocchio
»اليوم من المستحيل«، اعترض بينوكيو

"but don't worry, I will go another day"
"لكن لا تقلق ، سأذهب في يوم آخر"

"Another day it will be too late!" said the Fox
"يوم آخر سيكون قد فات الأوان "!قال الثعلب

"Why would it be too late?" asked Pinocchio
"لماذا يكون الأوان قد فات؟ "سأل بينوكيو

"Because the field has been bought by a gentleman"
"لأن الحقل قد تم شراؤه من قبل رجل نبيل"

"after tomorrow no one will be allowed to bury money there"
"بعد الغد لن يسمح لأحد بدفن الأموال هناك"

"How far off is the Field of Miracles?"
"كم يبعد ميدان المعجزات؟"

"It is less than two miles from here"
"إنه على بعد أقل من ميلين من هنا"

"Will you come with us?" asked the Fox
"هل ستأتي معنا؟ "سأل الثعلب

"In half an hour we can be there"

"في نصف ساعة يمكننا أن نكون هناك"
"You can bury your money straight away"
"يمكنك دفن أموالك على الفور"
"and in a few minutes you will collect two thousand coins"
"وفي بضع دقائق ستجمع ألفي قطعة نقدية"
"and this evening you will return with your pockets full"
"وهذا المساء ستعود وجيوبك ممتلئة"
"Will you come with us?" the Fox asked again
"هل ستأتي معنا؟" سأل الثعلب مرة أخرى
Pinocchio thought of the good Fairy
فكر بينوكيو في الجنية الجيدة
and Pinocchio thought of old Geppetto
وفكر بينوكيو في جيبيتو القديم
and he remembered the warnings of the talking little cricket
وتذكر تحذيرات الكريكيت الصغير المتكلم
and he hesitated a little before answering
وتردد قليلا قبل الإجابة
by now you know what kind of boy Pinocchio is
الآن أنت تعرف أي نوع من الصبي بينوكيو هو
Pinocchio is one of those boys without much sense
بينوكيو هو واحد من هؤلاء الأولاد دون معنى كبير
he ended by giving his head a little shake
انتهى بهز رأسه قليلا
and then he told the Fox and the Cat his plans
ثم أخبر الثعلب والقط بخططه
"Let us go: I will come with you"
"دعنا نذهب :سآتي معك"
and they went to the field of miracles
وذهبوا إلى ميدان المعجزات
they walked for half a day and reached a town
ساروا لمدة نصف يوم ووصلوا إلى بلدة
the town was the Trap for Blockheads
كانت المدينة فخ الرؤوس المحظورة
Pinocchio noticed something interesting about this town
لاحظ بينوكيو شيئا مثيرا للاهتمام حول هذه المدينة

everywhere where you looked there were dogs
في كل مكان نظرت فيه كانت هناك

all the dogs were yawning from hunger
كانت جميع تتثاءب من الجوع

and he saw shorn sheep trembling with cold
ورأى خروفا مقطوعة ترتجف من البرد

even the cockerels were begging for Indian corn
حتى الكعك كان يتوسل للحصول على الذرة الهندية

there were large butterflies that could no longer fly
كانت هناك فراشات كبيرة لم تعد قادرة على الطيران

because they had sold their beautiful coloured wings
لأنهم باعوا أجنحتهم الملونة الجميلة

there were peacocks that were ashamed to be seen
كانت هناك طاووس تخجل من رؤيتها

because they had sold their beautiful coloured tails
لأنهم باعوا ذيولهم الملونة الجميلة

and pheasants went scratching about in a subdued fashion
وذهب الدراجون يخدشون بطريقة خافتة

they were mourning for their gold and silver feathers
كانوا في حداد على ريشهم الذهبي والفضي

most were beggars and shamefaced creatures
كان معظمهم متسولين ومخلوقات مخزية

but among them some lordly carriage passed
ولكن من بينهم مرت بعض العربات الربانية

the carriages contained a Fox, or a thieving Magpie
احتوت العربات على ثعلب ، أو طائر العقعق السارق

or the carriage seated some other ravenous bird of prey
أو العربة تجلس بعض الطيور الجارحة المفترسة الأخرى

"And where is the Field of Miracles?" asked Pinocchio
"وأين هو مجال المعجزات؟" سأل بينوكيو

"It is here, not two steps from us"
"إنه هنا ، وليس خطوتين منا"

They crossed the town and and went over a wall
عبروا البلدة وتجاوزوا جدارا

and then they came to a solitary field
ثم جاءوا إلى حقل انفرادي

"Here we are," said the Fox to the puppet
"نحن هنا "، قال الثعلب للدمية

"Now stoop down and dig with your hands a little hole"
"الآن انحنى وحفر بيديك حفرة صغيرة"

"and put your gold pieces into the hole"
"وضع قطع الذهب الخاصة بك في حفرة"

Pinocchio obeyed what the fox had told him
أطاع بينوكيو ما قاله له الثعلب

He dug a hole and put into it the four gold pieces
حفر حفرة ووضع فيها القطع الذهبية الأربع

and then he filled up the hole with a little earth
ثم ملأ الحفرة بقليل من الأرض

"Now, then," said the Fox, "go to that canal close to us"
قال الثعلب": الآن ، إذن ، اذهب إلى تلك القناة القريبة منا"

"fetch a bucket of water from the canal"
"جلب دلو من الماء من القناة"

"water the ground where you have sowed the gold"
"سقي الأرض حيث زرعت الذهب"

Pinocchio went to the canal without a bucket
ذهب بينوكيو إلى القناة بدون دلو

as he had no bucket, he took off one of his old shoes
نظرا لأنه لم يكن لديه دلو ، فقد خلع أحد حذائه القديم

and he filled his shoe with water
وملأ حذاءه بالماء

and then he watered the ground over the hole
ثم سقى الأرض فوق الحفرة

He then asked, "Is there anything else to be done?
ثم سأل": هل هناك أي شيء آخر يجب القيام به؟

"you need not do anything else," answered the Fox
"لا تحتاج إلى فعل أي شيء آخر "، أجاب الثعلب

"there is no need for us to stay here"
"ليست هناك حاجة لنا للبقاء هنا"

"you can return in about twenty minutes"
"يمكنك العودة في حوالي عشرين دقيقة"

"and then you will find a shrub in the ground"

"وبعد ذلك ستجد شجيرة في الأرض"
"the tree's branches will be loaded with money"
"سيتم تحميل أغصان الشجرة بالمال"

The poor puppet was beside himself with joy
كانت الدمية المسكينة بجانبه بفرح

he thanked the Fox and the Cat a thousand times
شكر الثعلب والقط ألف مرة

and he promised them many beautiful presents
ووعدهم بالعديد من الهدايا الجميلة

"We wish for no presents," answered the two rascals
"لا نتمنى أي هدايا"، أجاب الأوغاد

"It is enough for us to have taught you how to enrich yourself"
"يكفينا أن نعلمك كيف تثري نفسك"

"there is nothing worse than seeing others do hard work"
"لا يوجد شيء أسوأ من رؤية الآخرين يقومون بعمل شاق"

"and we are as happy as people out for a holiday"
"ونحن سعداء مثل الناس لقضاء عطلة"

Thus saying, they took leave of Pinocchio
هكذا قالوا ، أخذوا إجازة من بينوكيو

and they wished him a good harvest
وتمنوا له حصادا جيدا

and then they went about their business
ثم ذهبوا إلى أعمالهم

Pinocchio is Robbed of his Money
بينوكيو يسرق من أمواله

The puppet returned to the town
عادت الدمية إلى المدينة

and he began to count the minutes one by one
وبدأ في عد الدقائق واحدة تلو الأخرى

and soon he thought he had counted long enough
وسرعان ما اعتقد أنه قد عد لفترة كافية

so he took the road leading to the Field of Miracles
لذلك سلك الطريق المؤدي إلى حقل المعجزات

And he walked along with hurried steps
ومشى بخطوات سريعة

and his heart beat fast with great excitement
وقلبه ينبض بسرعة مع إثارة كبيرة

like a drawing-room clock going very well
مثل ساعة غرفة الرسم تسير على ما يرام للغاية

Meanwhile he was thinking to himself:
في هذه الأثناء كان يفكر في نفسه :

"what if I don't find a thousand gold pieces?"
"ماذا لو لم أجد ألف قطعة ذهبية؟ "

"what if I find two thousand gold pieces instead?"
"ماذا لو وجدت ألفي قطعة ذهبية بدلا من ذلك؟ "

"but what if I don't find two thousand gold pieces?"
"ولكن ماذا لو لم أجد ألفي قطعة ذهبية؟ "

"what if I find five thousand gold pieces!"
"ماذا لو وجدت خمسة آلاف قطعة ذهبية "!

"what if I find a hundred thousand gold pieces??"
"ماذا لو وجدت مائة ألف قطعة ذهبية ؟؟ "

"Oh! what a fine gentleman I should then become!"
"أوه إيا له من رجل نبيل يجب أن أصبح بعد ذلك !

"I could live in a beautiful palace"
"يمكنني العيش في قصر جميل "

"and I would have a thousand little wooden horses"
"وسيكون لدي ألف حصان خشبي صغير "

"a cellar full of currant wine and sweet syrups"
"قبو مليء بنبيذ الكشمش والعصائر الحلوة "

"and a library quite full of candies and tarts"
"ومكتبة مليئة بالحلوى والفطائر "

"and I would have plum-cakes and macaroons"
"وأود أن يكون لديك كعك البرقوق والمعكرونة "

"and I would have biscuits with cream"
"وأود أن أتناول البسكويت مع كريمة "

he walked along building castles in the sky
مشى على طول بناء القلاع في السماء
and he build many of these castles in the sky
وبنى العديد من هذه القلاع في السماء
and eventually he arrived at the edge of the field
وفي النهاية وصل إلى حافة الحقل
and he stopped to look about for a tree
وتوقف للبحث عن شجرة
there were other trees in the field
كانت هناك أشجار أخرى في الحقل
but they had been there when he had left
لكنهم كانوا هناك عندما غادر
and he saw no money tree in all the field
ولم ير شجرة مال في كل الحقل
He walked along the field another hundred steps
مشى على طول الحقل مائة خطوة أخرى
but he couldn't find the tree he was looking for
لكنه لم يتمكن من العثور على الشجرة التي كان يبحث عنها
he then entered into the field
ثم دخل إلى الميدان
and he went up to the little hole
وصعد إلى الحفرة الصغيرة
the hole where he had buried his coins
الحفرة التي دفن فيها عملاته المعدنية
and he looked at the hole very carefully
ونظر إلى الحفرة بعناية فائقة
but there was definitely no tree growing there
ولكن بالتأكيد لم يكن هناك شجرة تنمو هناك
He then became very thoughtful
ثم أصبح مدروسا للغاية
and he forget the rules of society
وينسى قواعد المجتمع
and he didn't care for good manners for a moment
ولم يهتم بالأخلاق الحميدة للحظة
he took his hands out of his pocket
أخرج يديه من جيبه

and he gave his head a long scratch
وأعطى رأسه خدشا طويلا

At that moment he heard an explosion of laughter
في تلك اللحظة سمع انفجارا من الضحك

someone close by was laughing himself silly
شخص قريب كان يضحك نفسه سخيفا

he looked up one of the nearby trees
نظر إلى إحدى الأشجار القريبة

he saw a large Parrot perched on a branch
رأى ببغاء كبير يطفو على فرع

the parrot brushed the few feathers he had left
تم تنظيف الببغاء بالريش القليل الذي تركه

Pinocchio asked the parrot in an angry voice;
سأل بينوكيو الببغاء بصوت غاضب .

"Why are you here laughing so loud?"
"لماذا أنت هنا تضحك بصوت عال جدا؟ "

"I am laughing because in brushing my feathers"
"أنا أضحك لأنني في تنظيف ريشي "

"I was just brushing a little under my wings"
"كنت أنظف قليلا تحت جناحي "

"and while brushing my feathers I tickled myself"
"وبينما كنت أنظف ريشي دغدغت "

The puppet did not answer the parrot
الدمية لم تجب على الببغاء

but instead Pinocchio went to the canal
ولكن بدلا من ذلك ذهب بينوكيو إلى القناة

he filled his old shoe full of water again
ملأ حذاءه القديم بالماء مرة أخرى

and he proceeded to water the hole once more
وشرع في سقي الحفرة مرة أخرى

While he was busy doing this he heard more laughter
بينما كان مشغولا بالقيام بذلك سمع المزيد من الضحك

the laughter was even more impertinent than before
كان الضحك أكثر وقاحة من ذي قبل

it rang out in the silence of that solitary place
رن في صمت ذلك المكان الانفرادي

Pinocchio shouted out even angrier than before
صرخ بينوكيو أكثر غضبا من ذي قبل
"Once for all, may I know what you are laughing at?"
"مرة واحدة وإلى الأبد ، هل لي أن أعرف ما الذي تضحك عليه؟ "
"I am laughing at simpletons," answered the parrot
"أنا أضحك على البسطاء "، أجاب الببغاء
"simpletons who believe in foolish things
"البسطاء الذين يؤمنون بالأشياء الحمقاء
"the foolish things that people tell them"
" الأشياء الحمقاء التي يقولها لهم الناس "
"I laugh at those who let themselves be fooled"
"أضحك على أولئك الذين سمحوا لأنفسهم أن ينخدعوا "
"fooled by those more cunning than they are"
"ينخدع من قبل أولئك الأكثر دهاء مما هم عليه "
"Are you perhaps speaking of me?"
"هل تتحدث عني ربما؟ "
"Yes, I am speaking of you, poor Pinocchio"
"نعم ، أنا أتحدث عنك ، بينوكيو المسكين "
"you have believed a very foolish thing"
"لقد صدقت شيئا أحمق جدا "
"you believed that money can be grown in fields"
"كنت تعتقد أن المال يمكن زراعته في الحقول "
"you thought money can be grown like beans"
"كنت تعتقد أن المال يمكن زراعته مثل الفاصوليا "
"I also believed it once," admitted the parrot
«لقد صدقت ذلك أيضا مرة واحدة»، اعترف الببغاء
"and today I am suffering for having believed it"
"واليوم أعاني لأنني صدقت ذلك "
"but I have learned my lesson from that trick"
"لكنني تعلمت درسي من تلك الحيلة "
"I turned my efforts to honest work"
"حولت جهودي إلى العمل الصادق "
"and I have put a few pennies together"
"وقد وضعت بضعة بنسات معا "

"it is necessary to know how to earn your pennies"
"من الضروري معرفة كيفية كسب البنسات "

"you have to earn them either with your hands"
"عليك أن تكسبها إما بيديك "

"or you have to earn them with your brains"
"أو عليك أن تكسبها بعقولك "

"I don't understand you," said the puppet
"أنا لا أفهمك "، قالت الدمية

and he was already trembling with fear
وكان يرتجف بالفعل من الخوف

"Have patience!" rejoined the parrot
"تحلى بالصبر "!انضم إلى الببغاء

"I will explain myself better, if you let me"
"سأشرح بشكل أفضل ، إذا سمحت لي "

"there is something that you must know"
"هناك شيء يجب أن تعرفه "

"something happened while you were in the town"
"حدث شيء ما أثناء وجودك في المدينة "

"the Fox and the Cat returned to the field"
"عاد الثعلب والقط إلى الميدان "

"they took the money you had buried"
"أخذوا المال الذي دفنته "

"and then they fled from the scene of the crime"
"ثم فروا من مسرح الجريمة "

"And now he that catches them will be clever"
"والآن من يمسك بهم سيكون ذكيا "

Pinocchio remained with his mouth open
بقي بينوكيو وفمه مفتوح

and he chose not to believe the Parrot's words
واختار ألا يصدق كلام الببغاء

he began with his hands to dig up the earth
بدأ بيديه لحفر الأرض

And he dug deep into the ground
وحفر عميقا في الأرض

a rick of straw could have stood in the hole
ريك من القش كان يمكن أن يقف في الحفرة
but the money was no longer there
لكن المال لم يعد موجودا
He rushed back to the town in a state of desperation
هرع عائدا إلى البلدة في حالة يأس
and he went at once to the Courts of Justice
وذهب في الحال إلى محاكم العدل
and he spoke directly with the judge
وتحدث مباشرة مع القاضي
he denounced the two knaves who had robbed him
ندد بالسكاكين اللذين سرقاه
The judge was a big ape of the gorilla tribe
كان القاضي كبيرا من قبيلة الغوريلا
an old ape respectable because of his white beard
عجوز محترم بسبب لحيته البيضاء
and he was respectable for other reasons
وكان محترما لأسباب أخرى
because he had gold spectacles on his nose
لأنه كان لديه نظارات ذهبية على أنفه
although, his spectacles were without glass
على الرغم من أن نظاراته كانت بدون زجاج
but he was always obliged to wear them
لكنه كان دائما مضطرا لارتدائها
on account of an inflammation of the eyes
بسبب التهاب العينين

Pinocchio told him all about the crime
أخبره بينوكيو بكل شيء عن الجريمة

the crime of which he had been the victim of
الجريمة التي كان ضحية لها

He gave him the names and the surnames
أعطاه الأسماء والألقاب

and he gave all the details of the rascals
وأعطى كل تفاصيل الأوغاد

and he ended by demanding to have justice
وانتهى بالمطالبة بالعدالة

The judge listened with great benignity
استمع القاضي بلطف كبير

he took a lively interest in the story
اهتم بالقصة بشكل حيوي

he was much touched and moved by what he heard
لقد تأثر كثيرا وتأثر بما سمعه

finally the puppet had nothing further to say
أخيرا ، لم يكن لدى الدمية ما تقوله

and then the gorilla rang a bell

ثم دقت الغوريلا الجرس

two mastiffs appeared at the door

ظهر اثنان من الدرواس عند الباب

the dogs were dressed as gendarmes

كانت ترتدي زي الدرك

The judge then pointed to Pinocchio

ثم أشار القاضي إلى بينوكيو

"That poor devil has been robbed"

"لقد سرق هذا الشيطان المسكين"

"rascals took four gold pieces from him"

"أخذ الأوغاد منه أربع قطع ذهبية"

"take him away to prison immediately," he ordered

"خذوه إلى السجن على الفور"، أمر

The puppet was petrified on hearing this

تحجرت الدمية عند سماع هذا

it was not at all the judgement he had expected

لم يكن الحكم الذي توقعه على الإطلاق

and he tried to protest the judge

وحاول الاحتجاج على القاضي

but the gendarmes stopped his mouth

لكن رجال الدرك أوقفوا فمه

they didn't want to lose any time

لم يرغبوا في خسارة أي وقت

and they carried him off to the prison

وحملوه إلى السجن

And there he remained for four long months

وهناك بقي لمدة أربعة أشهر طويلة

and he would have remained there even longer

وكان سيبقى هناك لفترة أطول

but puppets do sometimes have good fortune too

لكن الدمى في بعض الأحيان لديها حظ جيد أيضا

a young King ruled over the Trap for Blockheads

ملك شاب حكم فخ الرؤوس المحظورة

he had won a splendid victory in battle

لقد حقق انتصارا رائعا في المعركة

because of this he ordered great public rejoicings

وبسبب هذا أمر بابتهاج شعبي كبير

There were illuminations and fireworks

كانت هناك إضاءات وألعاب نارية

and there were horse and velocipede races

وكانت هناك سباقات للخيول والسرعة

the King was so happy he released all prisoners

كان الملك سعيدا جدا لدرجة أنه أطلق سراح جميع السجناء

Pinocchio was very happy at this news

كان بينوكيو سعيدا جدا بهذا الخبر

"if they are freed, then so am I"

"إذا تم إطلاق سراحهم ، فأنا كذلك "

but the jailor had other orders

لكن السجان كان لديه أوامر أخرى

"No, not you," said the jailor

"لا ، ليس أنت "، قال السجان

"because you do not belong to the fortunate class"

"لأنك لا تنتمي إلى الطبقة المحظوظة "

"I beg your pardon," replied Pinocchio

»أستميحك العفو«، أجاب بينوكيو

"I am also a criminal," he proudly said

"أنا أيضا مجرم "، قال بفخر

the jailor looked at Pinocchio again

نظر السجان إلى بينوكيو مرة أخرى

"In that case you are perfectly right"

"في هذه الحالة أنت على حق تماما "

and he took off his hat

وخلع قبعته

and he bowed to him respectfully

وانحنى له باحترام

and he opened the prison doors

وفتح أبواب السجن

and he let the little puppet escape

وترك الدمية الصغيرة تهرب

Pinocchio Goes back to the Fairy's House
بينوكيو يعود إلى منزل الجنية

You can imagine Pinocchio's joy
يمكنك أن تتخيل فرحة بينوكيو
finally he was free after four months
أخيرا أصبح حرا بعد أربعة أشهر
but he didn't stop in order to celebrate
لكنه لم يتوقف من أجل الاحتفال
instead, he immediately left the town
بدلا من ذلك ، غادر المدينة على الفور
he took the road that led to the Fairy's house
أخذ الطريق المؤدي إلى منزل الجنية
there had been a lot of rain in recent days
كان هناك الكثير من الأمطار في الأيام الأخيرة
so the road had become a went boggy and marsh
لذلك أصبح الطريق مستنقعا ومستنقعا
and Pinocchio sank knee deep into the mud
وغرق بينوكيو ركبته في عمق الوحل

But the puppet was not one to give up
لكن الدمية لم تكن واحدة للاستسلام

he was tormented by the desire to see his father
كان يعذبه الرغبة في رؤية والده

and he wanted to see his little sister again too
وأراد أن يرى أخته الصغيرة مرة أخرى أيضا

and he ran through the marsh like a greyhound
وركض عبر المستنقع مثل السلوقي

and as he ran he was splashed with mud
وبينما كان يركض تم رشه بالطين

and he was covered from head to foot
وكان مغطى من الرأس إلى القدم

And he said to himself as he went along:
وقال لنفسه وهو يمضي:

"How many misfortunes have happened to me"
"كم عدد المصائب التي حدثت لي"

"But I deserved these misfortunes"
"لكنني أستحق هذه المصائب"

"because I am an obstinate, passionate puppet"
"لأنني دمية عنيدة وعاطفية"

"I am always bent upon having my own way"
"أنا عازم دائما على امتلاك طريقتي الخاصة"

"and I don't listen to those who wish me well"
"وأنا لا أستمع إلى أولئك الذين يتمنون لي التوفيق"

"they have a thousand times more sense than I!"
"لديهم إحساس أكثر مني بألف مرة"!

"But from now I am determined to change"
"لكن من الآن أنا مصمم على التغيير"

"I will become orderly and obedient"
"سأصبح منظما ومطيعا"

"because I have seen what happened"
"لأنني رأيت ما حدث"

"disobedient boys do not have an easy life"
"الأولاد العصاة ليس لديهم حياة سهلة"

"they come to no good and gain nothing"

"إنهم لا يأتون إلى أي خير ولا يكسبون شيئا"

"And has my papa waited for me?"

"وهل انتظرني أبي؟"

"Shall I find him at the Fairy's house?"

"هل أجده في منزل الجنية؟"

"it has been so long since I last saw him"

"لقد مر وقت طويل منذ أن رأيته آخر مرة"

"I am dying to embrace him again"

"أنا أموت لاحتضانه مرة أخرى"

"I can't wait to cover him with kisses!"

"لا استطيع الانتظار لتغطيته بالقبلات"!

"And will the Fairy forgive me my bad conduct?"

"وهل ستغفر لي الجنية سلوكي السيئ؟"

"To think of all the kindness I received from her"

"للتفكير في كل اللطف الذي تلقيته منها"

"oh how lovingly did she care for me"

"أوه كم كانت تهتم بي بمحبة"

"that I am now alive I owe to her!"

"أنني الآن على قيد الحياة أنا مدين لها"!

"could you find a more ungrateful boy"

"هل يمكن أن تجد صبيا أكثر امتنانا"

"is there a boy with less heart than I have?"

"هل هناك صبي بقلب أقل مني؟"

Whilst he was saying this he stopped suddenly

بينما كان يقول هذا توقف فجأة

he was frightened to death

كان خائفا حتى الموت

and he made four steps backwards

وقام بأربع خطوات إلى الوراء

What had Pinocchio seen?

ماذا رأى بينوكيو؟

He had seen an immense Serpent

لقد رأى ثعبانا هائلا

the snake was stretched across the road

امتد الثعبان عبر الطريق

the snake's skin was a grass green colour

كان جلد الثعبان بلون أخضر عشبي

and it had red eyes in its head

وكان لديه عيون حمراء في رأسه

and it had a long and pointed tail

وكان له ذيل طويل ومدبب

and the tail was smoking like a chimney

وكان الذيل يدخن مثل المدخنة

It would be impossible to imagine the puppet's terror

سيكون من المستحيل تخيل رعب الدمية

He walked away to a safe distance

مشى بعيدا إلى مسافة آمنة

and he sat on a heap of stones

وجلس على كومة من الحجارة

there he waited until the Serpent had finished

هناك انتظر حتى انتهى الثعبان

soon the Serpent's business should be done
قريبا يجب أن يتم عمل الثعبان
He waited an hour; two hours; three hours
انتظر ساعة .ساعتان ;ثلاث ساعات
but the Serpent was always there
لكن الثعبان كان دائما هناك
even from a distance he could see his fiery eyes
حتى من مسافة بعيدة كان يرى عينيه الناريتين
and he could see the column of smoke
وكان بإمكانه رؤية عمود الدخان
the smoke that ascended from the end of his tail
الدخان الذي صعد من نهاية ذيله
At last Pinocchio tried to feel courageous
أخيرا حاول بينوكيو أن يشعر بالشجاعة
and he approached to within a few steps
واقترب من خلال خطوات قليلة
he spoke to the Serpent in a little soft voice
تحدث إلى الثعبان بصوت ناعم قليلا
"Excuse me, Sir Serpent," he insinuated
"عفوا ، سيدي الثعبان "، ألمح
"would you be so good as to move a little?"
"هل ستكون جيدا بحيث تتحرك قليلا؟"
"just a step to the side, if you could"
"مجرد خطوة إلى الجانب ، إذا استطعت"
He might as well have spoken to the wall
ربما يكون قد تحدث أيضا إلى الحائط
He began again in the same soft voice:
بدأ مرة أخرى بنفس الصوت الناعم:
"please know, Sir Serpent, I am on my way home"
"من فضلك اعلم ، سيدي الثعبان ، أنا في طريقي إلى المنزل"
"my father is waiting for me"
"والدي ينتظرني"
"and it has been such a long time since I saw him!"
"وقد مر وقت طويل منذ أن رأيته"!
"Will you, therefore, allow me to continue?"

"هل ستسمح لي إذن بالاستمرار؟"

He waited for a sign in answer to this request

انتظر تسجيل الدخول ردا على هذا الطلب

but the snake made no answer

لكن الثعبان لم يقدم إجابة

up to that moment the serpent had been sprightly

حتى تلك اللحظة كان الثعبان رشيقا

up until then it had been full of life

حتى ذلك الحين كانت مليئة بالحياة

but now he became motionless and almost rigid

لكنه الآن أصبح بلا حراك وجامدة تقريبا

He shut his eyes and his tail ceased smoking

أغمض عينيه وتوقف ذيله عن التدخين

"Can he really be dead?" said Pinocchio

"هل يمكن أن يكون ميتا حقا؟" قال بينوكيو

and he rubbed his hands with delight

وفرك يديه بسرور

He decided to jump over him

قرر القفز فوقه

and then he could reach the other side of the road

وبعد ذلك يمكنه الوصول إلى الجانب الآخر من الطريق

Pinocchio took a little run up

أخذ بينوكيو القليل من الجري

and he went to jump over the snake

وذهب للقفز فوق الثعبان

but suddenly the Serpent raised himself on end

ولكن فجأة رفع الثعبان نفسه على النهاية

like a spring set in motion

مثل الربيع في الحركة

and the puppet stopped just in time

وتوقفت الدمية في الوقت المناسب

he stopped his feet from jumping

أوقف قدميه عن القفز

and he fell to the ground

وسقط على الأرض

he fell rather awkwardly into the mud

سقط بشكل محرج إلى حد ما في الوحل

his head got stuck in the mud

رأسه في الوحل

and his legs went into the air

وذهبت ساقيه في الهواء

the Serpent went into convulsions of laughter

دخل الثعبان في تشنجات من الضحك

it laughed until he broke a blood-vessel

ضحك حتى كسر وعاء دموي

and the snake died from all its laughter

ومات الثعبان من كل ضحكه

this time the snake really was dead

هذه المرة كان الثعبان ميتا حقا

Pinocchio then set off running again

ثم انطلق بينوكيو في الجري مرة أخرى

he hoped to reach the Fairy's house before dark

كان يأمل في الوصول إلى منزل الجنية قبل حلول الظلام

but soon he had other problems again

ولكن سرعان ما واجه مشاكل أخرى مرة أخرى

he began to suffer so dreadfully from hunger

بدأ يعاني بشكل مخيف من الجوع

and he could not bear the hunger any longer

ولم يعد بإمكانه تحمل الجوع بعد الآن

he jumped into a field by the wayside

قفز إلى حقل على جانب الطريق

perhaps there were some grapes he could pick

ربما كان هناك بعض العنب الذي يمكنه قطفه

Oh, if only he had never done it!

أوه ، لو لم يفعل ذلك أبدا!

He had scarcely reached the grapes

بالكاد وصل إلى العنب

and then there was a "cracking" sound

ثم كان هناك صوت" تكسير"

his legs were caught between something

علقت ساقيه بين شيء

he had stepped into two cutting iron bars

كان قد صعد إلى قضيبين من حديد القطع
poor Pinocchio became giddy with pain
أصبح بينوكيو المسكين دائخا من الألم
stars of every colour danced before his eyes
رقصت النجوم من كل لون أمام عينيه
The poor puppet had been caught in a trap
تم القبض على الدمية المسكينة في فخ
it had been put there to capture polecats
تم وضعه هناك للقبض على القطط القطبية

Pinocchio Becomes a Watch-Dog
بينوكيو يصبح حراسة

Pinocchio began to cry and scream
بدأ بينوكيو في البكاء والصراخ
but his tears and groans were useless
لكن دموعه وآهاته كانت عديمة الفائدة
because there was not a house to be seen
لأنه لم يكن هناك منزل يمكن رؤيته
nor did living soul pass down the road

ولم تمر الروح الحية على الطريق

At last the night had come on

أخيرا جاء الليل

the trap had cut into his leg

كان الفخ قد قطع ساقه

the pain brought him the point of fainting

جلب له الألم نقطة الإغماء

he was scared from being alone

كان خائفا من أن يكون وحيدا

he didn't like the darkness

لم يعجبه الظلام

Just at that moment he saw a Firefly

في تلك اللحظة فقط رأى اليراع

He called to the firefly and said:

نادى على اليراع وقال:

"Oh, little Firefly, will you have pity on me?"

"أوه ، اليراع الصغير ، هل ستشفق علي؟"

"please liberate me from this torture"

"أرجوكم حرروني من هذا التعذيب"

"Poor boy!" said the Firefly

"الولد المسكين "إقال اليراع

the Firefly stopped and looked at him with compassion

توقف اليراع ونظر إليه بشفقة

"your legs have been caught by those sharp irons"

"لقد تم القبض على ساقيك من قبل تلك المكواة الحادة"

"how did you get yourself into this trap?

"كيف أوقعت نفسك في هذا الفخ؟

"I came into the field to pick grapes"

"جئت إلى الحقل لقطف العنب"

"But where did you plant your grapes?"

"ولكن أين زرعت عنبك؟"

"No, they were not my grapes"

"لا ، لم يكونوا عنبي"

"who taught you to carry off other people's property?"

"من علمك أن تحمل ممتلكات الآخرين؟"

"I was so hungry," Pinocchio whimpered

"كنت جائعا جدا "، تذمر بينوكيو

"Hunger is not a good reason"

"الجوع ليس سببا وجيها"

"we cannot appropriated what does not belong to us"

"لا يمكننا الاستيلاء على ما لا يخصنا"

"That is true, that is true!" said Pinocchio, crying

"هذا صحيح ، هذا صحيح "،قال بينوكيو وهو يبكي

"I will never do it again," he promised

"لن أفعل ذلك مرة أخرى "، وعد

At this moment their conversation was interrupted

في هذه اللحظة انقطعت محادثتهم

there was a slight sound of approaching footsteps

كان هناك صوت طفيف لخطوات تقترب

It was the owner of the field coming on tiptoe

كان صاحب الحقل قادماً على رؤوس الأصابع

he wanted to see if he had caught a polecat

أراد أن يرى ما إذا كان قد قبض على قطب

the polecat that ate his chickens in the night

القطب الذي أكل دجاجه في الليل

but he was surprised by what was in his trap

لكنه فوجئ بما كان في فخه

instead of a polecat, a boy had been captured

بدلا من القط القطبي ، تم القبض على صبي

"Ah, little thief," said the angry peasant,

"آه ، لص صغير "، قال الفلاح الغاضب ،

"then it is you who carries off my chickens?"

"إذن أنت الذي تحمل دجاجاتي؟"

"No, I have not been carrying off your chickens"

"لا ، لم أحمل دجاجاتك"

"I only came into the field to take two grapes!"

"جئت إلى الحقل فقط لأخذ اثنين من العنب"!

"He who steals grapes can easily steal chicken"

"من يسرق العنب يمكنه بسهولة سرقة الدجاج"

"Leave it to me to teach you a lesson"

"اترك الأمر لي لأعلمك درسا"
"and you won't forget this lesson in a hurry"
"ولن تنسى هذا الدرس على عجل"
Opening the trap, he seized the puppet by the collar
فتح الفخ ، استولى على الدمية من ذوي الياقات البيضاء
and he carried him to his house like a young lamb
وحمله إلى بيته مثل حمل صغير
they reached the yard in front of the house
وصلوا إلى الفناء أمام المنزل
and he threw him roughly on the ground
وألقاه على الأرض تقريبا
he put his foot on his neck and said to him:
وضع قدمه على عنقه وقال له:
"It is late and I want to go to bed"
"الوقت متأخر وأريد أن أذهب إلى الفراش"
"we will settle our accounts tomorrow"
"سنقوم بتسوية حساباتنا غدا"
"the dog who kept guard at night died today"
"الذي ظل حارسا في الليل مات اليوم"
"you will live in his place from now"
"ستعيش في مكانه من الآن"
"You shall be my watch-dog from now"
"ستكون المراقبة الخاص بي من الآن"
he took a great dog collar covered with brass knobs
أخذ طوق كبير مغطى بمقابض نحاسية
and he strapped the dog collar around Pinocchio's neck
وربط طوق حول رقبة بينوكيو
it was so tight that he could not pull his head out
كان ضيقا لدرجة أنه لم يستطع سحب رأسه للخارج
the dog collar was attached to a heavy chain
تم ربط طوق بسلسلة ثقيلة
and the heavy chain was fastened to the wall
وتم تثبيت السلسلة الثقيلة على الحائط
"If it rains tonight you can go into the kennel"
"إذا هطل المطر الليلة يمكنك الذهاب إلى بيت"

"my poor dog had a little bed of straw in there"

"كلبي المسكين كان لديه سرير صغير من القش هناك"

"remember to keep your ears pricked for robbers"

"تذكر أن تبقي أذنيك وخز للصوص"

"and if you hear robbers, then bark loudly"

"وإذا سمعت اللصوص ، ثم النباح بصوت عال"

Pinocchio had received his orders for the night

تلقى بينوكيو أوامره ليلا

and the poor man finally went to bed

وأخيرا ذهب الرجل الفقير إلى الفراش

Poor Pinocchio remained lying on the ground

بقي بينوكيو المسكين ملقى على الأرض

he felt more dead than he felt alive

شعر بأنه ميت أكثر مما شعر بأنه على قيد الحياة

the cold, and hunger, and fear had taken all his energy

البرد والجوع والخوف قد أخذ كل طاقته

From time to time he put his hands angrily to the go collar

من وقت لآخر وضع يديه بغضب على طوق الذهاب

"It serves me right!" he said to himself
"إنه يخدمني بشكل صحيح "إقال لنفسه
"I was determined to be a vagabond"
"كنت مصمما على أن أكون متشردا"
"I wanted to live the life of a good-for-nothing"
"أردت أن أعيش حياة جيدة مقابل لا شيء"
"I used to listen to bad companions"
"كنت أستمع إلى الصحابة السيئين"
"and that is why I always meet with misfortunes"
"وهذا هو السبب في أنني دائما ما أقابل المصائب"
"if only I had been a good little boy"
"لو كنت صبيا صغيرا جيدا"
"then I would not be in the midst of the field"
"عندها لن أكون في وسط الميدان"
"I wouldn't be here if I had stayed at home"
"لم أكن لأكون هنا لو بقيت في المنزل"
"I wouldn't be a watch-dog if I had stayed with my papa"
"لن أكون حراسة إذا بقيت مع أبي"
"Oh, if only I could be born again!"
"أوه ، لو كان بإمكاني أن أولد من جديد"!
"But now it is too late to change anything"
"لكن الآن فات الأوان لتغيير أي شيء"
"the best thing to do now is having patience!"
"أفضل شيء نفعله الآن هو التحلي بالصبر"!
he was relieved by this little outburst
لقد شعر بالارتياح من هذا الانفجار الصغير
because it had come straight from his heart
لأنه جاء مباشرة من قلبه
and he went into the dog-kennel and fell asleep
وذهب إلى بيت ونام

Pinocchio Discovers the Robbers
بينوكيو يكتشف اللصوص

He had been sleeping heavily for about two hours
كان ينام بشدة لمدة ساعتين تقريبا

then he was aroused by a strange whispering
ثم أثاره همس غريب

the strange voices were coming from the courtyard
كانت الأصوات الغريبة قادمة من الفناء

he put the point of his nose out of the kennel
وضع نقطة أنفه من بيت

and he saw four little beasts with dark fur
ورأى أربعة وحوش صغيرة ذات فرو داكن

they looked like cats making a plan
بدوا مثل القطط التي تضع خطة

But they were not cats, they were polecats
لكنهم لم يكونوا قططا ، كانوا قططا قططا

what polecats are are carnivorous little animals
ما هي القطط هي صغيرة آكلة اللحوم

they are especially greedy for eggs and young chickens
هم جشعون بشكل خاص للبيض والدجاج الصغير

One of the polecats came to the opening of the kennel
جاء أحد القطبين إلى افتتاح بيت

he spoke in a low voice, "Good evening, Melampo"
تحدث بصوت منخفض ،" مساء الخير ، ميلامبو"

"My name is not Melampo," answered the puppet
»اسمي ليس ميلامبو«، أجاب الدمية

"Oh! then who are you?" asked the polecat
"أوه إثم من أنت؟ "سأل القطب

"I am Pinocchio," answered Pinocchio
"أنا بينوكيو "، أجاب بينوكيو

"And what are you doing here?"
"وماذا تفعل هنا؟"

"I am acting as watch-dog," confirmed Pinocchio
"أنا أتصرف ككلب حراسة "، أكد بينوكيو

"Then where is Melampo?" wondered the polecat
"إذن أين ميلامبو؟ "تساءل القطب
"Where is the old dog who lived in this kennel?"
"أين العجوز الذي عاش في بيت هذا؟"
"He died this morning," Pinocchio informed
"لقد مات هذا الصباح "، أبلغ بينوكيو
"Is he dead? Poor beast! He was so good"
"هل مات؟ الوحش المسكين !لقد كان جيدا جدا"
"but I would say that you were also a good dog"
"لكنني أود أن أقول إنك كنت أيضا جيدا"
"I can see it in your face"
"أستطيع أن أرى ذلك في وجهك"
"I beg your pardon, I am not a dog"
"أستميحك عذرا ، أنا لست"
"Not a dog? Then what are you?"
"ليس؟ ثم ما أنت؟"
"I am a puppet," corrected Pinocchio
"أنا دمية "، صحح بينوكيو
"And you are acting as watch-dog?"
"وأنت تتصرف ككلب حراسة؟"
"now you understand the situation"
"الآن أنت تفهم الوضع"
"I have been made to be a watch dog as a punishment"
"لقد خلقت لأكون مراقبة كعقاب"
"well, then we shall tell you what the deal is"
"حسنا ، سنخبرك ما هي الصفقة"
"the same deal we had with the deceased Melampo"
"نفس الصفقة التي أبرمناها مع المتوفى ميلامبو"
"I am sure you will be agree to the deal"
"أنا متأكد من أنك ستوافق على الصفقة"
"What are the conditions of this deal?"
"ما هي شروط هذه الصفقة؟"
"one night a week we will visit the poultry-yard"
"ليلة واحدة في الأسبوع سنزور ساحة الدواجن"

"and you will allow us to carry off eight chickens"
"وسوف تسمح لنا بحمل ثمانية دجاجات"
"Of these chickens seven are to be eaten by us"
"من هذه الدجاجات سبعة يجب أن نأكلها نحن"
"and we will give one chicken to you"
"وسنعطيك دجاجة واحدة"
"your end of the bargain is very easy"
"نهايتك من الصفقة سهلة للغاية"
"all you have to do is pretend to be asleep"
"كل ما عليك فعله هو التظاهر بأنك نائم"
"and don't get any ideas about barking"
"ولا تحصل على أي أفكار حول النباح"
"you are not to wake the peasant when we come"
"لا يجب أن توقظ الفلاح عندما نأتي"
"Did Melampo act in this manner?" asked Pinocchio
"هل تصرف ميلامبو بهذه الطريقة؟" سأل بينوكيو
"that is the deal we had with Melampo"
"هذه هي الصفقة التي أبرمناها مع ميلامبو"
"and we were always on the best terms with him
"وكنا دائما على أفضل علاقة معه"
"sleep quietly and let us do our business"
"نم بهدوء ودعونا نقوم بأعمالنا"
"and in the morning you will have a beautiful chicken"
"وفي الصباح سيكون لديك دجاجة جميلة"
"it will be ready plucked for your breakfast tomorrow"
"سيكون جاهزا لتناول الإفطار غدا"
"Have we understood each other clearly?"
"هل فهمنا بعضنا البعض بوضوح؟"
"Only too clearly!" answered Pinocchio
"فقط بوضوح شديد!" أجاب بينوكيو
and he shook his head threateningly
وهز رأسه مهددا
as if to say: "You shall hear of this shortly!"
كما لو كان يقول: "سوف تسمع عن هذا قريبا"!

the four polecats thought that they had a deal
اعتقدت القطبات الأربعة أن لديهم صفقة

so they continued to the poultry-yard
لذلك استمروا في ساحة الدواجن

first they opened the gate with their teeth
أولا فتحوا البوابة بأسنانهم

and then they slipped in one by one
ثم انزلقوا واحدا تلو الآخر

they hadn't been in the chicken-coup for long
لم يكونوا في انقلاب الدجاج لفترة طويلة

but then they heard the gate shut behind them
ولكن بعد ذلك سمعوا البوابة تغلق خلفهم

It was Pinocchio who had shut the gate
كان بينوكيو هو الذي أغلق البوابة

and Pinocchio took some extra security measures
واتخذ بينوكيو بعض التدابير الأمنية الإضافية

he put a large stone against the gate
وضع حجرا كبيرا على البوابة

this way the polecats couldn't get out again
بهذه الطريقة لم تستطع القطط الخروج مرة أخرى

and then Pinocchio began to bark like a dog
ثم بدأ بينوكيو ينبح مثل

and he barked exactly like a watch-dog barks
ونبح تماما مثل المراقبة ينبح

the peasant heard Pinocchio barking
سمع الفلاح بينوكيو ينبح

he quickly awoke and jumped out of bed
استيقظ بسرعة وقفز من السرير

with his gun he came to the window
بمسدسه جاء إلى النافذة

and from the window he called to Pinocchio
ومن النافذة دعا بينوكيو

"What is the matter?" he asked the puppet
"ما الأمر؟" سأل الدمية

"There are robbers!" answered Pinocchio
"هناك لصوص!" أجاب بينوكيو

"Where are they?" he wanted to know

"أين هم؟ "أراد أن يعرف

"they are in the poultry-yard," confirmed Pinocchio

"إنهم في ساحة الدواجن "، أكد بينوكيو

"I will come down directly," said the peasant

"سأنزل مباشرة "، قال الفلاح

and he came down in a great hurry

ونزل في عجلة من أمره

it would have taken less time to say "Amen"

"كان سيستغرق وقتا أقل لقول" آمين

He rushed into the poultry-yard

هرع إلى ساحة الدواجن

and quickly he caught all the polecats

وسرعان ما قبض على جميع القطط

and then he put the polecats into a sack

ثم وضع القططين في كيس

he said to them in a tone of great satisfaction:

قال لهم بنبرة ارتياح كبير:

"At last you have fallen into my hands!"

"أخيرا سقطت في يدي"!

"I could punish you, if I wanted to"

"يمكنني معاقبتك ، إذا أردت ذلك"

"but I am not so cruel," he comforted them

"لكنني لست قاسيا جدا "، عزاهم

"I will content myself in other ways"

"سأكتفي بطرق أخرى"

"I will carry you in the morning to the innkeeper"

"سأحملك في الصباح إلى صاحب النزل"

"he will skin and cook you like hares"

"سوف يسلخك ويطبخك مثل الأرانب"

"and you will be served with a sweet sauce"

"وسيتم تقديمك مع صلصة حلوة"

"It is an honour that you don't deserve"

"إنه لشرف لا تستحقه"

"you're lucky I am so generous with you"

"أنت محظوظ لأنني كريم جدا معك"

He then approached Pinocchio and stroked him

ثم اقترب من بينوكيو وداعبه

"How did you manage to discover the four thieves?"

"كيف تمكنت من اكتشاف اللصوص الأربعة؟"

"my faithful Melampo never found out anything!"

"لم يكتشف ميلامبو المؤمن أي شيء"!

The puppet could then have told him the whole story

كان بإمكان الدمية بعد ذلك أن تخبره القصة كاملة

he could have told him about the treacherous deal

كان بإمكانه أن يخبره عن الصفقة الغادرة

but he remembered that the dog was dead

لكنه تذكر أن قد مات

and the puppet thought to himself:

وفكرت الدمية في نفسها:

"of what use it it accusing the dead?"

"من أي فائدة يتهم الموتى؟"

"The dead are no longer with us"

"الموتى لم يعودوا معنا"

"it is best to leave the dead in peace!"

"من الأفضل ترك الموتى بسلام"!

the peasant went on to ask more questions

ذهب الفلاح لطرح المزيد من الأسئلة

"were you sleeping when the thieves came?"

"هل كنت نائما عندما جاء اللصوص؟"

"I was asleep," answered Pinocchio

"كنت نائما"، أجاب بينوكيو

"but the polecats woke me with their chatter"

"لكن القطط أيقظتني بثرثرتهم"

"one of the polecats came to the kennel"

"جاء أحد القطبين إلى بيت"

he tried to make a terrible deal with me

حاول عقد صفقة رهيبة معي

"promise not to bark and we'll give you fine chicken"

"وعد بعدم النباح وسنقدم لك دجاجة جيدة"
"I was offended by such an underhanded offer"
"لقد شعرت بالإهانة من مثل هذا العرض المخادع"
"I can admit that I am a naughty puppet"
"أستطيع أن أعترف بأنني دمية شقية"
"but there is one thing I will never be guilty of"
"ولكن هناك شيء واحد لن أكون مذنبا به أبدا"
"I will not make terms with dishonest people!"
"لن أتصالح مع أشخاص غير شريفين"!
"and I will not share their dishonest gains"
"ولن أشاركهم مكاسبهم غير الشريفة"
"Well said, my boy!" cried the peasant
"أحسنت القول يا ولدي "إصرخ الفلاح
and he patted Pinocchio on the shoulder
وربت بينوكيو على كتفه
"Such sentiments do you great honour, my boy"
"مثل هذه المشاعر شرف عظيم لك يا ولدي"
"let me show you proof of my gratitude to you"
"دعني أريكم دليلا على امتناني لك"
"I will at once set you at liberty"
"سأطلقك الحرية على الفور"
"and you may return home as you please"
"ويمكنك العودة إلى المنزل كما يحلو لك"
And he removed the dog-collar from Pinocchio
وأزال طوق من بينوكيو

Pinocchio Flies to the Seashore
بينوكيو يطير إلى شاطئ البحر

a dog-collar had hung around Pinocchio's neck
كان طوق معلقا حول رقبة بينوكيو
but now Pinocchio had his freedom again
ولكن الآن حصل بينوكيو على حريته مرة أخرى
and he wore the humiliating dog-collar no more
ولم يعد يرتدي طوق المهين
he ran off across the fields
ركض عبر الحقول
and he kept running until he reached the road
واستمر في الجري حتى وصل إلى الطريق
the road that led to the Fairy's house
الطريق المؤدي إلى منزل الجنية
in the woods he could see the Big Oak tree
في الغابة كان بإمكانه رؤية شجرة البلوط الكبيرة
the Big Oak tree to which he had been hung
شجرة البلوط الكبيرة التي عليها
Pinocchio looked around in every direction
نظر بينوكيو حوله في كل اتجاه
but he couldn't see his sister's house
لكنه لم يستطع رؤية منزل أخته
the house of the beautiful Child with blue hair
بيت الطفل الجميل ذو الشعر الأزرق
Pinocchio was seized with a sad presentiment
تم القبض على بينوكيو بشعور حزين
he began to run with all the strength he had left
بدأ يركض بكل القوة التي تركها
in a few minutes he reached the field
في بضع دقائق وصل إلى الميدان
he was where the little house had once stood
كان حيث كان المنزل الصغير يقف ذات مرة
But the little white house was no longer there
لكن البيت الأبيض الصغير لم يعد موجودا
Instead of the house he saw a marble stone

بدلا من المنزل رأى حجرا رخاميا

on the stone were engraved these sad words:

على الحجر نقشت هذه الكلمات الحزينة:

"Here lies the child with the blue hair"

"هنا يرقد الطفل ذو الشعر الأزرق"

"she was abandoned by her little brother Pinocchio"

"لقد تخلى عنها شقيقها الصغير بينوكيو"

"and from the sorrow she succumbed to death"

"ومن الحزن استسلمت للموت"

with difficulty he had read this epitaph

بصعوبة قرأ هذه المرثية

I leave you to imagine the puppet's feelings

أتركك لتتخيل مشاعر الدمية

He fell with his face on the ground

سقط ووجهه على الأرض

he covered the tombstone with a thousand kisses

غطى شاهد القبر بألف قبلة

and he burst into an agony of tears

وانفجر في عذاب من الدموع

He cried for all of that night

بكى طوال تلك الليلة

and when morning came he was still crying

وعندما جاء الصباح كان لا يزال يبكي

he cried although he had no tears left

بكى على الرغم من أنه لم يبق لديه دموع

his lamentations were heart-breaking

كانت رثاءه مفجعة

and his sobs echoed in the surrounding hills

وتردد صدى تنهداته في التلال المحيطة

And while he was weeping he said:

وبينما هو يبكي قال:

"Oh, little Fairy, why did you die?"

"أوه ، الجنية الصغيرة ، لماذا مت؟"

"Why did I not die instead of you?"

"لماذا لم أموت بدلا منك؟"

"I who am so wicked, whilst you were so good"

"أنا الشرير جدا ، بينما كنت جيدا جدا"

"And my papa? Where can he be?"

"وأبي؟ أين يمكن أن يكون؟"

"Oh, little Fairy, tell me where I can find him"

"أوه ، الجنية الصغيرة ، أخبرني أين يمكنني العثور عليه"

"for I want to remain with him always"

"لأني أريد أن أبقى معه دائما"

"and I never want to leave him ever again!"

"ولا أريد أن أتركه مرة أخرى"!

"tell me that it is not true that you are dead!"

"قل لي أنه ليس صحيحا أنك ميت"!

"If you really love your little brother, come to life again"

"إذا كنت تحب أخاك الصغير حقا ، تعال إلى الحياة مرة أخرى"

"Does it not grieve you to see me alone in the world?"

"ألا يحزنك أن تراني وحدي في العالم؟"

"does it not sadden you to see me abandoned by everybody?"

"ألا يحزنك أن تراني مهجورا من قبل الجميع؟"

"If assassins come they will hang me from the tree again"

"إذا جاء القتلة فسوف يعلقونني من الشجرة مرة أخرى"

"and this time I would die indeed"

"وهذه المرة سأموت حقا"

"What can I do here alone in the world?"

"ماذا يمكنني أن أفعل هنا وحدي في العالم؟"

"I have lost you and my papa"

"لقد فقدتك أنت وأبي"

"who will love me and give me food now?"

"من سيحبني ويعطيني الطعام الآن؟"

"Where shall I go to sleep at night?"

"أين أذهب للنوم ليلا؟"

"Who will make me a new jacket?"

"من سيصنع لي سترة جديدة؟"

"Oh, it would be better for me to die also!"

"أوه ، سيكون من الأفضل لي أن أموت أيضا"!
"not to live would be a hundred times better"
"عدم العيش سيكون أفضل مائة مرة"
"Yes, I want to die," he concluded
واختتم قائلا» :نعم، أريد أن أموت.«
And in his despair he tried to tear his hair
وفي يأسه حاول تمزيق شعره
but his hair was made of wood
لكن شعره كان مصنوعا من الخشب
so he could not have the satisfaction
لذلك لم يستطع الحصول على الرضا
Just then a large Pigeon flew over his head
عندها فقط طار حمامة كبيرة فوق رأسه
the pigeon stopped with distended wings
توقف الحمام بأجنحة منتفخة
and the pigeon called down from a great height
ونادى الحمام من ارتفاع كبير
"Tell me, child, what are you doing there?"
"قل لي ، يا طفل ، ماذا تفعل هناك؟"
"Don't you see? I am crying!" said Pinocchio
"ألا ترى؟ أنا أبكي "إقال بينوكيو
and he raised his head towards the voice
ورفع رأسه نحو الصوت
and he rubbed his eyes with his jacket
وفرك عينيه بسترته
"Tell me," continued the Pigeon
"أخبرني "، تابع الحمام
"do you happen to know a puppet called Pinocchio?"
"هل تعرف دمية تدعى بينوكيو؟"
"Pinocchio? Did you say Pinocchio?" repeated the puppet
"بينوكيو؟ هل قلت بينوكيو؟ "كررت الدمية
and he quickly jumped to his feet
وسرعان ما قفز على قدميه
"I am Pinocchio!" he exclaimed with hope
"أنا بينوكيو! "هتف بأمل

At this answer the Pigeon descended rapidly

في هذه الإجابة نزل الحمام بسرعة

He was larger than a turkey

كان أكبر من ديك رومي

"Do you also know Geppetto?" he asked

"هل تعرف أيضا جيبيتو؟" سأل

"Do I know him! He is my poor papa!"

"هل أعرفه !إنه بابا المسكين"!

"Has he perhaps spoken to you of me?"

"هل ربما كلمك عني؟"

"Will you take me to him?"

"هل ستأخذني إليه؟"

"Is he still alive?"

"هل ما زال على قيد الحياة؟"

"Answer me, for pity's sake"

"أجبني ، من أجل الشفقة"

"is he still alive??"

"هل لا يزال على قيد الحياة ؟؟"

"I left him three days ago on the seashore"

"تركته قبل ثلاثة أيام على شاطئ البحر"

"What was he doing?" Pinocchio had to know

"ماذا كان يفعل؟ "كان على بينوكيو أن يعرف

"He was building a little boat for himself"

"كان يبني قاربا صغيرا لنفسه"

"he was going to cross the ocean"

"كان سيعبر المحيط"

"that poor man has been going all round the world"

"هذا الرجل الفقير كان يذهب في جميع أنحاء العالم"

"he has been looking for you"

"لقد كان يبحث عنك"

"but he had no success in finding you"

"لكنه لم ينجح في العثور عليك"

"so now he will go to the distant countries"

"حتى الآن سوف يذهب إلى البلدان البعيدة"

"he will search for you in the New World"

"سوف يبحث عنك في العالم الجديد"

"How far is it from here to the shore?"

"كم يبعد من هنا إلى الشاطئ؟"

"More than six hundred miles"

"أكثر من ستمائة ميل"

"Six hundred miles?" echoed Pinocchio

"ستمائة ميل؟ "ردد بينوكيو

"Oh, beautiful Pigeon," pleaded Pinocchio

"أوه ، حمامة جميلة "، ناشد بينوكيو

"what a fine thing it would be to have your wings!"

"يا له من شيء جيد أن يكون لديك أجنحتك"!

"If you wish to go, I will carry you there"

"إذا كنت ترغب في الذهاب ، سأحملك إلى هناك"

"How could you carry me there?"

"كيف يمكنك حملي إلى هناك؟"

"I can carry you on my back"

"أستطيع أن أحملك على ظهري"

"Do you weigh much?"

"هل تزن كثيرا؟"

"I weigh next to nothing"

"أنا لا أزن شيئا تقريبا"

"I am as light as a feather"

"أنا خفيف مثل الريشة"

Pinocchio didn't hesitate for another moment

لم يتردد بينوكيو للحظة أخرى

and he jumped at once on the Pigeon's back

وقفز في الحال على ظهر الحمام

he put a leg on each side of the pigeon

وضع ساق على كل جانب من الحمام

just like men do when they're riding horseback

تماما كما يفعل الرجال عندما يركبون الخيل

and Pinocchio exclaimed joyfully:

وصرخ بينوكيو بفرح:

"Gallop, gallop, my little horse"

"بالفرس ، العدو ، حصاني الصغير"

"because I am anxious to arrive quickly!"

"لأنني حريص على الوصول بسرعة"!

The Pigeon took flight into the air

أخذت حمامة الطيران في الهواء

and in a few minutes they almost touched the clouds

وفي بضع دقائق كادوا يلمسون الغيوم

now the puppet was at an immense height

الآن كانت الدمية على ارتفاع هائل

and he became more and more curious

وأصبح فضوليا أكثر فأكثر

so he looked down to the ground

لذلك نظر إلى الأرض

but his head spun round in dizziness

لكن رأسه يدور في دوخة

he became ever so frightened of the height

أصبح خائفا جدا من الارتفاع

and he had to save himself from the danger of falling
وكان عليه أن ينقذ نفسه من خطر السقوط

and so held tightly to his feathered steed
وهكذا تمسك بإحكام بفرسه الريش

They flew through the skies all of that day
طاروا في السماء طوال ذلك اليوم

Towards evening the Pigeon said:
قرب المساء قال الحمام:

"I am very thirsty from all this flying!"
"أنا عطشان جدا من كل هذا الطيران"!

"And I am very hungry!" agreed Pinocchio
"وأنا جائع جدا "!وافق بينوكيو

"Let us stop at that dovecote for a few minutes"
"دعونا نتوقف عند تلك الحمامة لبضع دقائق"

"and then we will continue our journey"
"وبعد ذلك سنواصل رحلتنا"

"then we may reach the seashore by dawn tomorrow"
"ثم قد نصل إلى شاطئ البحر بحلول فجر الغد"

They went into a deserted dovecote
ذهبوا إلى حمامة مهجورة

here they found nothing but a basin full of water
هنا لم يجدوا سوى حوض مليء بالماء

and they found a basket full of vetch
ووجدوا سلة مليئة بالبيقية

The puppet had never in his life been able to eat vetch
لم تكن الدمية في حياته قادرة على أكل البيقية

according to him it made him sick
وفقا له جعله مريضا

That evening, however, he ate to repletion
في ذلك المساء ، أكل حتى الملء

and he nearly emptied the basket of it
وكاد يفرغ السلة منها

and then he turned to the Pigeon and said to him:
ثم التفت إلى الحمامة وقال له:

"I never could have believed that vetch was so good!"

"لم أكن أصدق أبدا أن البيقية كانت جيدة جدا"!

"Be assured, my boy," replied the Pigeon

"كن مطمئنا يا ولدي "، أجاب الحمام

"when hunger is real even vetch becomes delicious"

"عندما يكون الجوع حقيقيا ، يصبح البيقية لذيذا"

"Hunger knows neither caprice nor greediness"

"الجوع لا يعرف النزوة ولا الجشع"

the two quickly finished their little meal

أنهى الاثنان بسرعة وجبتهما الصغيرة

and they recommenced their journey and flew away

واستأنفوا رحلتهم وطاروا بعيدا

The following morning they reached the seashore

في صباح اليوم التالي وصلوا إلى شاطئ البحر

The Pigeon placed Pinocchio on the ground

وضعت الحمامة بينوكيو على الأرض

the pigeon did not wish to be troubled with thanks

الحمام لا يرغب في أن ينزعج من الشكر

it was indeed a good action he had done

لقد كان بالفعل عملا جيدا قام به

but he had done it out the goodness of his heart

لكنه فعل ذلك بطيبة قلبه

and Pinocchio had no time to lose

ولم يكن لدى بينوكيو وقت يضيعه

so he flew quickly away and disappeared

لذلك طار بسرعة بعيدا واختفى

The shore was crowded with people

كان الشاطئ مزدحما بالناس

the people were looking out to sea

كان الناس ينظرون إلى البحر

they shouting and gesticulating at something

يصرخون ويشيرون إلى شيء ما

"What has happened?" asked Pinocchio of an old woman

"ماذا حدث؟ "سأل بينوكيو عن امرأة عجوز

"there is a poor father who has lost his son"

"هناك أب فقير فقد ابنه"

"he has gone out to sea in a little boat"
"لقد خرج إلى البحر في قارب صغير"

"he will search for him on the other side of the water"
"سيبحث عنه على الجانب الآخر من الماء"

"and today the sea is most tempestuous"
"واليوم البحر هو الأكثر عاصفة"

"and the little boat is in danger of sinking"
"والقارب الصغير في خطر الغرق"

"Where is the little boat?" asked Pinocchio
"أين القارب الصغير؟" سأل بينوكيو

"It is out there in a line with my finger"
"إنه موجود في خط بإصبعي"

and she pointed to a little boat
وأشارت إلى قارب صغير

and the little boat looked like a little nutshell
وبدا القارب الصغير وكأنه باختصار صغير

a little nutshell with a very little man in it
باختصار مع رجل صغير جدا في ذلك

Pinocchio fixed his eyes on the little nutshell
ثبت بينوكيو عينيه على الخلاصة الصغيرة

after looking attentively he gave a piercing scream:
بعد أن نظر باهتمام أطلق صرخة خارقة:

"It is my papa! It is my papa!"
"إنه بابا! إنه أبي"!

The boat, meanwhile, was being beaten by the fury of the waves
في غضون ذلك ، كان القارب يتعرض للضرب من غضب الأمواج

at one moment it disappeared in the trough of the sea
في لحظة واحدة اختفى في حوض البحر

and in the next moment the boat came to the surface again
وفي اللحظة التالية ظهر القارب على السطح مرة أخرى

Pinocchio stood on the top of a high rock
وقف بينوكيو على قمة صخرة عالية

and he kept calling to his father
وظل ينادي والده

and he made every kind of signal to him
وقدم له كل نوع من الإشارات

he waved his hands, his handkerchief, and his cap
لوح بيديه ومنديله وقبعته

Pinocchio was very far away from him
كان بينوكيو بعيدا جدا عنه

but Geppetto appeared to recognize his son
لكن يبدو أن جيبيتو يتعرف على ابنه

and he also took off his cap and waved it
وخلع أيضا قبعته ولوح بها

he tried by gestures to make him understand
حاول بالإيماءات أن يجعله يفهم

"I would have returned if it were possible"
"كنت سأعود لو كان ذلك ممكنا"

"but the sea is most tempestuous"
"لكن البحر هو الأكثر عاصفة"

"and my oars won't take me to the shores again"
"ولن تأخذني مجاديفي إلى الشواطئ مرة أخرى"

Suddenly a tremendous wave rose out of the sea
فجأة ارتفعت موجة هائلة من البحر

and then the the little nutshell disappeared
ثم اختفى الاختصار الصغير

They waited, hoping the boat would come again to the surface
انتظروا ، على أمل أن يأتي القارب مرة أخرى إلى السطح

but the little boat was seen no more
لكن القارب الصغير لم يعد يرى

the fisherman had assembled at the shore
كان الصياد قد تجمع على الشاطئ

"Poor man!" they said of him, and murmured a prayer
"رجل مسكين "إقالوا عنه ، وتمتم صلاة

and then they turned to go home
ثم التفتوا للعودة إلى ديارهم

Just then they heard a desperate cry
عندها فقط سمعوا صرخة يائسة

looking back, they saw a little boy

بالنظر إلى الوراء ، رأوا صبيا صغيرا

"I will save my papa," the boy exclaimed

"سأنقذ بابا "، هتف الصبي

and he jumped from a rock into the sea

وقفز من صخرة إلى البحر

as you know Pinocchio was made of wood

كما تعلمون بينوكيو كان مصنوعا من الخشب

so he floated easily on the water

لذلك طاف بسهولة على الماء

and he swam as well as a fish

وسبح وكذلك سمكة

At one moment they saw him disappear under the water

في لحظة واحدة رأوه يختفي تحت الماء

he was carried down by the fury of the waves

حمله غضب الأمواج

and in the next moment he reappeared to the surface of the water

وفي اللحظة التالية ظهر مرة أخرى على سطح الماء

he struggled on swimming with a leg or an arm

كافح في السباحة بساق أو ذراع

but at last they lost sight of him

لكن في النهاية فقدوا رؤيته

and he was seen no more

ولم يعد يرى

and they offered another prayer for the puppet

وقدموا صلاة أخرى للدمية

Pinocchio Finds the Fairy Again
بينوكيو يجد الجنية مرة أخرى

Pinocchio wanted to be in time to help his father
أراد بينوكيو أن يكون في الوقت المناسب لمساعدة والده

so he swam all through the night
لذلك سبح طوال الليل

And what a horrible night it was!
ويا لها من ليلة رهيبة!

The rain came down in torrents
نزل المطر في السيول

it hailed and the thunder was frightful
هتف وكان الرعد مخيفا

the flashes of lightning made it as light as day
ومضات البرق جعلته خفيفا مثل النهار

Towards morning he saw a long strip of land

قرب الصباح رأى شريطا طويلا من الأرض

It was an island in the midst of the sea

كانت جزيرة في وسط البحر

He tried his utmost to reach the shore

لقد بذل قصارى جهده للوصول إلى الشاطئ

but his efforts were all in vain

لكن جهوده ذهبت سدى

The waves raced and tumbled over each other

تسابقت الأمواج وهبطت فوق بعضها البعض

and the torrent knocked Pinocchio about

وطرق السيل بينوكيو حول

it was as if he had been a wisp of straw

كان الأمر كما لو كان خصلة من القش

At last, fortunately for him, a billow rolled up

أخيرا ، لحسن حظه ، تدحرجت خوار

it rose with such fury that he was lifted up

ارتفع بغضب شديد لدرجة أنه تم رفعه

and finally he was thrown on to the sands

وأخيرا تم إلقاؤه على الرمال

the little puppet crashed onto the ground

تحطمت الدمية الصغيرة على الأرض

and all his joints cracked from the impact

وجميع مفاصله متشققة من الارتطام

but he comforted himself, saying:

لكنه عزى نفسه قائلا:

"This time also I have made a wonderful escape!"

"هذه المرة أيضا قمت بهروب رائع"!

Little by little the sky cleared

شيئا فشيئا صفت السماء

the sun shone out in all his splendour

أشرقت الشمس بكل روعته

and the sea became as quiet and smooth as oil

وأصبح البحر هادئا وسلسا مثل النفط

The puppet put his clothes in the sun to dry

وضعت الدمية ملابسه في الشمس لتجف

and he began to look in every direction

وبدأ ينظر في كل اتجاه

somewhere on the water there must be a little boat

في مكان ما على الماء يجب أن يكون هناك قارب صغير

and in the boat he hoped to see a little man

وفي القارب كان يأمل أن يرى رجلا صغيرا

he looked out to sea as far as he could see

نظر إلى البحر بقدر ما يستطيع أن يرى

but all he saw was the sky and the sea

لكن كل ما رآه هو السماء والبحر

"If I only knew what this island was called!"

"لو كنت أعرف فقط ما كانت تسمى هذه الجزيرة"!

"If I only knew whether it was inhabited"

"إذا كنت أعرف فقط ما إذا كانت مأهولة"

"perhaps civilized people do live here"

"ربما يعيش الناس المتحضرون هنا"

"people who do not hang boys from trees"

"الناس الذين لا يعلقون الأولاد من الأشجار"

"but whom can I ask if there is nobody?"

"ولكن من يمكنني أن أسأل إذا لم يكن هناك أحد؟"

Pinocchio didn't like the idea of being all alone

لم يعجب بينوكيو بفكرة أن يكون وحيدا

and now he was alone on a great uninhabited country

والآن كان وحيدا في بلد عظيم غير مأهول

the idea of it made him melancholy

فكرة ذلك جعلته حزينا

he was just about to to cry

كان على وشك البكاء

But at that moment he saw a big fish swimming by

ولكن في تلك اللحظة رأى سمكة كبيرة تسبح بجانبها

the big fish was only a short distance from the shore

كانت السمكة الكبيرة على بعد مسافة قصيرة من الشاطئ

the fish was going quietly on its own business

كانت السمكة تسير بهدوء في عملها الخاص

and it had its head out of the water

وكان رأسه من الماء

Not knowing its name, the puppet called to the fish
لا يعرف اسمها ، دعا الدمية إلى الأسماك

he called out in a loud voice to make himself heard:
صرخ بصوت عال ليجعل نفسه مسموعا:

"Eh, Sir Fish, will you permit me a word with you?"
"إيه ، سيدي فيش ، هل تسمح لي بكلمة معك؟"

"Two words, if you like," answered the fish
"كلمتان ، إذا أردت "، أجاب السمكة

the fish was in fact not a fish at all
لم تكن السمكة في الواقع سمكة على الإطلاق

what the fish was was a Dolphin
ما كانت السمكة كان دولفين

and you couldn't have found a politer dolphin
ولم يكن بإمكانك العثور على دولفين مهذب

"Would you be kind enough to tell:"
"هل ستكون لطيفا بما يكفي لتقول":

"is there are villages in this island?"
"هل هناك قرى في هذه الجزيرة؟"

"and might there be something to eat in these villages?"
"وهل يمكن أن يكون هناك شيء للأكل في هذه القرى؟"

"and is there any danger in these villages?"
"وهل هناك أي خطر في هذه القرى؟"

"might one get eaten in these villages?"
"هل يمكن للمرء أن يأكل في هذه القرى؟"

"there certainly are villages," replied the Dolphin
"هناك بالتأكيد قرى "، أجاب دولفين

"Indeed, you will find one village quite close by"
"في الواقع ، ستجد قرية واحدة قريبة جدا"

"And what road must I take to go there?"
"وما الطريق الذي يجب أن أسلكه للذهاب إلى هناك؟"

"You must take that path to your left"
"يجب أن تأخذ هذا الطريق إلى يسارك"

"and then you must follow your nose"
"وبعد ذلك يجب أن تتبع أنفك"

"Will you tell me another thing?"

"هل ستخبرني بشيء آخر؟"

"You swim about the sea all day and night"

"أنت تسبح حول البحر طوال النهار والليل"

"have you by chance met a little boat"

"هل قابلت بالصدفة قاربا صغيرا"

"a little boat with my papa in it?"

"قارب صغير مع بابا بداخله؟"

"And who is your papa?"

"ومن هو والدك؟"

"He is the best papa in the world"

"إنه أفضل بابا في العالم"

"but it would be difficult to find a worse son than I am"

"لكن سيكون من الصعب العثور على ابن أسوأ مني"

The fish regretted to tell him what he feared

ندمت السمكة على إخباره بما يخشاه

"you saw the terrible storm we had last night"

"لقد رأيت العاصفة الرهيبة التي شهدناها الليلة الماضية"

"the little boat must have gone to the bottom"

"يجب أن يكون القارب الصغير قد ذهب إلى القاع"

"And my papa?" asked Pinocchio

"وأبي؟" سأل بينوكيو

"He must have been swallowed by the terrible Dog-Fish"

"يجب أن يكون قد ابتلعه السمك الرهيب"

"of late he has been swimming on our waters"

"في الآونة الأخيرة كان يسبح في مياهنا"

"and he has been spreading devastation and ruin"

"وكان ينشر الخراب والخراب"

Pinocchio was already beginning to quake with fear

كان بينوكيو قد بدأ بالفعل في الاهتزاز من الخوف

"Is this Dog-Fish very big?" asked Pinocchio

"هل هذه السمكة الكبيرة جدا؟ "سأل بينوكيو

"oh, very big!" replied the Dolphin

"أوه ، كبير جدا "!أجاب دولفين

"let me tell you about this fish"
"دعني أخبرك عن هذه السمكة"

"then you can form some idea of his size"
"ثم يمكنك تكوين فكرة عن حجمه"

"he is bigger than a five-storied house"
"إنه أكبر من منزل من خمسة طوابق"

"and his mouth is more enormous than you've ever seen"
"وفمه أضخم مما رأيته من قبل"

"a railway train could pass down his throat"
"قطار سكة حديد يمكن أن يمر في حلقه"

"Mercy upon us!" exclaimed the terrified puppet
"ارحمنا!" هتف الدمية المرعوبة

and he put on his clothes with the greatest haste
وألبس ثيابه بأكبر قدر من التسرع

"Good-bye, Sir Fish, and thank you"
"وداعا سيدي فيش ، وشكرا لك"

"excuse the trouble I have given you"
"عذرا على المتاعب التي سببتها لك"

"and many thanks for your politeness"
"وشكرا جزيلا على أدبك"

He then took the path that had been pointed out to him
ثم سلك الطريق الذي أشار إليه

and he began to walk as fast as he could
وبدأ يمشي بأسرع ما يمكن

he walked so fast, indeed, that he was almost running
مشى بسرعة كبيرة ، في الواقع ، لدرجة أنه كان يركض تقريبا

And at the slightest noise he turned to look behind him
وعند أدنى ضجيج التفت لينظر خلفه

he feared that he might see the terrible Dog-Fish
كان يخشى أن يرى سمكة الرهيبة

and he imagined a railway train in its mouth
وتخيل قطار سكة حديد في فمه

a half-hour walk took him to a little village
أخذه نصف ساعة سيرا على الأقدام إلى قرية صغيرة

the village was The Village of the Industrious Bees

كانت القرية قرية النحل الكادح

The road was alive with people

كان الطريق ينبض بالحياة مع الناس

and they were running here and there

وكانوا يركضون هنا وهناك

and they all had to attend to their business

وكان عليهم جميعا الاهتمام بأعمالهم

all were at work, all had something to do

كانوا جميعا في العمل ، وكان لديهم جميعا ما يفعلونه

You could not have found an idler or a vagabond

لا يمكن أن تجد العاطل أو المتشرد

even if you searched for him with a lighted lamp

حتى لو بحثت عنه بمصباح مضاء

"Ah!" said that lazy Pinocchio at once

"آه!"قال ذلك بينوكيو كسول في الحال

"I see that this village will never suit me!"

"أرى أن هذه القرية لن تناسبني أبدا"!

"I wasn't born to work!"

"لم أولد للعمل"!

In the meanwhile he was tormented by hunger

في غضون ذلك كان يعذبه الجوع

he had eaten nothing for twenty-four hours

لم يأكل شيئا لمدة أربع وعشرين ساعة

he had not even eaten vetch

لم يأكل حتى البيقية

What was poor Pinocchio to do?

ماذا كان بينوكيو المسكين يفعل؟

There were only two ways to obtain food

كانت هناك طريقتان فقط للحصول على الطعام

he could either get food by asking for a little work

يمكنه إما الحصول على الطعام عن طريق طلب القليل من العمل

or he could get food by way of begging

أو يمكنه الحصول على الطعام عن طريق التسول

someone might be kind enough to throw him a nickel

قد يكون شخص ما لطيفا بما يكفي لرميه بالنيكل

or they might give him a mouthful of bread

أو قد يعطونه فم من الخبز

generally Pinocchio was ashamed to beg

بشكل عام ، كان بينوكيو يخجل من التسول

his father had always preached him to be industrious

كان والده يعظه دائما ليكون مجتهدا

he taught him no one had a right to beg

علمه أنه لا يحق لأحد أن يتسول

except the aged and the infirm

باستثناء المسنين والعجزة

The really poor in this world deserve compassion

الفقراء حقا في هذا العالم يستحقون الرحمة

the really poor in this world require assistance

الفقراء حقا في هذا العالم يحتاجون إلى المساعدة

only those who are aged or sick

فقط أولئك الذين هم في سن أو مرضى

those who are no longer able to earn their own bread

أولئك الذين لم يعودوا قادرين على كسب خبزهم

It is the duty of everyone else to work

من واجب الجميع العمل

and if they don't labour, so much the worse for them

وإذا لم يعملوا ، فهذا أسوأ بكثير بالنسبة لهم

let them suffer from their hunger

دعهم يعانون من جوعهم

At that moment a man came down the road

في تلك اللحظة نزل رجل على الطريق

he was tired and panting for breath

كان متعبا ويلهث لالتقاط الأنفاس

He was dragging two carts full of charcoal

كان يجر عربتين مملوءتين بالفحم

Pinocchio judged by his face that he was a kind man

حكم بينوكيو من وجهه أنه كان رجلا طيبا

so Pinocchio approached the charcoal man

لذلك اقترب بينوكيو من رجل الفحم

he cast down his eyes with shame

ألقى عينيه بخجل

and he said to him in a low voice:

فقال له بصوت منخفض:

"Would you have the charity to give me a nickel?"

"هل لديك جمعية خيرية لتعطيني نيكل؟"

"because, as you can see, I am dying of hunger"

"لأنني ، كما ترون ، أموت من الجوع"

"You shall have not only a nickel," said the man

"لن يكون لديك نيكل فقط "، قال الرجل

"I will give you a dime"

"سأعطيك عشرة سنتات"

"but for the dime you must do some work"

"ولكن بالنسبة للعشرة سنتات ، يجب عليك القيام ببعض الأعمال"

"help me to drag home these two carts of charcoal"

"ساعدني في سحب عربتي الفحم هاتين إلى المنزل"

"I am surprised at you!" answered the puppet

"أنا مندهش منك"! أجابت الدمية

and there was a tone of offense in his voice

وكانت هناك نبرة إهانة في صوته

"Let me tell you something about myself"

"دعني أخبرك شيئا عن"

"I am not accustomed to do the work of a donkey"

"لست معتادا على القيام بعمل حمار"

"I have never drawn a cart!"

"لم أرسم عربة قط"!

"So much the better for you," answered the man

"هذا أفضل بكثير بالنسبة لك "، أجاب الرجل

"my boy, I see how you are dying of hunger"

"يا ولدي ، أرى كيف تموت من الجوع"

"eat two fine slices of your pride"

"أكل شريحتين رائعتين من كبريائك"

"and be careful not to get indigestion"

"واحرص على عدم الإصابة بعسر الهضم"

A few minutes afterwards a mason passed by

بعد بضع دقائق مر بناء

he was carrying a basket of mortar

كان يحمل سلة من الهاون

"Would you have the charity to give me a nickel?"

"هل لديك جمعية خيرية لتعطيني نيكل؟"

"me, a poor boy who is yawning for want of food"

"أنا ، صبي فقير يتثاءب بسبب نقص الطعام"

"Willingly," answered the man

"عن طيب خاطر "، أجاب الرجل

"Come with me and carry the mortar"

"تعال معي واحمل الهاون"

"and instead of a nickel I will give you a dime"

"وبدلا من النيكل سأعطيك عشرة سنتات"

"But the mortar is heavy," objected Pinocchio

"لكن الهاون ثقيل "، اعترض بينوكيو

"and I don't want to tire myself"

"ولا أريد أن أتعب"

"I see you you don't want to tire yourself"

"أراك أنك لا تريد أن تتعب نفسك"

"then, my boy, go amuse yourself with yawning"

"إذن ، يا ولدي ، اذهب واستمتع بالتثاؤب"

In less than half an hour twenty other people went by

في أقل من نصف ساعة مر عشرون شخصا آخر

and Pinocchio asked charity of them all

وطلب بينوكيو الصدقة منهم جميعا

but they all gave him the same answer

لكنهم جميعا أعطوه نفس الإجابة

"Are you not ashamed to beg, young boy?"

"ألا تخجل من التسول أيها الفتى الصغير؟"

"Instead of idling about, look for a little work"

"بدلا من التباطؤ ، ابحث عن القليل من العمل"

"you have to learn to earn your bread"

"عليك أن تتعلم أن تكسب خبزك"

finally a nice little woman walked by

أخيرا مرت امرأة صغيرة لطيفة

she was carrying two cans of water

كانت تحمل علبتين من الماء

Pinocchio asked her for charity too

طلب منها بينوكيو الصدقة أيضا

"Will you let me drink a little of your water?"

"هل ستسمح لي بشرب القليل من الماء؟"

"because I am burning with thirst"

"لأنني أحترق من العطش"

the little woman was happy to help

كانت المرأة الصغيرة سعيدة للمساعدة

"Drink, my boy, if you wish it!"

"اشرب يا ولدي ، إذا كنت ترغب في ذلك"!

and she set down the two cans

ووضعت العلبتين

Pinocchio drank like a fish

شرب بينوكيو مثل السمكة

and as he dried his mouth he mumbled:

وبينما كان يجفف فمه تمتم:

"I have quenched my thirst"

"لقد أطفأت عطشي"

"If I could only appease my hunger!"

"إذا كان بإمكاني فقط إرضاء جوعي"!

The good woman heard Pinocchio's pleas

سمعت المرأة الطيبة نداءات بينوكيو

and she was only too willing to oblige

وكانت فقط على استعداد تام للالتزام

"help me to carry home these cans of water"

"ساعدني في حمل علب الماء هذه إلى المنزل"

"and I will give you a fine piece of bread"

"وسأعطيك قطعة خبز جيدة"

Pinocchio looked at the cans of water

نظر بينوكيو إلى علب الماء

and he answered neither yes nor no

ولم يجب بنعم ولا لا

and the good woman added more to the offer

وأضافت المرأة الطيبة المزيد إلى العرض

"As well as bread you shall have cauliflower"

"وكذلك الخبز يكون لديك القرنبيط"

Pinocchio gave another look at the can

ألقى بينوكيو نظرة أخرى على العلبة

and he answered neither yes nor no

ولم يجب بنعم ولا لا

"And after the cauliflower there will be more"

"وبعد القرنبيط سيكون هناك المزيد"

"I will give you a beautiful syrup bonbon"

"سأعطيك شراب بونبون جميل"

The temptation of this last dainty was great

كان إغراء هذا اللذيذ الأخير عظيما

finally Pinocchio could resist no longer

أخيرا ، لم يعد بإمكان بينوكيو المقاومة

with an air of decision he said:

بجو من القرار قال:

"I must have patience!"

"يجب أن أتحلى بالصبر"!

"I will carry the water to your house"

"سأحمل الماء إلى منزلك"

The water was too heavy for Pinocchio

كانت المياه ثقيلة جدا بالنسبة لبينوكيو

he could not carry it with his hands

لم يستطع حملها بيديه

so he had to carry it on his head

لذلك كان عليه أن يحملها على رأسه

Pinocchio did not enjoy doing the work

لم يستمتع بينوكيو بالقيام بالعمل

but soon they reached the house

ولكن سرعان ما وصلوا إلى المنزل

and the good little woman offered Pinocchio a seat

وعرضت المرأة الصغيرة الطيبة على بينوكيو مقعدا

the table had already been laid

تم وضع الطاولة بالفعل

and she placed before him the bread

ووضعت أمامه الخبز

and then he got the cauliflower and the bonbon

ثم حصل على القرنبيط والبونبون

Pinocchio did not eat his food, he devoured it

بينوكيو لم يأكل طعامه ، لقد التهمه

His stomach was like an empty apartment

كانت معدته مثل شقة فارغة

an apartment that had been left uninhabited for months

شقة تركت غير مأهولة لعدة أشهر

but now his ravenous hunger was somewhat appeased

ولكن الآن تم تهدئة جوعه المفترس إلى حد ما

he raised his head to thank his benefactress

رفع رأسه ليشكر محسنته

then he took a better look at her

ثم ألقى نظرة أفضل عليها

he gave a prolonged "Oh!" of astonishment

أعطى "أوه" إمن الدهشة لفترة طويلة

and he continued staring at her with wide open eyes

واستمر في التحديق فيها بعيون مفتوحة على مصراعيها

his fork was in the air

كانت شوكته في الهواء

and his mouth was full of cauliflower

وكان فمه ممتلئا بالقرنبيط

it was as if he had been bewitched

كان الأمر كما لو كان قد سحر

the good woman was quite amused

كانت المرأة الطيبة مسلية جدا

"What has surprised you so much?"

"ما الذي فاجأك كثيرا؟"

"It is..." answered the puppet

"إنه "... أجاب الدمية

"it's just that you are like..."

"كل ما في الأمر أنك مثل"...

"it's just that you remind me of someone"

"كل ما في الأمر أنك تذكرني بشخص ما"

"yes, yes, yes, the same voice"

"نعم ، نعم ، نعم ، نفس الصوت"
"and you have the same eyes and hair"
"ولديك نفس العيون والشعر"
"yes, yes, yes. you also have blue hair"
"نعم ، نعم ، نعم .لديك أيضا شعر أزرق"
"Oh, little Fairy! tell me that it is you!"
"أوه ، الجنية الصغيرة !قل لي أنه أنت!"
"Do not make me cry anymore!"
"لا تجعلني أبكي بعد الآن"!
"If only you knew how much I've cried"
"لو كنت تعرف كم بكيت"
"and I have suffered so much"
"وقد عانيت كثيرا"
And Pinocchio threw himself at her feet
وألقى بينوكيو بنفسه عند قدميها
and he embraced the knees of the mysterious little woman
واحتضن ركبتي المرأة الصغيرة الغامضة
and he began to cry bitterly
وبدأ يبكي بمرارة

Pinocchio Promises the Fairy he'll be a Good Boy Again
بينوكيو يعد الجنية بأنه سيكون فتى جيدا مرة أخرى

At first the good little woman played innocent
في البداية لعبت المرأة الصغيرة الطيبة دور بريئة
she said she was not the little Fairy with blue hair
قالت إنها لم تكن الجنية الصغيرة ذات الشعر الأزرق
but Pinocchio could not be tricked
لكن بينوكيو لا يمكن خداعه
she had continued the comedy long enough
لقد واصلت الكوميديا لفترة كافية
and so she ended by making herself known
وهكذا انتهت بالتعريف بنفسها
"You naughty little rogue, Pinocchio"
"أيها المشاغب الصغير المارق ، بينوكيو"
"how did you discover who I was?"
"كيف اكتشفت من أكون؟"
"It was my great affection for you that told me"
"لقد كانت عاطفتي الكبيرة لك هي التي أخبرتني"
"Do you remember when you left me?"
"هل تتذكر عندما تركتني؟"
"I was still a child back then"
"كنت لا أزال طفلا في ذلك الوقت"
"and now I have become a woman"
"والآن أصبحت امرأة"
"a woman almost old enough to be your mamma"
"امرأة تبلغ من العمر ما يكفي لتكون أمك"
"I am delighted at that"
"أنا سعيد بذلك"
"I will not call you little sister anymore"
"لن أتصل بك أختي الصغيرة بعد الآن"
"from now I will call you mamma"
"من الآن سأتصل بك ماما"
"all the other boys have a mamma"

"جميع الأولاد الآخرين لديهم ماما"
"and I have always wished to also have a mamma"
"ولطالما تمنيت أن يكون لدي ماما أيضا"
"But how did you manage to grow so fast?"
"ولكن كيف تمكنت من النمو بهذه السرعة؟"
"That is a secret," said the fairy
"هذا سر "، قالت الجنية
Pinocchio wanted to know, "teach me your secret"
أراد بينوكيو أن يعرف ،" علمني سرك"
"because I would also like to grow"
"لأنني أود أيضا أن أنمو"
"Don't you see how small I am?"
"ألا ترى كم أنا صغير؟"
"I always remain no bigger than a ninepin"
"أنا دائما لا أبقى أكبر من تسعة دبوس"
"But you cannot grow," replied the Fairy
"لكن لا يمكنك أن تنمو "، أجابت الجنية
"Why can't I grow?" asked Pinocchio
"لماذا لا أستطيع النمو؟ "سأل بينوكيو
"Because puppets never grow"
"لأن الدمى لا تنمو أبدا"
"when they are born they are puppets"
"عندما يولدون هم دمى"
"and they live their lives as puppets"
"ويعيشون حياتهم كدمى"
"and when they die they die as puppets"
"وعندما يموتون يموتون كدمى"
Pinocchio game himself a slap
بينوكيو لعبة نفسه صفعة
"Oh, I am sick of being a puppet!"
"أوه ، لقد سئمت من كوني دمية"!
"It is time that I became a man"
"لقد حان الوقت لأن أصبح رجلا"
"And you will become a man," promised the fairy

"وسوف تصبح رجلا "، وعدت الجنية

"but you must know how to deserve it"

"لكن يجب أن تعرف كيف تستحق ذلك"

"Is this true?" asked Pinocchio

"هل هذا صحيح؟ "سأل بينوكيو

"And what can I do to deserve to be a man?"

"وماذا يمكنني أن أفعل لأستحق أن أكون رجلا؟"

"it is a very easy thing to deserve to be a man"

"من السهل جدا أن تستحق أن تكون رجلا"

"all you have to do is learn to be a good boy"

"كل ما عليك فعله هو أن تتعلم أن تكون فتى جيدا"

"And you think I am not a good boy?"

"وهل تعتقد أنني لست ولدا جيدا؟"

"You are quite the opposite of a good boy"

"أنت على العكس تماما من صبي جيد"

"Good boys are obedient, and you..."

"الأولاد الطيبون مطيعون ، وأنت"...

"And I never obey," confessed Pinocchio

"وأنا لا أطيع أبدا "، اعترف بينوكيو

"Good boys like to learn and to work, and you..."

"الأولاد الطيبون يحبون التعلم والعمل ، وأنت"...

"And I instead lead an idle, vagabond life"

"وأنا بدلا من ذلك أعيش حياة خاملة ومتشردة"

"Good boys always speak the truth"

"الأولاد الطيبون يقولون الحقيقة دائما"

"And I always tell lies," admitted Pinocchio

»وأنا دائما أقول الأكاذيب«، اعترف بينوكيو

"Good boys go willingly to school"

"الأولاد الطيبون يذهبون عن طيب خاطر إلى المدرسة"

"And school gives me pain all over the body"

"والمدرسة تعطيني الألم في جميع أنحاء الجسم"

"But from today I will change my life"

"لكن من اليوم سأغير حياتي"

"Do you promise me?" asked the Fairy

"هل تعدني؟ "سألت الجنية

"I promise that I will become a good little boy"

"أعدك بأنني سأصبح ولدا صغيرا جيدا"

"and I promise be the consolation of my papa"

"وأعدك أن يكون عزاء أبي"

"Where is my poor papa at this moment?"

"أين بابا المسكين في هذه اللحظة؟"

but the fairy didn't know where his papa was

لكن الجنية لم تكن تعرف مكان بابا

"Shall I ever have the happiness of seeing him again?"

"هل سأشعر بالسعادة لرؤيته مرة أخرى؟"

"will I ever kiss him again?"

"هل سأقبله مرة أخرى؟"

"I think so; indeed, I am sure of it"

"أعتقد ذلك. في الواقع ، أنا متأكد من ذلك"

At this answer Pinocchio was delighted

في هذه الإجابة كان بينوكيو سعيدا

he took the Fairy's hands

أخذ يدي الجنية

and he began to kiss her hands with great fervour

وبدأ في تقبيل يديها بحماس كبير

he seemed beside himself with joy

بدا بجانبه بفرح

Then Pinocchio raised his face

ثم رفع بينوكيو وجهه

and he looked at her lovingly

ونظر إليها بمحبة

"Tell me, little mamma:"

"قل لي ، ماما الصغيرة":

"then it was not true that you were dead?"

"إذن لم يكن صحيحا أنك ميت؟"

"It seems not," said the Fairy, smiling

"يبدو أنه ليس كذلك "، قالت الجنية وهي تبتسم

"If you only knew the sorrow I felt"

"إذا كنت تعرف فقط الحزن الذي شعرت به"

"you can't imagined the tightening of my throat"

"لا يمكنك تخيل شد حلقي"

"reading what was on that stone almost broke my heart"

"قراءة ما كان على هذا الحجر كاد أن يكسر قلبي"

"I know what it did to you"

"أنا أعرف ما فعلته بك"

"and that is why I have forgiven you"

"ولهذا السبب غفرت لك"

"I saw it from the sincerity of your grief"

"رأيت ذلك من صدق حزنك"

"I saw that you have a good heart"

"رأيت أن لديك قلبا طيبا"

"boys with good hearts are not lost"

"الأولاد ذوو القلوب الطيبة لا يضيعون"

"there is always something to hope for"

"هناك دائما شيء نأمله"

"even if they are scamps"

"حتى لو كانوا ساخرين"

"and even if they have got bad habits"

"وحتى لو كان لديهم عادات سيئة"

"there is always hope they change their ways"

"هناك دائما أمل في أن يغيروا طرقهم"

"That is why I came to look for you here"

"لهذا السبب جئت للبحث عنك هنا"

"I will be your mamma"

"سأكون أمك"

"Oh, how delightful!" shouted Pinocchio

"أوه ، كم هو ممتع" إصاح بينوكيو

and the little puppet jumped for joy

وقفزت الدمية الصغيرة من الفرح

"You must obey me, Pinocchio"

"يجب أن تطيعني يا بينوكيو"

"and you must do everything that I bid you"

"ويجب أن تفعل كل ما أودعك إليه"

"I will willingly obey you"

"سأطيعك عن طيب خاطر"

"and I will do as I'm told!"

"وسأفعل ما قيل لي"!

"Tomorrow you will begin to go to school"

"غدا ستبدأ في الذهاب إلى المدرسة"

Pinocchio became at once a little less joyful

أصبح بينوكيو في الحال أقل بهجة

"Then you must choose a trade to follow"

"ثم يجب عليك اختيار التجارة لمتابعة"

"you most choose a job according to your wishes"

"أنت تختار وظيفة وفقا لرغباتك"

Pinocchio became very grave at this

أصبح بينوكيو خطيرا جدا في هذا

the Fairy asked him in an angry voice:

سألته الجنية بصوت غاضب:

"What are you muttering between your teeth?"

"ماذا تتمتم بين أسنانك؟"

"I was saying..." moaned the puppet in a low voice

"كنت أقول "... أنين الدمية بصوت منخفض

"it seems to me too late for me to go to school now"

"يبدو لي أن الأوان قد فات بالنسبة لي للذهاب إلى المدرسة الآن"

"No, sir, it is not too late for you to go to school"

"لا يا سيدي ، لم يفت الأوان بعد للذهاب إلى المدرسة"

"Keep it in mind that it is never too late"

"ضع في اعتبارك أنه لم يفت الأوان بعد"

"we can always learn and instruct ourselves"

"يمكننا دائما التعلم وتعليم أنفسنا"

"But I do not wish to follow a trade"

"لكنني لا أرغب في متابعة التجارة"

"Why do you not wish to follow an trade?"

"لماذا لا ترغب في متابعة التجارة؟"

"Because it tires me to work"

"لأنه يتعبني للعمل"

"My boy," said the Fairy lovingly

"يا ولدي "، قالت الجنية بمحبة

"there are two kinds of people who talk like that"

"هناك نوعان من الناس يتحدثون هكذا"

"there are those that are in prison"

"هناك من هم في السجن"

"and there are those that are in hospital"

"وهناك من هم في المستشفى"

"Let me tell you one thing, Pinocchio;"

"دعني أخبرك بشيء واحد ، بينوكيو ؛"

"every man, rich or poor, is obliged work"

"كل إنسان، غني أو فقير، ملزم بالعمل"

"he has to occupy himself with something"

"عليه أن يشغل نفسه بشيء ما"

"Woe to those who lead slothful lives"

"ويل لأولئك الذين يعيشون حياة كسولة"

"Sloth is a dreadful illness"

"الكسل مرض مروع"

"it must be cured at once, in childhood"

"يجب علاجه مرة واحدة ، في مرحلة الطفولة"

"because it can never be cured once you are old"

"لأنه لا يمكن علاجه أبدا بمجرد أن تكبر"

Pinocchio was touched by these words

تأثر بينوكيو بهذه الكلمات

lifting his head quickly, he said to the Fairy:

رفع رأسه بسرعة ، وقال للجنية:

"I will study and I will work"

"سأدرس وسأعمل"

"I will do all that you tell me"

"سأفعل كل ما تقوله لي"

"for indeed I have become weary of being a puppet"

"لأني حقا سئمت من أن أكون دمية"

"and I wish at any price to become a boy"

"وأتمنى بأي ثمن أن أصبح صبيا"

"You promised me that I can become a boy, did you not?"

"لقد وعدتني بأنني أستطيع أن أصبح صبيا ، أليس كذلك؟"

"I did promise you that you can become a boy"

"لقد وعدتك أنه يمكنك أن تصبح صبيا"

"and whether you become a boy now depends upon yourself"

"وما إذا كنت ستصبح صبيا الآن يعتمد على نفسك"

The Terrible Dog-Fish
الرهيب السمك

The following day Pinocchio went to school
في اليوم التالي ذهب بينوكيو إلى المدرسة
you can imagine the delight of all the little rogues
يمكنك أن تتخيل فرحة جميع المحتالين الصغار
a puppet had walked into their school!
دخلت دمية إلى مدرستهم!
They set up a roar of laughter that never ended
أقاموا هدير من الضحك الذي لم ينته
They played all sorts of tricks on him
لعبوا كل أنواع الحيل عليه
One boy carried off his cap
حمل صبي قبعته
another boy pulled Pinocchio's jacket over him
سحب صبي آخر سترة بينوكيو فوقه
one tried to give him a pair of inky mustachios
حاول أحدهم أن يعطيه زوجا من الشوارب المحبرة
another boy attempted to tie strings to his feet and hands
حاول صبي آخر ربط الخيوط إلى قدميه ويديه
and then he tried to make him dance
ثم حاول أن يجعله يرقص
For a short time Pinocchio pretended not to care
لفترة قصيرة تظاهر بينوكيو بعدم الاهتمام
and he got on as well with school as he could
واستمر في المدرسة قدر استطاعته
but at last he lost all his patience
لكنه في النهاية فقد كل صبره
he turned to those who were teasing him most
التفت إلى أولئك الذين كانوا يضايقونه أكثر
"Beware, boys!" he warned them
"احذروا أيها الأولاد" "إحذرهم
"I have not come here to be your buffoon"
"لم آت إلى هنا لأكون مهرجك"
"I respect others," he said

قال" :أنا أحترم الآخرين."

"and I intend to be respected"

"وأعتزم أن أحترم"

"Well said, boaster!" howled the young rascals

"أحسنت القول ، متهور "!إعوى الأوغاد الشباب

"You have spoken like a book!"

"لقد تحدثت مثل كتاب"!

and they convulsed with mad laughter

وتشنجوا من الضحك المجنون

there was one boy more impertinent than the others

كان هناك صبي واحد أكثر وقاحة من الآخرين

he tried to seize the puppet by the end of his nose

حاول الاستيلاء على الدمية بنهاية أنفه

But he could not do so quickly enough

لكنه لم يستطع القيام بذلك بسرعة كافية

Pinocchio stuck his leg out from under the table

أمسك بينوكيو ساقه من تحت الطاولة

and he gave him a great kick on his shins

وأعطاه ركلة عظيمة على ساقيه

the boy roared in pain

زأر الصبي من الألم

"Oh, what hard feet you have!"

"أوه ، ما هي أقدامك الصلبة"!

and he rubbed the bruise the puppet had given him

وفرك الكدمة التي أعطتها له الدمية

"And what elbows you have!" said another

"وما المرفقين لديك "!قال آخر

"they are even harder than his feet!"

"إنها أصعب من قدميه"!

this boy had also played rude tricks on him

كان هذا الصبي قد لعب أيضا حيلا وقحة عليه

and he had received a blow in the stomach

وكان قد تلقى ضربة في المعدة

But, nevertheless, the kick and the blow acquired sympathy

ولكن ، مع ذلك ، اكتسبت الركلة والضربة تعاطفا.

and Pinocchio earned the esteem of the boys
وحصل بينوكيو على تقدير الأولاد

They soon all made friends with him
سرعان ما أقاموا جميعا صداقات معه

and soon they liked him heartily
وسرعان ما أحبوه بحرارة

And even the master praised him
وحتى السيد مدحه

because Pinocchio was attentive in class
لأن بينوكيو كان منتبها في الفصل

he was a studious and intelligent student
كان طالبا مجتهدا وذكيا

and he was always the first to come to school
وكان دائما أول من يأتي إلى المدرسة

and he was always the last to leave when school was over
وكان دائما آخر من يغادر عندما تنتهي المدرسة

But he had one fault; he made too many friends
لكن كان لديه خطأ واحد. لقد كون الكثير من الأصدقاء

and amongst his friends were several rascals
وكان من بين أصدقائه العديد من الأوغاد

these boys were well known for their dislike of study
كان هؤلاء الأولاد معروفين بكراهيتهم للدراسة

and they especially loved to cause mischief
وأحبوا بشكل خاص التسبب في الأذى

The master warned him about them every day
حذره السيد منهم كل يوم

even the good Fairy never failed to tell him:
حتى الجنية الطيبة لم تفشل أبدا في إخباره:

"Take care, Pinocchio, with your friends!"
"اعتن بنفسك ، بينوكيو ، مع أصدقائك"!

"Those bad school-fellows of yours are trouble"
"هؤلاء الزملاء السيئون في المدرسة هم مشكلة"

"they will make you lose your love of study"
"سوف يجعلونك تفقد حبك للدراسة"

"they may even bring upon you some great misfortune"

"قد يجلبون لك بعض المحنة الكبيرة"

"There is no fear of that!" answered the puppet

"لا خوف من ذلك "أجابت الدمية

and he shrugged his shoulders and touched his forehead

وهز كتفيه ولمس جبهته

"There is so much sense here!"

"هناك الكثير من المعنى هنا"!

one fine day Pinocchio was on his way to school

في أحد الأيام الجميلة كان بينوكيو في طريقه إلى المدرسة

and he met several of his usual companions

والتقى بالعديد من رفاقه المعتادين

coming up to him, they asked:

عندما اقتربوا منه ، سألوه:

"Have you heard the great news?"

"هل سمعت الأخبار العظيمة؟"

"No, I have not heard the great news"

"لا ، لم أسمع الأخبار السارة"

"In the sea near here a Dog-Fish has appeared"

"في البحر بالقرب من هنا ظهرت سمكة"
"he is as big as a mountain"
"إنه كبير مثل الجبل"
"Is it true?" asked Pinocchio
"هل هذا صحيح؟ "سأل بينوكيو
"Can it be the same Dog-Fish?"
"هل يمكن أن يكون نفس السمكة؟"
"The Dog-Fish that was there when my papa drowned"
"سمكة التي كانت هناك عندما غرق أبي"
"We are going to the shore to see him"
"نحن ذاهبون إلى الشاطئ لرؤيته"
"Will you come with us?"
"هل ستأتي معنا؟"
"No; I am going to school"
"لا .أنا ذاهب إلى المدرسة"
"of what great importance is school?"
"ما هي أهمية المدرسة؟"
"We can go to school tomorrow"
"يمكننا الذهاب إلى المدرسة غدا"
"one lesson more or less doesn't matter"
"درس واحد أكثر أو أقل لا يهم"
"we shall always remain the same donkeys"
"سنبقى دائما نفس الحمير"
"But what will the master say?"
"ولكن ماذا سيقول السيد؟"
"The master may say what he likes"
"قد يقول السيد ما يحلو له"
"He is paid to grumble all day"
"يتم الدفع له مقابل التذمر طوال اليوم"
"And what will my mamma say?"
"وماذا ستقول أمي؟"
"Mammas know nothing," answered the bad little boys
"الأمهات لا يعرفن شيئا "، أجاب الأولاد الصغار السيئون
"Do you know what I will do?" said Pinocchio

"هل تعرف ماذا سأفعل؟ "قال بينوكيو
"I have reasons for wishing to see the Dog-Fish"
"لدي أسباب لرغبتي في رؤية سمكة"
"but I will go and see him when school is over"
"لكنني سأذهب لرؤيته عندما تنتهي المدرسة"
"Poor donkey!" exclaimed one of the boys
"حمار مسكين"! إهتف أحد الأولاد
"Do you suppose a fish of that size will wait your convenience?"
"هل تفترض أن سمكة بهذا الحجم ستنتظر راحتك؟"
"when he is tired of being here he will go another place"
"عندما يتعب من وجوده هنا سيذهب إلى مكان آخر"
"and then it will be too late"
"وبعد ذلك سيكون الأوان قد فات"
the Puppet had to think about this
كان على الدمية أن تفكر في هذا
"How long does it take to get to the shore?"
"كم من الوقت يستغرق الوصول إلى الشاطئ؟"
"We can be there and back in an hour"
"يمكننا أن نكون هناك ونعود في غضون ساعة"
"Then off we go!" shouted Pinocchio
"ثم نذهب "!إصاح بينوكيو
"and he who runs fastest is the best!"
"ومن يركض أسرع هو الأفضل"!
and the boys rushed off across the fields
واندفع الأولاد عبر الحقول
and Pinocchio was always the first
وكان بينوكيو دائما الأول
he seemed to have wings on his feet
بدا أن لديه أجنحة على قدميه
From time to time he turned to jeer at his companions
من وقت لآخر كان يلجأ إلى السخرية من رفاقه
they were some distance behind
كانوا على مسافة وراء
he saw them panting for breath

رآهم يلهثون لالتقاط الأنفاس

and they were covered with dust

وكانت مغطاة بالغبار

and their tongues were hanging out of their mouths

وكانت ألسنتهم تتدلى من أفواههم

and Pinocchio laughed heartily at the sight

وضحك بينوكيو بحرارة على المنظر

The unfortunate boy did not know what was to come

لم يعرف الصبي التعيس ما سيأتي

the terrors and horrible disasters that were coming!

الأهوال والكوارث الرهيبة التي كانت قادمة!

Pinocchio is Arrested by the Gendarmes
اعتقال بينوكيو من قبل رجال الدرك

Pinocchio arrived at the shore

وصل بينوكيو إلى الشاطئ

and he looked out to sea

ونظر إلى البحر

but he saw no Dog-Fish

لكنه لم ير سمكة

The sea was as smooth as a great crystal mirror

كان البحر سلسا مثل مرآة كريستالية رائعة

"Where is the Dog-Fish?" he asked

"أين سمكة؟" سأل

and he turned to his companions

والتفت إلى أصحابه

all the boys laughed together

ضحك جميع الأولاد معا

"He must have gone to have his breakfast"

"لا بد أنه ذهب لتناول وجبة الإفطار"

"Or he has thrown himself on to his bed"

"أو ألقى بنفسه على سريره"

"yes, he's having a little nap"

"نعم ، إنه يأخذ قيلولة صغيرة"

and they laughed even louder

وضحكوا بصوت أعلى

their answers seemed particularly absurd

بدت إجاباتهم سخيفة بشكل خاص

and their laughter was very silly

وكان ضحكهم سخيفا جدا

Pinocchio looked around at his friends

نظر بينوكيو حوله إلى أصدقائه

his companions seemed to be making a fool of him

بدا أن رفاقه يخدعونه

they had induced him to believe a tale

لقد حثوه على تصديق حكاية

but there was no truth to the tale

لكن لم يكن هناك حقيقة في الحكاية

Pinocchio did not take the joke well

بينوكيو لم يأخذ النكتة جيدا

and he spoke angrily with the boys

وتحدث بغضب مع الأولاد

"And now??" he shouted

"والآن؟؟" صرخ

"you told me a story of the Dog-Fish"

"لقد أخبرتني قصة سمكة"

"but what fun did you find in deceiving me?"

"ولكن ما هي المتعة التي وجدتها في خداعي؟"

"Oh, it was great fun!" answered the little rascals

"أوه ، لقد كان ممتعا للغاية "إأجاب الأوغاد الصغار

"And in what did this fun consist of?"

"وفي ماذا تتكون هذه المتعة؟"

"we made you miss a day of school"

"جعلناك تفوتك يوما من المدرسة"

"and we persuaded you to come with us"

"وأقنعناك أن تأتي معنا"

"Are you not ashamed of your conduct?"

"ألا تخجل من سلوكك؟"

"you are always so punctual to school"

"أنت دائما دقيق جدا في المدرسة"

"and you are always so diligent in class"

"وأنت دائما مجتهد جدا في الفصل"

"Are you not ashamed of studying so hard?"

"ألا تخجل من الدراسة بجد؟"

"so what if I study hard?"

"إذن ماذا لو درست بجد؟"

"what concern is it of yours?"

"ما هو قلقك؟"

"It concerns us excessively"

"إنه يهمنا بشكل مفرط"

"because it makes us appear in a bad light"

"لأنه يجعلنا نظهر في ضوء سيء"

"Why does it make you appear in a bad light?"

"لماذا يجعلك تظهر في ضوء سيء؟"

"there are those of us who have no wish to study"

"هناك من منا ليس لديه رغبة في الدراسة"

"we have no desire to learn anything"

"ليس لدينا رغبة في تعلم أي شيء"

"good boys make us seem worse by comparison"

"الأولاد الطيبون يجعلوننا نبدو أسوأ بالمقارنة"

"And that is too bad for you"

"وهذا سيء للغاية بالنسبة لك"

"We, too, have our pride!"

"نحن أيضا لدينا فخرنا"!

"Then what must I do to please you?"

"إذن ماذا علي أن أفعل لإرضائك؟"

"You must follow our example"

"يجب أن تحذو حذونا"

"you must hate school like us"

"يجب أن تكره المدرسة مثلنا"

"you must rebel in the lessons"

"يجب أن تتمرد في الدروس"

"and you must disobey the master"
"ويجب أن تعصي السيد"

"those are our three greatest enemies"
"هؤلاء هم أكبر ثلاثة أعداء"

"And if I wish to continue my studies?"
"وإذا كنت أرغب في مواصلة دراستي؟"

"In that case we will have nothing more to do with you"
"في هذه الحالة لن يكون لدينا أي علاقة أخرى بك"

"and at the first opportunity we will make you pay for it"
"وفي أول فرصة سنجعلك تدفع ثمنها"

"Really," said the puppet, shaking his head
"حقا "، قال الدمية وهو يهز رأسه

"you make me inclined to laugh"
"أنت تجعلني أميل إلى الضحك"

"Eh, Pinocchio," shouted the biggest of the boys
"إيه ، بينوكيو "، صاح أكبر الأولاد

and he confronted Pinocchio directly
وواجه بينوكيو مباشرة

"None of your superiority works here"
"لا شيء من تفوقك يعمل هنا"

"don't come here to crow over us"
"لا تأتي إلى هنا لتبكي علينا"

"if you are not afraid of us, we are not afraid of you"
"إذا لم تكن خائفا منا ، فنحن لسنا خائفين منك"

"Remember that you are one against seven"
"تذكر أنك واحد ضد سبعة"

"Seven, like the seven deadly sins," said Pinocchio
"سبعة ، مثل الخطايا السبع المميتة "، قال بينوكيو

and he shouted with laughter
وصرخ ضاحكا

"Listen to him! He has insulted us all!"
"استمع إليه !لقد أهاننا جميعا"!

"He called us the seven deadly sins!"
"لقد دعانا بالخطايا السبع المميتة"!

"Take that to begin with," said one of the boys
"خذ هذا لتبدأ "، قال أحد الأولاد
"and keep it for your supper tonight"
"واحتفظ بها لعشائك الليلة"
And, so saying, he punched him on the head
وهكذا قال ، لكمه على رأسه
But it was a give and take
لكنه كان أخذ وعطاء
because the puppet immediately returned the blow
لأن الدمية أعادت الضربة على الفور
this was no big surprise
لم تكن هذه مفاجأة كبيرة
and the fight quickly got desperate
وسرعان ما أصبحت المعركة يائسة
it is true that Pinocchio was alone
صحيح أن بينوكيو كان وحيدا
but he defended himself like a hero
لكنه دافع عن نفسه كبطل
He used his feet, which were of the hardest wood
استخدم قدميه ، التي كانت من أصعب الأخشاب
and he kept his enemies at a respectful distance
وأبقى أعداءه على مسافة محترمة
Wherever his feet touched they left a bruise
أينما لمست قدميه تركوا كدمة
The boys became furious with him
غضب الأولاد منه
hand to hand they couldn't match the puppet
يدا بيد لم يتمكنوا من مطابقة الدمية
so they took other weapons into their hands
لذلك أخذوا أسلحة أخرى في أيديهم
the boys loosened their satchels
أرخى الأولاد حقائبهم
and they threw their school-books at him
وألقوا كتبهم المدرسية عليه
grammars, dictionaries, and spelling-books
القواعد والقواميس وكتب الإملاء

geography books and other scholastic works

كتب الجغرافيا والأعمال الدراسية الأخرى

But Pinocchio was quick to react

لكن بينوكيو كان سريعا في الرد

and he had sharp eyes for these things

وكان لديه عيون حادة لهذه الأشياء

he always managed to duck in time

تمكن دائما من الانحناء في الوقت المناسب

so the books passed over his head

فمرت الكتب فوق رأسه

and instead the books fell into the sea

وبدلا من ذلك سقطت الكتب في البحر

Imagine the astonishment of the fish!

تخيل دهشة السمكة!

they thought the books were something to eat

اعتقدوا أن الكتب كانت شيئا للأكل

and they all arrived in large shoals of fish

ووصلوا جميعا في مياه ضحلة كبيرة من الأسماك

but they tasted a couple of the pages

and they quickly spat the paper out again
لكنهم تذوقوا بضع صفحات
وسرعان ما بصقوا الورقة مرة أخرى
and the fish made wry faces
وجعلت الأسماك وجوها ساخرة
"this isn't food for us at all"
"هذا ليس طعاما لنا على الإطلاق"
"we are accustomed to something much better!"
"لقد اعتدنا على شيء أفضل بكثير"!
The battle meantime had become fiercer than ever
أصبحت المعركة في هذه الأثناء أكثر ضراوة من أي وقت مضى
a big crab had come out of the water
خرج سلطعون كبير من الماء
and he had climbed slowly up on the shore
وكان قد صعد ببطء على الشاطئ
he called out in a hoarse voice
نادى بصوت أجش
it sounded like a trumpet with a bad cold
بدا وكأنه بوق مع نزلة برد سيئة
"enough of your fighting, you young ruffians"
"كفى قتالكم أيها الشباب التافهون"
"because you are nothing other than ruffians!"
"لأنك لست سوى روفيان"!
"These fights between boys seldom finish well"
"هذه المعارك بين الأولاد نادرا ما تنتهي بشكل جيد"
"Some disaster is sure to happen!"
"من المؤكد أن تحدث بعض الكوارث"!
but the poor crab should have saved himself the trouble
لكن السلطعون المسكين كان يجب أن ينقذ نفسه من المتاعب
He might as well have preached to the wind
ربما كان قد بشر للريح
Even that young rascal, Pinocchio, turned around
حتى ذلك الوغد الشاب، بينوكيو، استدار
he looked at him mockingly and said rudely:
نظر إليه بسخرية وقال بوقاحة:

"Hold your tongue, you tiresome crab!"

"امسك لسانك ، أيها السلطعون المتعب"!

"You had better suck some liquorice lozenges"

"كان من الأفضل أن تمتص بعض معينات عرق السوس"

"cure that cold in your throat"

"علاج هذا البرد في حلقك"

Just then the boys had no more books

عندها فقط لم يكن لدى الأولاد المزيد من الكتب

at least, they had no books of their own

على الأقل ، لم يكن لديهم كتب خاصة بهم

they spied at a little distance Pinocchio's bag

تجسسوا على مسافة صغيرة حقيبة بينوكيو

and they took possession of his things

واستولوا على أغراضه

Amongst his books there was one bound in card

من بين كتبه كان هناك واحد مجلدة في بطاقة

It was a Treatise on Arithmetic

كانت رسالة في الحساب

One of the boys seized this volume

استولى أحد الأولاد على هذا المجلد

and he aimed the book at Pinocchio's head

ووجه الكتاب إلى رأس بينوكيو

he threw it at him with all his strength

رماها عليه بكل قوته

but the book did not hit the puppet

لكن الكتاب لم يضرب الدمية

instead the book hit a companion on the head

بدلا من ذلك ، ضرب الكتاب رفيقا على رأسه

the boy turned as white as a sheet

تحول الصبي إلى اللون الأبيض مثل ملاءة

"Oh, mother! help, I am dying!"

"يا أمي !ساعديني ، أنا أموت!"

and he fell his whole length on the sand

وسقط طوله كله على الرمال

the boys must have thought he was dead

لا بد أن الأولاد اعتقدوا أنه مات

and they ran off as fast as their legs could run
وهربوا بأسرع ما يمكن أن تركض أرجلهم

in a few minutes they were out of sight
في بضع دقائق كانوا بعيدين عن الأنظار

But Pinocchio remained with the boy
لكن بينوكيو بقي مع الصبي

although he would have rather ran off too
على الرغم من أنه كان يفضل الهرب أيضا

because his fear was also great
لأن خوفه كان كبيرا أيضا

nevertheless, he ran over to the sea
ومع ذلك ، ركض إلى البحر

and he soaked his handkerchief in the water
ونقع منديله في الماء

he ran back to his poor school-fellow
ركض عائدا إلى زميله الفقير في المدرسة

and he began to bathe his forehead
وبدأ يستحم جبهته

he cried bitterly in despair
بكى بمرارة في يأس

and he kept calling him by name
وظل يناديه بالاسم

and he said many things to him:
وقال له أشياء كثيرة:

"Eugene! my poor Eugene!"
"يوجين !يوجين المسكين"!

"Open your eyes and look at me!"
"افتح عينيك وانظر إلي"!

"Why do you not answer?"
"لماذا لا تجيب؟"

"I did not do it to you"
"لم أفعل ذلك لك"

"it was not I that hurt you so!"
"لم أكن أنا من آذاك هكذا"!

"believe me, it was not me!"

"صدقوني ، لم أكن أنا"!

"Open your eyes, Eugene"

"افتح عينيك ، يوجين"

"If you keep your eyes shut I shall die, too"

"إذا أغمضت عينيك فسوف أموت أيضا"

"Oh! what shall I do?"

"أوه إماذا أفعل؟"

"how shall I ever return home?"

"كيف سأعود إلى المنزل؟"

"How can I ever have the courage to go back to my good mamma?"

"كيف يمكنني امتلاك الشجاعة للعودة إلى أمي الطيبة؟"

"What will become of me?"

"ماذا سيحدث لي؟"

"Where can I fly to?"

"إلى أين يمكنني أن أسافر؟"

"had I only gone to school!"

"لو ذهبت إلى المدرسة فقط"!

"Why did I listen to my companions?"

"لماذا استمعت إلى رفاقي؟"

"they have been my ruin"

"لقد كانوا خرابي"

"The master said it to me"

"قال لي السيد"

"and my mamma repeated it often"

"وكررت أمي ذلك كثيرا"

'Beware of bad companions!'

"احذر من الصحابة السيئين"!

"Oh, dear! what will become of me?"

"أوه ، عزيزي إماذا سيحدث لي؟"

And Pinocchio began to cry and sob

وبدأ بينوكيو في البكاء والبكاء

and he struck his head with his fists

وضرب رأسه بقبضتيه

Suddenly he heard the sound of footsteps

فجأة سمع صوت خطى

He turned and saw two soldiers

التفت ورأى جنديين

"What are you doing there?"

"ماذا تفعل هناك؟"

"why are you lying on the ground?"

"لماذا ترقد على الأرض؟"

"I am helping my school-fellow"

"أنا أساعد زميلي في المدرسة"

"Has he been hurt?"

"هل أصيب بأذى؟"

"It seems he has been hurt"

"يبدو أنه أصيب"

"Hurt indeed!" said one of them

"مؤلم حقا "!قال أحدهم

and he stooped down to examine Eugene closely

وانحنى لفحص يوجين عن كثب

"This boy has been wounded on the head"

"أصيب هذا الصبي في رأسه"

"Who wounded him?" they asked Pinocchio

"من جرحه؟ "سألوا بينوكيو

"Not I," stammered the puppet breathlessly

"لست أنا "، تلعثم الدمية لاهثا

"If it was not you, who then did it?"

"إذا لم تكن أنت ، فمن فعل ذلك بعد ذلك؟"

"Not I," repeated Pinocchio

"لست أنا "، كرر بينوكيو

"And with what was he wounded?"

"وبماذا جرح؟"

"he was hurt with this book"

"لقد أصيب بهذا الكتاب"

And the puppet picked up from the ground his book

والتقطت الدمية من الأرض كتابه

the Treatise on Arithmetic

الرسالة في الحساب

and he showed the book to the soldier

وأظهر الكتاب للجندي

"And to whom does this belong?"

"ولمن ينتمي هذا؟"

"It belongs to me," answered Pinocchio, honestly

"إنه ملك لي "، أجاب بينوكيو ، بصراحة

"That is enough, nothing more is wanted"

"هذا يكفي ، لا شيء أكثر من ذلك"

"Get up and come with us at once"

"انهض وتعال معنا في الحال"

"But I..." Pinocchio tried to object

"لكنني "... حاول بينوكيو الاعتراض

"Come along with us!" they insisted

"تعال معنا"! أصروا

"But I am innocent" he pleaded

"لكنني بريء"

but they didn't listen. "Come along with us!"

لكنهم لم يستمعوا". تعال معنا"!

Before they left, the soldiers called a passing fishermen

قبل أن يغادروا ، اتصل الجنود بصياد عابر

"We give you this wounded boy"

"نعطيك هذا الفتى الجريح"

"we leave him in your care"

"نتركه في رعايتك"

"Carry him to your house and nurse him"

"احمله إلى منزلك وأرضعه"

"Tomorrow we will come and see him"

"غدا سنأتي ونراه"

They then turned to Pinocchio

ثم تحولوا إلى بينوكيو

"Forward! and walk quickly"

"إلى الأمام !والمشي بسرعة"

"or it will be the worse for you"

"أو سيكون أسوأ بالنسبة لك"

Pinocchio did not need to be told twice

لم يكن بينوكيو بحاجة إلى إخباره مرتين

the puppet set out along the road leading to the village

انطلقت الدمية على طول الطريق المؤدي إلى القرية

But the poor little Devil hardly knew where he was

لكن الشيطان الصغير المسكين بالكاد عرف مكانه

He thought he must be dreaming

اعتقد أنه يجب أن يحلم

and what a dreadful dream it was!

ويا له من حلم مروع!

He saw double and his legs shook

رأى ضعف ورجلاه اهتزت

his tongue clung to the roof of his mouth

تشبث لسانه بسقف فمه

and he could not utter a word

ولم يستطع أن ينطق بكلمة

And yet, in the midst of his stupefaction and apathy

ومع ذلك ، في خضم غبله ولامبالاته

his heart was pierced by a cruel thorn

اخترقت شوكة قاسية قلبه

he knew where he had to walk past

كان يعرف أين يجب أن يمشي في الماضي

under the windows of the good Fairy's house

تحت نوافذ منزل الجنية الجيدة

and she was going see him with the soldiers

وكانت ذاهبة لرؤيته مع الجنود

He would rather have died

كان يفضل أن يموت

soon they reached the village

سرعان ما وصلوا إلى القرية

a gust of wind blew Pinocchio's cap off his head

هبت عاصفة من الرياح قبعة بينوكيو عن رأسه

"Will you permit me?" said the puppet to the soldiers

"هل تسمحون لي؟" قالت الدمية للجنود

"can I go and get my cap?"

"هل يمكنني الذهاب والحصول على قبعتي؟"

"Go, then; but be quick about it"

"اذهب إذن. لكن كن سريعا في ذلك"

The puppet went and picked up his cap

ذهبت الدمية والتقطت قبعته

but he didn't put the cap on his head

لكنه لم يضع الغطاء على رأسه

he put the cap between his teeth

وضع الغطاء بين أسنانه

and began to run as fast as he could

وبدأ في الجري بأسرع ما يمكن

he was running back towards the seashore!

كان يركض عائدا نحو شاطئ البحر!

The soldiers thought it would be difficult to overtake him

اعتقد الجنود أنه سيكون من الصعب تجاوزه

so they sent after him a large mastiff

لذلك أرسلوا بعده الدرواس الكبير

he had won the first prizes at all the dog races

كان قد فاز بالجوائز الأولى في جميع سباقات

Pinocchio ran, but the dog ran faster

ركض بينوكيو، لكن ركض بشكل أسرع

The people came to their windows

جاء الناس إلى نوافذهم

and they crowded into the street

واحتشدوا في الشارع

they wanted to see the end of the desperate race

أرادوا أن يروا نهاية السباق اليائس

Pinocchio Runs the Danger of being Fried in a Pan like a Fish
بينوكيو يواجه خطر القلي في مقلاة مثل السمكة

the race was not going well for the puppet
لم يكن السباق يسير على ما يرام بالنسبة للدمية

and Pinocchio thought he had lost
واعتقد بينوكيو أنه خسر

Alidoro, the mastiff, had run swiftly
كان أليدورو ، الدرواس ، قد ركض بسرعة

and he had nearly caught up with him
وكان قد كاد يلحق به

the dreadful beast was very close behind him
كان الوحش المروع قريبا جدا خلفه

he could hear the panting of the dog
كان يسمع لهث

there was not a hand's breadth between them
لم يكن هناك اتساع يد بينهما

he could even feel the dog's hot breath
يمكنه حتى أن يشعر بأنفاس الساخنة

Fortunately the shore was close
لحسن الحظ كان الشاطئ قريبا

and the sea was but a few steps off
وكان البحر على بعد خطوات قليلة

soon they reached the sands of the beach
سرعان ما وصلوا إلى رمال الشاطئ

they got there almost at the same time
وصلوا إلى هناك في نفس الوقت تقريبا

but the puppet made a wonderful leap
لكن الدمية حققت قفزة رائعة

a frog could have done no better
الضفدع لا يمكن أن يفعل أفضل

and he plunged into the water
وسقط في الماء

Alidoro, on the contrary, wished to stop himself
أليدورو ، على العكس من ذلك ، رغب في إيقاف نفسه

but he was carried away by the impetus of the race

لكنه انجرف بعيدا بزخم السباق

he also went into the sea

ذهب أيضا إلى البحر

The unfortunate dog could not swim

المؤسف لا يستطيع السباحة

but he made great efforts to keep himself afloat

لكنه بذل جهودا كبيرة للحفاظ على نفسه واقفا على قدميه

and he swam as well as he could with his paws

وسبح بقدر ما استطاع بمخالبه

but the more he struggled the farther he sank

ولكن كلما كافح أكثر كلما غرق

and soon his head was under the water

وسرعان ما كان رأسه تحت الماء

his head rose above the water for a moment

ارتفع رأسه فوق الماء للحظة

and his eyes were rolling with terror

وكانت عيناه تتدحرجان من الرعب

and the poor dog barked out:

ونبح المسكين:

"I am drowning! I am drowning!"

"أنا أغرق !وأنا أغرق"!

"Drown!" shouted Pinocchio from a distance

"غرق "!صاح بينوكيو من مسافة بعيدة

he knew that he was in no more danger

كان يعلم أنه لم يعد في خطر

"Help me, dear Pinocchio!"

"ساعدني يا عزيزي بينوكيو"!

"Save me from death!"

"أنقذني من الموت"!

in reality Pinocchio had an excellent heart

في الواقع كان بينوكيو قلبا ممتازا

he heard the agonizing cry from the dog

سمع صرخة مؤلمة من

and the puppet was moved with compassion

وتحركت الدمية برحمة

he turned to the dog, and said:

التفت إلى وقال:

"I will save you," said Pinocchio

"سأنقذك "، قال بينوكيو

"but do you promise to give me no further annoyance?"

"لكن هل تعدني بعدم إعطائي المزيد من الإزعاج؟"

"I promise! I promise!" barked the dog

"أعدك !أعدك "إنبح

"Be quick, for pity's sake"

"كن سريعا ، من أجل الشفقة"

"if you delay another half-minute I shall be dead"

"إذا تأخرت نصف دقيقة أخرى سأكون ميتا"

Pinocchio hesitated for a moment

تردد بينوكيو للحظة

but then he remembered what his father had often told him

لكنه تذكر بعد ذلك ما قاله له والده في كثير من الأحيان.

"a good action is never lost"

"العمل الجيد لا يضيع أبدا"

he quickly swam over to Alidoro

سبح بسرعة إلى أليدورو

and he took hold of his tail with both hands

وأمسك ذيله بكلتا يديه

soon they were on dry land again

سرعان ما كانوا على اليابسة مرة أخرى

and Alidoro was safe and sound

وكان أليدورو آمنا وسليما

The poor dog could not stand

المسكين لا يستطيع الوقوف

He had drunk a lot of salt water

كان قد شرب الكثير من الماء المالح

and now he was like a balloon

والآن كان مثل البالون

The puppet, however, didn't entirely trust him

الدمية ، ومع ذلك ، لم تثق به تماما

he thought it more prudent to jump again into the water

كان يعتقد أنه من الحكمة القفز مرة أخرى في الماء

he swam a little distance into the water

سبح مسافة صغيرة في الماء

and he called out to his friend he had rescued

ونادى على صديقه الذي أنقذه

"Good-bye, Alidoro; a good journey to you"

"وداعا يا أليدورو. رحلة جيدة لك"

"and take my compliments to all at home"

"وأخذ تحياتي للجميع في المنزل"

"Good-bye, Pinocchio," answered the dog

"وداعا بينوكيو "، أجاب

"a thousand thanks for having saved my life"

"ألف شكر لإنقاذ حياتي"

"You have done me a great service"

"لقد قدمت لي خدمة عظيمة"

"and in this world what is given is returned"

"وفي هذا العالم ما يعطى يرجع"

"If an occasion offers I shall not forget it"

"إذا أتيحت مناسبة لن أنساها"

Pinocchio swam along the shore

سبح بينوكيو على طول الشاطئ

At last he thought he had reached a safe place

في النهاية اعتقد أنه وصل إلى مكان آمن

so he gave a look along the shore

لذلك ألقى نظرة على طول الشاطئ

he saw amongst the rocks a kind of cave

رأى بين الصخور نوعا من الكهف

from the cave there was a cloud of smoke

من الكهف كان هناك سحابة من الدخان

"In that cave there must be a fire"

"في هذا الكهف يجب أن يكون هناك حريق"

"So much the better," thought Pinocchio

"هذا أفضل بكثير "، فكر بينوكيو

"I will go and dry and warm myself"

"سأذهب وأجفف وأدفئ"

"and then?" Pinocchio wondered

"وبعد ذلك؟ "تساءل بينوكيو

"and then we shall see," he concluded

واختتم قائلا" :وبعد ذلك سنرى."

Having taken the resolution he swam landwards

بعد أن اتخذ القرار سبح إلى اليابسة

he was was about to climb up the rocks

كان على وشك تسلق الصخور

but he felt something under the water

لكنه شعر بشيء تحت الماء

whatever it was rose higher and higher

مهما كان ارتفع أعلى وأعلى

and it carried him into the air

وحملته في الهواء

He tried to escape from it

حاول الهرب منه

but it was too late to get away

ولكن بعد فوات الأوان للهروب

he was extremely surprised when he saw what it was

لقد فوجئ للغاية عندما رأى ما كان عليه

he found himself enclosed in a great net

وجد نفسه محاطا بشبكة كبيرة

he was with a swarm of fish of every size and shape

كان مع سرب من الأسماك من كل حجم وشكل

they were flapping and struggling around

كانوا يرفرفون ويكافحون

like a swarm of despairing souls

مثل سرب من النفوس اليائسة

At the same moment a fisherman came out of the cave

في نفس اللحظة خرج صياد من الكهف

the fisherman was horribly ugly

كان الصياد قبيحا بشكل فظيع

and he looked like a sea monster

وبدا وكأنه وحش البحر

his head was not covered in hair

لم يكن رأسه مغطى بالشعر

instead he had a thick bush of green grass

بدلا من ذلك كان لديه شجيرة سميكة من العشب الأخضر

his skin was green and his eyes were green

كانت بشرته خضراء وعيناه خضراء

and his long beard came down to the ground

ونزلت لحيته الطويلة على الأرض

and of course his beard was also green

وبالطبع كانت لحيته خضراء أيضا

He had the appearance of an immense lizard

كان لديه مظهر سحلية ضخمة

a lizard standing on its hind-paws

سحلية تقف على مخالبها الخلفية

the fisherman pulled his net out of the sea

سحب الصياد شبكته من البحر

"Thank Heaven!" he exclaimed greatly satisfied

"شكرا للسماء" إهتف راضيا جدا

"Again today I shall have a splendid feast of fish!"

"مرة أخرى اليوم سيكون لدي وليمة رائعة من الأسماك"!

Pinocchio thought to himself for a moment
فكر بينوكيو في نفسه للحظة
"What a mercy that I am not a fish!"
"يا لها من رحمة أنني لست سمكة"!
and he regained a little courage
واستعاد القليل من الشجاعة
The netful of fish was carried into the cave
تم نقل شبكة الأسماك إلى الكهف
and the cave was dark and smoky
وكان الكهف مظلما ودخانيا
In the middle of the cave was a large frying-pan
في منتصف الكهف كانت مقلاة كبيرة
and the frying-pan was full of oil
وكانت المقلاة مليئة بالزيت
there was a suffocating smell of mushrooms
كانت هناك رائحة خانقة من الفطر
but the fisherman was very excited
لكن الصياد كان متحمسا جدا
"Now we will see what fish we have taken!"
"الآن سنرى ما هي الأسماك التي أخذناها"!
and he put into the net an enormous hand
ووضع في الشبكة يدا هائلة
his hand had the proportions of a baker's shovel
كان ليده نسب مجرفة الخباز
and he pulled out a handful of fish
وأخرج حفنة من السمك
"These fish are good!" he said
"هذه الأسماك جيدة "!قال
and he smelled the fish complacently
وشم رائحة السمك راضيا
And then he threw the fish into a pan without water
ثم ألقى السمك في مقلاة بدون ماء
He repeated the same operation many times
كرر نفس العملية عدة مرات
and as he drew out the fish his mouth watered
وبينما كان يخرج السمكة يسيل فمه

and the Fisherman chuckled to himself

وضحك الصياد لنفسه

"What exquisite sardines I've caught!"

"يا له من سردين رائع أمسكته"!

"These mackerel are going to be delicious!"

"هذه الماكريل ستكون لذيذة"!

"And these crabs will be excellent!"

"وهذه السرطانات ستكون ممتازة"!

"What dear little anchovies they are!"

"يا لها من أنشوجة صغيرة عزيزة"!

The last to remain in the fisher's net was Pinocchio

آخر من بقي في شبكة الصياد كان بينوكيو

his big green eyes opened with astonishment

فتحت عيناه الخضراوتان الكبيرتان بدهشة

"What species of fish is this??"

"ما هي أنواع الأسماك هذه؟؟"

"Fish of this kind I don't remember to have eaten"

"سمكة من هذا النوع لا أتذكر أنني أكلتها"

And he looked at him again attentively

ونظر إليه مرة أخرى باهتمام

and he examined him well all over

وفحصه جيدا في كل مكان

"I know: he must be a craw-fish"

"أنا أعلم: يجب أن يكون جراد البحر"

Pinocchio was mortified at being mistaken for a craw-fish

شعر بينوكيو بالخزي من الخلط بينه وبين جراد البحر

"Do you take me for a craw-fish?"

"هل تأخذني لصيد جراد البحر؟"

"that's no way to treat your guests!"

"هذه ليست طريقة لمعاملة ضيوفك"!

"Let me tell you that I am a puppet"

"دعني أخبرك أنني دمية"

"A puppet?" replied the fisherman

"دمية؟ "أجاب الصياد

"then I must tell you the truth"

- 217 -

"إذن يجب أن أقول لك الحقيقة"
"a puppet is quite a new fish to me"
"الدمية هي سمكة جديدة تماما بالنسبة لي"
"but that is even better!"
"لكن هذا أفضل"!
"I shall eat you with greater pleasure"
"سوف آكلك بسرور أكبر"
"you can eat me all you want"
"يمكنك أن تأكلني كما تريد"
"but will you understand that I am not a fish?"
"ولكن هل ستفهم أنني لست سمكة؟"
"Do you not hear that I talk?"
"ألا تسمع أنني أتكلم؟"
"can you not see that I reason as you do?"
"ألا ترى أنني أفكر كما تفعل؟"
"That is quite true," said the fisherman
"هذا صحيح تماما "، قال الصياد
"you are indeed a fish with the talent of talking"
"أنت بالفعل سمكة تتمتع بموهبة التحدث"
"and you are a fish that can reason as I do"
"وأنت سمكة يمكن أن تفكر كما أفعل"
"I must treat you with appropriate attention"
"يجب أن أعاملك بالاهتمام المناسب"
"And what would this attention be?"
"وماذا سيكون هذا الاهتمام؟"
"let me give you a token of my friendship"
"دعني أعطيك عربون صداقتي"
"and let me show my particular regard"
"واسمحوا لي أن أظهر احترامي الخاص"
"I will let you choose how you would like to be cooked"
"سأسمح لك باختيار الطريقة التي تريد أن تطبخ بها"
"Would you like to be fried in the frying-pan?
"هل ترغب في أن تقلى في المقلاة؟
"or would you prefer to be stewed with tomato sauce?"

"أو هل تفضل أن تطهى مع صلصة الطماطم؟"

"let me tell you the truth," answered Pinocchio

"دعني أقول لك الحقيقة "، أجاب بينوكيو

"if I had to choose, I would like to be set free"

"إذا كان علي أن أختار ، أود أن أتحرر"

"You are joking!" laughed the fisherman

"أنت تمزح "إضحك الصياد"

"why would I lose the opportunity to taste such a rare fish?"

"لماذا أفقد الفرصة لتذوق مثل هذه السمكة النادرة؟"

"I can assure you puppet fish are rare here"

"يمكنني أن أؤكد لكم أن أسماك الدمى نادرة هنا"

"one does not catch a puppet fish every day"

"لا يصطاد المرء سمكة دمية كل يوم"

"Let me make the choice for you"

"دعني أختار لك"

"you will be with the other fish"

"سوف تكون مع الأسماك الأخرى"

"I will fry you in the frying-pan"

"سأقليك في المقلاة"

"and you will be quite satisfied"

"وسوف تكون راضيا تماما"

"It is always consolation to be fried in company"

"من العزاء دائما أن تكون مقليا في الشركة"

At this speech the unhappy Pinocchio began to cry

في هذا الخطاب بدأ بينوكيو التعيس في البكاء

he screamed and implored for mercy

صرخ وتوسل للرحمة

"How much better it would have been if I had gone to school!"

"كم كان من الأفضل لو ذهبت إلى المدرسة"!

"I shouldn't have listened to my companions"

"ما كان يجب أن أستمع إلى رفاقي"

"and now I am paying for it"

"والآن أنا أدفع ثمنها"

And he wriggled like an eel
وكان يتلوى مثل ثعبان البحر
and he made indescribable efforts to slip out
وبذل جهودا لا توصف للتسلل
but he was tight in clutches of the green fisherman
لكنه كان مشدودا في براثن الصياد الأخضر
and all of Pinocchio's efforts were useless
وكانت كل جهود بينوكيو عديمة الفائدة
the fisherman took a long strip of rush
أخذ الصياد شريطا طويلا من الاندفاع
and he bound the puppets hands and feet
وربط أيدي الدمى وأقدامها
Poor Pinocchio was tied up like a sausage
تم ربط بينوكيو المسكين مثل النقانق
and he threw him into the pan with the other fish
وألقاه في المقلاة مع السمكة الأخرى
He then fetched a wooden bowl full of flour
ثم أحضر وعاء خشبيا مليئا بالدقيق
and one by one he began to flour each fish
وواحدا تلو الآخر بدأ في طحين كل سمكة
soon all the little fish were ready
سرعان ما كانت جميع الأسماك الصغيرة جاهزة
and he threw them into the frying-pan
وألقاهم في المقلاة
The first to dance in the boiling oil were the poor whitings
أول من رقص في الزيت المغلي كان البياض الفقير
the crabs were next to follow the dance
كانت السرطانات بجانب متابعة الرقصة
and then the sardines came too
ثم جاء السردين أيضا
and finally the anchovies were thrown in
وأخيرا تم إلقاء الأنشوجة في
at last it had come to Pinocchio's turn
أخيرا جاء دور بينوكيو
he saw the horrible death waiting for him
رأى الموت الرهيب في انتظاره

and you can imagine how frightened he was
ويمكنك أن تتخيل مدى خوفه

he trembled violently and with great effort
ارتجف بعنف وبجهد كبير

and he had neither voice nor breath left for further entreaties
ولم يتبق له صوت ولا نفس لمزيد من التوسلات

But the poor boy implored with his eyes!
لكن الصبي المسكين توسل بعينيه!

The green fisherman, however, didn't care the least
ومع ذلك ، لم يهتم الصياد الأخضر على الأقل

and he plunged him five or six times in the flour
وأغرقه خمس أو ست مرات في الدقيق

finally he was white from head to foot
أخيرا كان أبيض من الرأس إلى القدم

and he looked like a puppet made of plaster
وبدا وكأنه دمية مصنوعة من الجص

Pinocchio Returns to the Fairy's House
بينوكيو يعود إلى منزل الجنية

Pinocchio was dangling over the frying pan
كان بينوكيو يتدلى فوق المقلاة

the fisherman was just about to throw him in
كان الصياد على وشك رميه

but then a large dog entered the cave
ولكن بعد ذلك دخل كبير الكهف

the dog had smelled the savoury odour of fried fish
كان قد شم رائحة السمك المقلي اللذيذة

and he had been enticed into the cave
وقد تم إغرائه إلى الكهف

"Get out!" shouted the fisherman
"اخرج "إصاح الصياد

he was holding the floured puppet in one hand
كان يحمل الدمية المطحونة بيد واحدة

and he threatened the dog with the other hand

و هدد باليد الأخرى

But the poor dog was as hungry as a wolf

لكن المسكين كان جائعا مثل الذئب

and he whined and wagged his tail

وأنين وهز ذيله

if he could have talked he would have said:

لو كان بإمكانه التحدث لقال:

"Give me some fish and I will leave you in peace"

"أعطني بعض السمك وسأتركك بسلام"

"Get out, I tell you!" repeated the fisherman

"اخرج ، أقول لك "!كرر الصياد

and he stretched out his leg to give him a kick

ومد ساقه ليعطيه ركلة

But the dog would not stand trifling

لكن لن يقف تافها

he was too hungry to be denied the food

كان جائعا جدا بحيث لا يحرم من الطعام

he started growling at the fisherman

بدأ يهدر على الصياد

and he showed his terrible teeth

وأظهر أسنانه الرهيبة

At that moment a little feeble voice called out

في تلك اللحظة نادى صوت ضعيف قليلا

"Save me, Alidoro, please!"

"أنقذني ، أليدورو ، من فضلك"!

"If you do not save me I shall be fried!"

"إذا لم تنقذني سأكون مقليا"!

The dog recognized Pinocchio's voice

تعرف على صوت بينوكيو

all he saw was the floured bundle in the fisherman's hand

كل ما رآه هو حزمة الدقيق في يد الصياد

that must be where the voice had come from

يجب أن يكون هذا هو المكان الذي جاء منه الصوت

So what do you think he did?

إذن ماذا تعتقد أنه فعل؟

Alidoro sprung up to the fisherman

انطلق أليدورو إلى الصياد

and he seized the bundle in his mouth

واستولى على الحزمة في فمه

he held the bundle gently in his teeth

أمسك الحزمة برفق في أسنانه

and he rushed out of the cave again

وهرع من الكهف مرة أخرى

and then he was gone like a flash of lightning

ثم ذهب مثل وميض البرق

The fisherman was furious

كان الصياد غاضبا

the rare puppet fish had been snatched from him

تم خطف السمكة الدمية النادرة منه

and he ran after the dog

وركض وراء

he tried to get his fish back

حاول استعادة سمكته

but the fisherman did not run far

لكن الصياد لم يركض بعيدا

because he had been taken by a fit of coughing

لأنه أصيب بنوبة من السعال

Alidoro ran almost to the village

ركض أليدورو تقريبا إلى القرية

when he got to the path he stopped

عندما وصل إلى الطريق توقف

he put his friend Pinocchio gently on the ground

وضع صديقه بينوكيو برفق على الأرض

"How much I have to thank you for!" said the puppet

"كم يجب أن أشكرك على "!قالت الدمية

"There is no necessity," replied the dog

"لا توجد ضرورة "، أجاب

"You saved me and I have now returned it"

"لقد أنقذتني وأعدتها الآن"

"You know that we must all help each other in this world"

"أنت تعلم أنه يجب علينا جميعا مساعدة بعضنا البعض في هذا العالم"

Pinocchio was happy to have saved Alidoro

كان بينوكيو سعيدا بإنقاذ أليدورو

"But how did you get into the cave?"

"ولكن كيف دخلت الكهف؟"

"I was lying on the shore more dead than alive"

"كنت مستلقيا على الشاطئ ميتا أكثر من حي"

"then the wind brought to me the smell of fried fish"

"ثم جلبت لي الريح رائحة السمك المقلي"

"The smell excited my appetite"

"الرائحة أثارت شهيتي"

"and I followed my nose"

"واتبعت أنفي"

"If I had arrived a second later..."

"إذا كنت قد وصلت بعد ثانية"...

"Do not mention it!" sighed Pinocchio

"لا تذكر ذلك "إتنهد بينوكيو

he was still trembling with fright

كان لا يزال يرتجف من الخوف

"I would be a fried puppet by now"

"سأكون دمية مقلية الآن"

"It makes me shudder just to think of it!"

"يجعلني أرتجف لمجرد التفكير في الأمر"!

Alidoro laughed a little at the idea

ضحك أليدورو قليلا على الفكرة

but he extended his right paw to the puppet

لكنه مد مخلبه الأيمن إلى الدمية

Pinocchio shook his paw heartily

هز بينوكيو مخلبه بحرارة

and then they went their separate ways

ثم ذهبوا في طريقهم المنفصل

The dog took the road home

أخذ الطريق إلى المنزل

and Pinocchio went to a cottage not far off

وذهب بينوكيو إلى كوخ ليس بعيدا

there was a little old man warming himself in the sun

كان هناك رجل عجوز صغير يسخن نفسه في الشمس

Pinocchio spoke to the little old man

تحدث بينوكيو إلى الرجل العجوز الصغير

"Tell me, good man," he started

"قل لي ، رجل جيد "، بدأ

"do you know anything of a poor boy called Eugene?"

"هل تعرف أي شيء عن صبي فقير يدعى يوجين؟"

"he was wounded in the head"

"أصيب في رأسه"

"The boy was brought by some fishermen to this cottage"

"تم إحضار الصبي من قبل بعض الصيادين إلى هذا الكوخ"

"and now I do not know what happened to him"

"والآن لا أعرف ماذا حدث له"

"And now he is dead!" interrupted Pinocchio with great sorrow

"والآن مات "إقاطع بينوكيو بحزن شديد

"No, he is alive," interrupted the fisherman

»لا، إنه على قيد الحياة«، قاطع الصياد

"and he has been returned to his home"

"وقد أعيد إلى منزله"

"Is it true?" cried the puppet

"هل هذا صحيح؟" صرخت الدمية

and Pinocchio danced with delight

ورقص بينوكيو بسرور

"Then the wound was not serious?"

"إذن لم يكن الجرح خطيرا؟"

the little old man answered Pinocchio

أجاب الرجل العجوز الصغير بينوكيو

"It might have been very serious"

"ربما كان الأمر خطيرا جدا"

"it could even have been fatal"

"كان من الممكن أن يكون قاتلا"

"they threw a thick book at his head"

"ألقوا كتابا سميكا على رأسه"

"And who threw it at him?"

"ومن رماها عليه؟"

"One of his school-fellows, by the name of Pinocchio"

"أحد زملائه في المدرسة، باسم بينوكيو"

"And who is this Pinocchio?" asked the puppet

"ومن هو بينوكيو هذا؟" سألت الدمية

and he pretended his ignorance as best he could

وتظاهر بجهله قدر استطاعته

"They say that he is a bad boy"

"يقولون إنه ولد سيء"

"a vagabond, a regular good-for-nothing"

"متشرد، سلعة عادية مقابل لا شيء"

"Calumnies! all calumnies!"

"افتراءات!كل الافتراءات"!

"Do you know this Pinocchio?"

"هل تعرف هذا بينوكيو؟"

"By sight!" answered the puppet

"عن طريق البصر" أجاب الدمية

"And what is your opinion of him?" asked the little man

"وما رأيك فيه؟" سأل الرجل الصغير

"He seems to me to be a very good boy"

"يبدو لي أنه فتى جيد جدا"

"he is anxious to learn," added Pinocchio

"إنه حريص على التعلم "، أضاف بينوكيو

"and he is obedient and affectionate to his father and family"

"وهو مطيع وحنون لأبيه وعائلته"

the puppet fired off a bunch of lies

أطلقت الدمية مجموعة من الأكاذيب

but then he remembered to touch his nose

ولكن بعد ذلك تذكر أن يلمس أنفه

his nose seemed to have grown by more than a hand

يبدو أن أنفه قد نما بأكثر من يد

Very much alarmed he began to cry:

منزعجا جدا بدأ في البكاء:

"Don't believe me, good man"

"لا تصدقني أيها الرجل الطيب"

"what I said were all lies"

"ما قلته كان كله أكاذيب"

"I know Pinocchio very well"

"أعرف بينوكيو جيدا"

"and I can assure you that he is a very bad boy"

"ويمكنني أن أؤكد لكم أنه فتى سيء للغاية"

"he is disobedient and idle"

"إنه غير مطيع وعاطل"

"instead of going to school, he runs off with his companions"

"بدلا من الذهاب إلى المدرسة، يهرب مع رفاقه"

He had hardly finished speaking when his nose became shorter

كان قد انتهى من الكلام بالكاد عندما أصبح أنفه أقصر

and finally his nose returned to the old size

وأخيرا عاد أنفه إلى الحجم القديم

the little old man noticed the boys' colour

لاحظ الرجل العجوز الصغير لون الأولاد

"And why are you all covered with white?"

"ولماذا أنتم جميعا مغطون باللون الأبيض؟"

"I will tell you why," said Pinocchio

"سأخبرك لماذا"، قال بينوكيو

"Without observing it I rubbed myself against a wall"

"دون أن ألاحظ ذلك فركت على الحائط"

"little did I know that the wall had been freshly whitewashed"

"لم أكن أعرف أن الجدار قد تم تبييضه حديثا"

he was ashamed to confess the truth

كان يخجل من الاعتراف بالحقيقة

in fact he had been floured like a fish

في الواقع كان قد تم طحنه بالدقيق مثل السمكة

"And what have you done with your jacket?"

"وماذا فعلت بسترتك؟"

"where are your trousers, and your cap?"

"أين سروالك وقبعتك؟"

"I met some robbers on my journey"

"قابلت بعض اللصوص في رحلتي"

"and they took all my things from me"

"وأخذوا مني كل شيء"

"Good old man, I have a favour to ask"

"رجل عجوز جيد، لدي معروف لأطلبه"

"could you perhaps give me some clothes to return home in?"

"هل يمكن أن تعطيني بعض الملابس لأعود بها إلى المنزل؟"

"My boy, I would like to help you"

"ابني، أود مساعدتك"

"but I have nothing but a little sack"

"لكن ليس لدي سوى كيس صغير"

"it is but a sack in which I keep beans"

"إنه مجرد كيس أحتفظ فيه بالفاصوليا"

"but if you have need of it, take it"

"ولكن إذا كنت بحاجة إليها، خذها"

Pinocchio did not wait to be asked twice

He took the sack at once

لم ينتظر بينوكيو حتى يطلب منه مرتين

أخذ الكيس في الحال

and he borrowed a pair of scissors

واستعار مقصا

and he cut a hole at the end of the sack

وقطع حفرة في نهاية الكيس

at each side, he cut out small holes for his arms

في كل جانب ، قطع ثقوبا صغيرة لذراعيه

and he put the sack on like a shirt

ووضع الكيس مثل القميص

And with his new clothing he set off for the village

وبملابسه الجديدة انطلق إلى القرية

But as he went he did not feel at all comfortable

ولكن عندما ذهب لم يشعر بالراحة على الإطلاق

for each step forward he took another step backwards

لكل خطوة إلى الأمام اتخذ خطوة أخرى إلى الوراء

"How shall I ever present myself to my good little Fairy?"

"كيف سأقدم لجنيتي الصغيرة الطيبة؟"

"What will she say when she sees me?"

"ماذا ستقول عندما تراني؟"

"Will she forgive me this second escapade?"

"هل ستسامحني هذه المغامرة الثانية؟"

"Oh, I am sure that she will not forgive me!"

"أوه ، أنا متأكد من أنها لن تسامحني"!

"And it serves me right, because I am a rascal"

"وهذا يخدمني بشكل صحيح ، لأنني وغد"

"I am always promising to correct myself"

"أنا دائما أعد بتصحيح"

"but I never keep my word!"

"لكنني لا أفي بكلمتي أبدا"!

When he reached the village it was night

عندما وصل إلى القرية كان الليل

and it had gotten very dark

وقد أصبح الظلام شديدا

A storm had come in from the shore
جاءت عاصفة من الشاطئ
and the rain was coming down in torrents
وكان المطر ينزل في السيول
he went straight to the Fairy's house
ذهب مباشرة إلى منزل الجنية
he was resolved to knock at the door
كان مصمما على طرق الباب
But when he was there his courage failed him
ولكن عندما كان هناك خذلته شجاعته
instead of knocking he ran away some twenty paces
بدلا من أن يطرق هرب حوالي عشرين خطوة
He returned to the door a second time
عاد إلى الباب مرة ثانية
and he held the door knocker in his hand
وأمسك مطرقة الباب في يده
trembling, he gave a little knock at the door
يرتجف ، أعطى طرقا صغيرا على الباب
He waited and waited for his mother to open the door
انتظر وانتظر أن تفتح والدته الباب
Pinocchio must have waited no less than half an hour
يجب أن يكون بينوكيو قد انتظر ما لا يقل عن نصف ساعة
At last a window on the top floor was opened
أخيرا تم فتح نافذة في الطابق العلوي
the house was four stories high
كان المنزل بارتفاع أربعة طوابق
and Pinocchio saw a big Snail
ورأى بينوكيو حلزونا كبيرا
it had a lighted candle on her head to look out
كان لديها شمعة مضاءة على رأسها لتنظر إلى الخارج
"Who is there at this hour?"
"من هناك في هذه الساعة؟"
"Is the Fairy at home?" asked the puppet
"هل الجنية في المنزل؟" سألت الدمية
"The Fairy is asleep," answered the snail
"الجنية نائمة "، أجاب الحلزون

"and she must not be awakened"
"ويجب ألا تستيقظ"

"but who are you?" asked the Snail
"ولكن من أنت؟ "سأل الحلزون

"It is I," answered Pinocchio
"إنه أنا "، أجاب بينوكيو

"Who is I?" asked the Snail
"من أنا؟ "سأل الحلزون

"It is I, Pinocchio," answered Pinocchio
"أنا ، بينوكيو "، أجاب بينوكيو

"And who is Pinocchio?" asked the Snail
"ومن هو بينوكيو؟ "سأل الحلزون

"The puppet who lives in the Fairy's house"
"الدمية التي تعيش في منزل الجنية"

"Ah, I understand!" said the Snail
"آه ، أنا أفهم "إقال الحلزون

"Wait for me there"
"انتظرني هناك"

"I will come down and open the door"
"سأنزل وأفتح الباب"

"Be quick, for pity's sake"
"كن سريعا ، من أجل الشفقة"

"because I am dying of cold"
"لأنني أموت من البرد"

"My boy, I am a snail"
"يا ولدي ، أنا حلزون"

"and snails are never in a hurry"
"والقواقع ليست في عجلة من أمرها"

An hour passed, and then two
مرت ساعة ، ثم ساعتان

and the door was still not opened
وكان الباب لا يزال غير مفتوح

Pinocchio was wet through and through
كان بينوكيو مبللا من خلال وعبر

and he was trembling from cold and fear
وكان يرتجف من البرد والخوف

at last he had the courage to knock again
في النهاية كان لديه الشجاعة للطرق مرة أخرى

this time he knocked louder than before
هذه المرة طرق بصوت أعلى من ذي قبل

At this second knock a window on the lower story opened
في هذه الضربة الثانية ، فتحت نافذة على الطابق السفلي

and the same Snail appeared at the window
وظهر نفس الحلزون في النافذة

"Beautiful little Snail," cried Pinocchio
"الحلزون الصغير الجميل "، صرخ بينوكيو

"I have been waiting for two hours!"
"لقد كنت أنتظر لمدة ساعتين"!

"two hours on such a night seems longer than two years"
"ساعتان في مثل هذه الليلة تبدو أطول من عامين"

"Be quick, for pity's sake"
"كن سريعا ، من أجل الشفقة"

"My boy," answered the calm little animal
"ابني "، أجاب الصغير الهادئ

"you know that I am a snail"
"أنت تعرف أنني حلزون"

"and snails are never in a hurry"
"والقواقع ليست في عجلة من أمرها"

And the window was shut again
وأغلقت النافذة مرة أخرى

Shortly afterwards midnight struck
بعد ذلك بوقت قصير ضرب منتصف الليل

then one o'clock, then two o'clock
ثم الساعة الواحدة ثم الساعة الثانية

and the door still remained unopened
وظل الباب غير مفتوح

Pinocchio finally lost all patience
أخيرا فقد بينوكيو كل صبره

he seized the door knocker in a rage

he intended bang the door as hard as he could

استولى على مطرقة الباب في غضب

كان ينوي طرق الباب بأقصى ما يستطيع

a blow that would resound through the house

ضربة من شأنها أن تدوي في المنزل

the door knocker was made from iron

مطرقة الباب مصنوعة من الحديد

but suddenly it turned into an eel

ولكن فجأة تحولت إلى ثعبان البحر

and the eel slipped out of Pinocchio's hand

وانزلق ثعبان البحر من يد بينوكيو

down the street was a stream of water

أسفل الشارع كان هناك تيار من الماء

and the eel disappeared down the stream

واختفى ثعبان البحر أسفل التيار

Pinocchio was blinded with rage

كان بينوكيو أعمى من الغضب

"Ah! so that's the way it is?"

"آه! إذن هذا هو الحال؟"

"then I will kick with all my might"

"ثم سأركل بكل قوتي"

Pinocchio took a little run up to the door

أخذ بينوكيو يركض قليلا إلى الباب

and he kicked the door with all his might

وركل الباب بكل قوته

it was indeed a mighty strong kick

لقد كانت بالفعل ركلة قوية قوية

and his foot went through the door

ودخلت قدمه من الباب

Pinocchio tried to pull his foot out

حاول بينوكيو سحب قدمه للخارج

but then he realized his predicament

ولكن بعد ذلك أدرك مأزقه

it was as if his foot had been nailed down

كان الأمر كما لو أن قدمه قد تم تسميرها

Think of poor Pinocchio's situation!

فكر في وضع بينوكيو المسكين!

He had to spend the rest of the night on one foot

كان عليه أن يقضي بقية الليل على قدم واحدة

and the other foot was in the air

وكانت القدم الأخرى في الهواء

after many hours daybreak finally came

بعد ساعات عديدة جاء الفجر أخيرا

and at last the door was opened

وأخيرا فتح الباب

it had only taken the Snail nine hours

استغرق الحلزون تسع ساعات فقط

he had come all the way from the fourth story

لقد جاء على طول الطريق من القصة الرابعة

It is evident that her exertions must have been great

من الواضح أن جهودها يجب أن تكون كبيرة

but she was equally confused by Pinocchio

لكنها كانت مرتبكة بنفس القدر من بينوكيو

"What are you doing with your foot in the door?"

"ماذا تفعل بقدمك في الباب؟"

"It was an accident," answered the puppet

"لقد كان حادثا "، أجابت الدمية

"oh beautiful snail, please help me"

"يا حلزون جميل ، الرجاء مساعدتي"

"try and get my foot out the door"

"حاول إخراج قدمي من الباب"

"My boy, that is the work of a carpenter""

"يا ولدي ، هذا عمل نجار"

"and I have never been a carpenter"

"ولم أكن نجارا أبدا"

"in that case please get the Fairy for me!"

"في هذه الحالة ، يرجى الحصول على الجنية من أجلي"!

"The Fairy is still asleep"

"الجنية لا تزال نائمة"

"and she must not be awakened"

"ويجب ألا تستيقظ"

"But what can I do with me foot stuck in the door?"

"ولكن ماذا يمكنني أن أفعل بقدمي عالقة في الباب؟"

"there are many ants in this area"

"هناك العديد من النمل في هذا المجال"

"Amuse yourself by counting all the little ants"

"يروق نفسك من خلال عد كل النمل الصغير"

"Bring me at least something to eat"

"أحضر لي شيئا على الأقل لأكله"

"because I am quite exhausted and hungry"

"لأنني مرهق وجائع جدا"

"At once," said the Snail

"في الحال "، قال الحلزون

it was in fact almost as fast as she had said

كان في الواقع تقريبا بالسرعة التي قالت بها

after three hours she returned to Pinocchio

بعد ثلاث ساعات عادت إلى بينوكيو

and on her head was a silver tray

وعلى رأسها صينية فضية

The tray contained a loaf of bread

احتوت الصينية على رغيف خبز

and there was a roast chicken

وكان هناك دجاج مشوي

and there were four ripe apricots

وكان هناك أربعة مشمش ناضج

"Here is the breakfast that the Fairy has sent you"

"هذا هو الإفطار الذي أرسلته لك الجنية"

these were all things Pinocchio liked to eat

كانت هذه كل الأشياء التي أحب بينوكيو تناولها

The puppet felt very much comforted at the sight

شعرت الدمية براحة كبيرة عند المنظر

But then he began to eat the food

ولكن بعد ذلك بدأ يأكل الطعام

and he was most disgusted by the taste

وكان أكثر الاشمئزاز من الذوق

he discovered that the bread was plaster

اكتشف أن الخبز كان جصا
the chicken was made of cardboard
كان الدجاج مصنوعا من الورق المقوى
and the four apricots were alabaster
وكان المشمش الأربعة من المرمر
Poor Pinocchio wanted to cry
أراد بينوكيو المسكين أن يبكي
In his desperation he tried to throw away the tray
في يأسه حاول التخلص من الدرج
perhaps it was because of his grief
ربما كان بسبب حزنه
or it could have been that he was exhausted
أو ربما كان مرهقا
and the little puppet fainted from the effort
وأغمي على الدمية الصغيرة من الجهد
eventually he regained consciousness
في النهاية استعاد وعيه
and he found that he was lying on a sofa
ووجد أنه كان مستلقيا على أريكة
and the good Fairy was beside him
وكانت الجنية الطيبة بجانبه
"I will pardon you once more," the Fairy said
"سأعفو عنك مرة أخرى"، قالت الجنية
"but woe to you if you behave badly a third time!"
"لكن ويل لك إذا تصرفت بشكل سيء مرة ثالثة"!
Pinocchio promised and swore that he would study
وعد بينوكيو وأقسم أنه سيدرس
and he swore he would always conduct himself well
وأقسم أنه سيتصرف دائما بشكل جيد
And he kept his word for the remainder of the year
وحافظ على كلمته لبقية العام
Pinocchio got very good grades at school
حصل بينوكيو على درجات جيدة جدا في المدرسة
and he had the honour of being the best student
وكان له شرف كونه أفضل طالب
his behaviour in general was very praiseworthy

كان سلوكه بشكل عام جديرا بالثناء
and the Fairy was very much pleased with him
وكانت الجنية سعيدة جدا به
"Tomorrow your wish shall be gratified"
"غدا ستكون رغبتك مرضية"
"what wish was that?" asked Pinocchio
"ما هي الأمنية التي كانت تلك؟" سأل بينوكيو
"Tomorrow you shall cease to be a wooden puppet"
"غدا ستتوقف عن أن تكون دمية خشبية"
"and you shall finally become a boy"
"وستصبح أخيرا صبيا"
you could not have imagined Pinocchio's joy
لم يكن بإمكانك تخيل فرحة بينوكيو
and Pinocchio was allowed to have a party
وسمح لبينوكيو بإقامة حفلة
All his school-fellows were to be invited
كان من المقرر دعوة جميع زملائه في المدرسة
there would be a grand breakfast at the Fairy's house
سيكون هناك إفطار كبير في منزل الجنية
together they would celebrate the great event
معا سيحتفلون بالحدث العظيم
The Fairy had prepared two hundred cups of coffee and milk
أعدت الجنية مائتي كوب من القهوة والحليب
and four hundred rolls of bread were cut
وتم قطع أربعمائة لفافة خبز
and all the bread was buttered on each side
وكان كل الخبز بالزبدة على كل جانب
The day promised to be most happy and delightful
وعد اليوم بأن يكون أكثر سعادة ومتعة
but...
لكن...

Unfortunately in the lives of puppets there is always a "but" that spoils everything
لسوء الحظ في حياة الدمى هناك دائما "لكن" يفسد كل شيء

The Land of the Boobie Birds
أرض الطيور المغفلة

Of course Pinocchio asked the Fairy's permission
بالطبع طلب بينوكيو إذن الجنية
"may I go round the town to give out the invitations?"
"هل لي أن أذهب في جولة في المدينة لإعطاء الدعوات؟"
and the Fairy said to him:
فقالت له الجنية:
"Go, if you like, you have my permission"
"اذهب ، إذا أردت ، لديك إذني"
"invite your companions for the breakfast tomorrow"
"ادع رفاقك لتناول الإفطار غدا"
"but remember to return home before dark"
"لكن تذكر أن تعود إلى المنزل قبل حلول الظلام"
"Have you understood?" she checked
"هل فهمت؟ "فحصت
"I promise to be back in an hour"
"أعدك بالعودة في غضون ساعة"
"Take care, Pinocchio!" she cautioned him
"اعتن بنفسك ، بينوكيو "إحذرته
"Boys are always very ready to promise"
"الأولاد دائما مستعدون جدا للوعد"
"but generally boys struggle to keep their word"
"لكن بشكل عام يكافح الأولاد للحفاظ على كلمتهم"
"But I am not like other boys"
"لكنني لست مثل الأولاد الآخرين"
"When I say a thing, I do it"
"عندما أقول شيئا ، أفعله"
"We shall see if you will keep your promise"
"سنرى ما إذا كنت ستفي بوعدك"
"If you are disobedient, so much the worse for you"
"إذا كنت غير مطيع ، فهذا أسوأ بكثير بالنسبة لك"
"Why would it be so much the worse for me?"

"لماذا سيكون الأمر أسوأ بكثير بالنسبة لي؟"
"there are boys who do not listen to the advice"
"هناك أولاد لا يستمعون إلى النصيحة"
"advice from people who know more than them"
"نصيحة من الناس الذين يعرفون أكثر منهم"
"and they always meet with some misfortune or other"
"ويجتمعون دائما مع بعض المحن أو غيرها"
"I have experienced that," said Pinocchio
"لقد اختبرت ذلك "، قال بينوكيو
"but I shall never make that mistake again"
"لكنني لن أرتكب هذا الخطأ مرة أخرى"
"We shall see if that is true"
"سنرى ما إذا كان هذا صحيحا"
and the puppet took leave of his good Fairy
وأخذت الدمية إجازة من جنيته الطيبة
the good Fairy was now like a mamma to him
كانت الجنية الطيبة الآن مثل ماما بالنسبة له
and he went out of the house singing and dancing
وخرج من المنزل يغني ويرقص
In less than an hour all his friends were invited
في أقل من ساعة تمت دعوة جميع أصدقائه
Some accepted at once heartily
قبل البعض في وقت واحد بحرارة
others at first required some convincing
البعض الآخر في البداية يتطلب بعض الإقناع
but then they heard that there would be coffee
ولكن بعد ذلك سمعوا أنه سيكون هناك قهوة
and the bread was going to be buttered on both sides
وكان الخبز على وشك الزبدة على كلا الجانبين
"We will come also, to do you a pleasure"
"سوف نأتي أيضا ، لنفعل لك متعة"

Now I must tell you that Pinocchio had many friends
الآن يجب أن أخبرك أن بينوكيو كان لديه العديد من الأصدقاء

and there were many boys he went to school with
وكان هناك العديد من الأولاد الذين ذهب معهم إلى المدرسة

but there was one boy he especially liked
ولكن كان هناك صبي واحد كان يحبه بشكل خاص

This boy's name was Romeo
كان اسم هذا الصبي روميو

but he always went by his nickname
لكنه كان دائما يذهب بلقبه

all the boys called him Candle-wick
جميع الأولاد أطلقوا عليه اسم شمعة الفتيل

because he was so thin, straight and bright
لأنه كان نحيفا جدا ومستقيما ومشرقا

like the new wick of a little nightlight
مثل الفتيل الجديد لضوء الليل الصغير

Candle-wick was the laziest of the boys
كان شمعة الفتيل هو الأكثر كسلا بين الأولاد

and he was naughtier than the other boys too

وكان أكثر شقاوة من الأولاد الآخرين أيضا

but Pinocchio was devoted to him

لكن بينوكيو كان مكرسا له

he had gone to Candle-wick's house before the others

كان قد ذهب إلى منزل كاندل ويك قبل الآخرين

but he had not found him

لكنه لم يجده

He returned a second time, but Candle-wick was not there

عاد مرة ثانية ، لكن كاندل ويك لم يكن هناك

He went a third time, but it was in vain

ذهب مرة ثالثة ، لكن عبثا

Where could he search for him?

أين يمكن أن يبحث عنه؟

He looked here, there, and everywhere

نظر هنا وهناك وفي كل مكان

and at last he found his friend Candle-wick

وأخيرا وجد صديقه كاندل ويك

he was hiding on the porch of a peasant's cottage

كان يختبئ على شرفة كوخ الفلاح

"What are you doing there?" asked Pinocchio

"ماذا تفعل هناك؟ "سأل بينوكيو

"I am waiting for midnight"

"أنا في انتظار منتصف الليل"

"I am going to run away"

"سأهرب"

"And where are you going?"

"وإلى أين أنت ذاهب؟"

"I am going to live in another country"

"سأعيش في بلد آخر"

"the most delightful country in the world"

"البلد الأكثر متعة في العالم"

"a real land of sweetmeats!"

"أرض حقيقية من الحلويات"!

"And what is it called?"

"وماذا يسمى؟"

"It is called the Land of Boobies"

"تسمى أرض المغفلين"

"Why do you not come, too?"

"لماذا لا تأتي أنت أيضاً؟"

"I? No, even if I wanted to!"

"أنا؟ لا ، حتى لو أردت ذلك!"

"You are wrong, Pinocchio"

"أنت مخطئ يا بينوكيو"

"If you do not come you will repent it"

"إذا لم تأت فسوف تتوب عنه"

"Where could you find a better country for boys?"

"أين يمكنك أن تجد بلدا أفضل للأولاد؟"

"There are no schools there"

"لا توجد مدارس هناك"

"there are no masters there"

"لا يوجد سادة هناك"

"and there are no books there"

"ولا توجد كتب هناك"

"In that delightful land nobody ever studies"

"في تلك الأرض المبهجة لا أحد يدرس أبدا"

"On Saturday there is never school"

"يوم السبت لا توجد مدرسة أبدا"

"every week consists of six Saturdays"

"كل أسبوع يتكون من ستة أيام سبت"

"and the remainder of the week are Sundays"

"وبقية الأسبوع هي أيام الأحد"

"think of all the time there is to play"

"فكر في كل الوقت المتاح للعب"

"the autumn holidays begin on the first of January"

"تبدأ عطلة الخريف في الأول من يناير"

"and they finish on the last day of December"

"وينتهون في اليوم الأخير من شهر ديسمبر"

"That is the country for me!"

"هذا هو البلد بالنسبة لي"!

"That is what all civilized countries should be like!"

"هذا ما يجب أن تكون عليه جميع الدول المتحضرة"!

"But how are the days spent in the Land of Boobies?"

"ولكن كيف هي الأيام التي تقضيها في أرض المغفلين؟"

"The days are spent in play and amusement"

"تقضي الأيام في اللعب والتسلية"

"you enjoy yourself from morning till night"

"تستمتع بنفسك من الصباح حتى الليل"

"and when night comes you go to bed"

"وعندما يأتي الليل تذهب إلى الفراش"

"and then you recommence the fun the next day"

"ثم تستأنف المرح في اليوم التالي"

"What do you think of it?"

"ما رأيك في ذلك؟"

"Hum!" said Pinocchio thoughtfully

"همهمة "إقال بينوكيو بعناية

and he shook his head slightly

وهز رأسه قليلا

the gesture did seem to say something

يبدو أن الإيماءة تقول شيئا ما

"That is a life that I also would willingly lead"

"هذه هي الحياة التي سأعيشها أيضا عن طيب خاطر"

but he had not accepted the invitation yet

لكنه لم يقبل الدعوة بعد

"Well, will you go with me?"

"حسنا ، هل ستذهب معي؟"

"Yes or no? Resolve quickly"

"نعم أم لا؟ حل سريع"

"No, no, no, and no again"

"لا ، لا ، لا ، ولا مرة أخرى"

"I promised my good Fairy to be good boy"

"لقد وعدت جنيتي الجيدة بأن أكون فتى صالحا"

"and I will keep my word"

"وسأحافظ على كلمتي"

"the sun will soon be setting"

"ستغرب الشمس قريبا"

"so I must leave you and run away"

"لذلك يجب أن أتركك وأهرب"

"Good-bye, and a pleasant journey to you"

"وداعا ، ورحلة ممتعة لك"

"Where are you rushing off to in such a hurry?"

"إلى أين تهرع في عجلة من أمرك؟"

"I am going home," said Pinocchio

"أنا ذاهب إلى المنزل "، قال بينوكيو

"My good Fairy wishes me to be back before dark"

"جنيتي الطيبة تتمنى لي أن أعود قبل حلول الظلام"

"Wait another two minutes"

"انتظر دقيقتين أخريين"

"It will make me too late"

"سيجعلني متأخرا جدا"

"Only two minutes," Candle-wick pleaded

"دقيقتان فقط "، ناشد كاندل ويك

"And if the Fairy scolds me?"

"وإذا وبخني الجنية؟"

"Let her scold you," he suggested

"دعها توبخك "، اقترح

Candle-wick was quite a persuasive rascal

كان شمعة الفتيل وغد مقنعا تماما

"When she has scolded well she will hold her tongue"

"عندما توبخ جيدا ستمسك لسانها"

"And what are you going to do?"

"وماذا ستفعل؟"

"Are you going alone or with companions?"

"هل ستذهب بمفردك أم مع رفاق؟"

"oh don't worry about that Pinocchio"

"أوه لا تقلق بشأن ذلك بينوكيو"

"I will not be alone in the Land of Boobies"

"لن أكون وحدي في أرض المغفلين"

"there will be more than a hundred boys"
"سيكون هناك أكثر من مائة ولد"
"And do you make the journey on foot?"
"وهل تقوم بالرحلة سيرا على الأقدام؟"
"A coach will pass by shortly"
"مدرب سيمر قريبا"
"the carriage will take me to that happy country"
"ستأخذني العربة إلى ذلك البلد السعيد"
"What would I not give for the coach to pass by now!"
"ما الذي لن أعطيه للمدرب ليمر الآن"!
"Why do you want the coach to come by so badly?"
"لماذا تريد أن يأتي المدرب بشكل سيء للغاية؟"
"so that I can see you all go together"
"حتى أتمكن من رؤيتكم جميعا تذهبون معا"
"Stay here a little longer, Pinocchio"
"ابق هنا لفترة أطول قليلا ، بينوكيو"
"stay a little longer and you will see us"
"ابق لفترة أطول قليلا وسوف ترانا"
"No, no, I must go home"
"لا ، لا ، يجب أن أعود إلى المنزل"
"just wait another two minutes"
"فقط انتظر دقيقتين أخريين"
"I have already delayed too long"
"لقد تأخرت بالفعل لفترة طويلة"
"The Fairy will be anxious about me"
"الجنية ستكون قلقة علي"
"Is she afraid that the bats will eat you?"
"هل تخشى أن تأكلك الخفافيش؟"
Pinocchio had grown a little curious
كان بينوكيو قد نما فضوليا بعض الشيء
"are you certain that there are no schools?"
"هل أنت متأكد من عدم وجود مدارس؟"
"there is not even the shadow of a school"
"لا يوجد حتى ظل مدرسة"

- 245 -

"And are there no masters either?"

"وألا يوجد سادة أيضاً؟"

"the Land of the Boobies is free of masters"

"أرض المغفلين خالية من الأسياد"

"And no one is ever made to study?"

"ولا أحد يجبر على الدراسة؟"

"Never, never, and never again!"

"أبدا ، أبدا ، وأبدا مرة أخرى"!

Pinocchio's mouth watered at the idea

دمعن فم بينوكيو من الفكرة

"What a delightful country!" said Pinocchio

"يا له من بلد مبهج"!قال بينوكيو

"I have never been there," said Candle-wick

"لم أكن هناك من قبل "، قال كاندل ويك

"but I can imagine it perfectly well"

"لكن يمكنني أن أتخيلها جيدا"

"Why will you not come also?"

"لماذا لا تأتي أيضا؟"

"It is useless to tempt me"

"لا جدوى من إغرائي"

"I made a promise to my good Fairy"

"لقد قطعت وعدا لجنيتي الطيبة"

"I will become a sensible boy"

"سأصبح فتى عاقلا"

"and I will not break my word"

"ولن أكسر كلمتي"

"Good-bye, then," said Candle-wick

"وداعا ، إذن "، قال كاندل ويك

"give my compliments to all the boys at school"

"أتقدم بتحياتي لجميع الأولاد في المدرسة"

"Good-bye, Candle-wick; a pleasant journey to you"

"وداعا ، شمعة الفتيل .رحلة ممتعة لك"

"amuse yourself in this pleasant land"

"يروق نفسك في هذه الأرض الممتعة"

"and think sometimes of your friends"

"وفكر أحيانا في أصدقائك"

Thus saying, the puppet made two steps to go

هكذا يقول ، قامت الدمية بخطوتين للذهاب

but then he stopped halfway in his track

ولكن بعد ذلك توقف في منتصف الطريق في مساره

and, turning to his friend, he inquired:

والتفت إلى صديقه واستفسر قائلا:

"But are you quite certain about all this?"

"لكن هل أنت متأكد تماما من كل هذا؟"

"in that country all the weeks consist of six Saturdays?"

"في ذلك البلد ، تتكون جميع الأسابيع من ستة أيام سبت؟"

"and the rest of the week consists of Sundays?"

"وبقية الأسبوع يتكون من أيام الأحد؟"

"all the weekdays most certainly consist of six Saturdays"

"جميع أيام الأسبوع تتكون بالتأكيد من ستة أيام سبت"

"and the rest of the days are indeed Sundays"

"وبقية الأيام هي بالفعل أيام الأحد"

"and are you quite sure about the holidays?"

"وهل أنت متأكد تماما من العطلات؟"

"the holidays definitely begin on the first of January?"

"تبدأ العطلات بالتأكيد في الأول من يناير؟"

"and you're sure the holidays finish on the last day of December?"

"وأنت متأكد من أن العطلات تنتهي في اليوم الأخير من شهر ديسمبر؟"

"I am assuredly certain that this is how it is"

"أنا متأكد بالتأكيد من أن هذا هو الحال"

"What a delightful country!" repeated Pinocchio

"يا له من بلد مبهج "!كرر بينوكيو

and he was enchanted by all that he had heard

وكان مسحورا بكل ما سمعه

this time Pinocchio spoke more resolute

هذه المرة تحدث بينوكيو بشكل أكثر حزما

"This time really good-bye"

- 247 -

"هذه المرة وداعا حقا"
"I wish you pleasant journey and life"
"أتمنى لك رحلة ممتعة والحياة"
"Good-bye, my friend," bowed Candle-wick
"وداعا يا صديقي "، انحنى شمعة الفتيل
"When do you start?" inquired Pinocchio
"متى تبدأ؟ "استفسر بينوكيو
"I will be leaving very soon"
"سأغادر قريبا جدا"
"What a pity that you must leave so soon!"
"يا للأسف أن تغادر قريبا"!
"I would almost be tempted to wait"
"سأكاد أميل إلى الانتظار"
"And the Fairy?" asked Candle-wick
"والجنية؟ "سأل كاندل ويك
"It is already late," confirmed Pinocchio
"لقد فات الأوان بالفعل "، أكد بينوكيو
"I can return home an hour sooner"
"يمكنني العودة إلى المنزل قبل ساعة"
"or I can return home an hour later"
"أو يمكنني العودة إلى المنزل بعد ساعة"
"really it will be all the same"
"حقا سيكون كل نفس"
"but what if the Fairy scolds you?"
"ولكن ماذا لو وبختك الجنية؟"
"I must have patience!"
"يجب أن أتحلى بالصبر"!
"I will let her scold me"
"سأتركها توبخني"
"When she has scolded well she will hold her tongue"
"عندما توبخ جيدا ستمسك لسانها"
In the meantime night had come on
في هذه الأثناء كان الليل قد حل
and by now it had gotten quite dark

والآن أصبح الظلام مظلما تماما
Suddenly they saw in the distance a small light moving
فجأة رأوا في المسافة ضوءا صغيرا يتحرك

they heard a noise of talking

سمعوا ضجيج الحديث

and there was the sound of a trumpet

وكان هناك صوت بوق

but the sound was still small and feeble

لكن الصوت كان لا يزال صغيرا وضعيفا

so the sound still resembled the hum of a mosquito

لذلك لا يزال الصوت يشبه همهمة البعوض

"Here it is!" shouted Candle-wick, jumping to his feet

"ها هو" إصاح شمعدان الفتيل ، وقفز على قدميه

"What is it?" asked Pinocchio in a whisper

"ما هذا؟" سأل بينوكيو في همس

"It is the carriage coming to take me"

"إنها العربة القادمة لتأخذني"

"so will you come, yes or no?"

"إذن هل ستأتي ، نعم أم لا؟"

"But is it really true?" asked the puppet

"ولكن هل هذا صحيح حقا؟" "سألت الدمية

"in that country boys are never obliged to study?"

"في هذا البلد لا يجبر الأولاد أبدا على الدراسة؟"

"Never, never, and never again!"

"أبدا ، أبدا ، وأبدا مرة أخرى"!

"What a delightful country!"

"يا له من بلد مبهج"!

Pinocchio Enjoys Six Months of Happiness
بينوكيو يتمتع بستة أشهر من السعادة

At last the wagon finally arrived

أخيرا وصلت العربة أخيرا

and it arrived without making the slightest noise

ووصلت دون أن تصدر أدنى ضجيج

because its wheels were bound with flax and rags

لأن عجلاتها كانت مربوطة بالكتان والخرق

It was drawn by twelve pairs of donkeys

تم رسمها بواسطة اثني عشر زوجا من الحمير

all the donkeys were the same size

كانت جميع الحمير بنفس الحجم

but each donkey was a different colour

لكن كل حمار كان لونه مختلفا

Some of the donkeys were gray

كانت بعض الحمير رمادية اللون

and some of the donkeys were white

وكانت بعض الحمير بيضاء

and some donkeys were brindled like pepper and salt

وكانت بعض الحمير مشوشة مثل الفلفل والملح

and other donkeys had large stripes of yellow and blue

والحمير الأخرى لديها خطوط كبيرة من الأصفر والأزرق

But there was something most extraordinary about them

ولكن كان هناك شيء غير عادي عنهم
they were not shod like other beasts of burden
لم يكونوا مبتذلين مثل وحوش العبء الأخرى
on their feet the donkeys had men's boots
على أقدامهم كان للحمير أحذية رجالية
"And the coachman?" you may ask
"والمدرب؟" "قد تسأل
Picture to yourself a little man broader than long
صورة لنفسك رجل صغير أوسع من طويل
flabby and greasy like a lump of butter
مترهل ودهني مثل كتلة من الزبدة
with a small round face like an orange
مع وجه مستدير صغير مثل البرتقال
a little mouth that was always laughing
فم صغير كان يضحك دائما
and a soft, caressing voice of a cat
وصوت قطة ناعم ومداعب
All the boys fought for their place in the coach
قاتل جميع الأولاد من أجل مكانهم في المدرب
they all wanted to be conducted to the Land of Boobies
كلهم أرادوا أن يتم نقلهم إلى أرض المغفلين
The carriage was, in fact, quite full of boys
كانت العربة ، في الواقع ، مليئة بالأولاد
and all the boys were between eight and fourteen years
وكان جميع الأولاد بين ثمانية وأربعة عشر عاما
the boys were heaped one upon another
كان الأولاد ينهالون واحدا تلو الآخر
just like herrings are squeezed into a barrel
تماما مثل الرنجة يتم ضغطها في برميل
They were uncomfortable and packed closely together
كانت غير مريحة ومعبأة معا بشكل وثيق
and they could hardly breathe
وبالكاد يستطيعون التنفس
but not one of the boys thought of grumbling
لكن لم يفكر أحد من الأولاد في التذمر
they were consoled by the promises of their destination

تم مواساتهم بوعود وجهتهم

a place with no books, no schools, and no masters
مكان بلا كتب ولا مدارس ولا سادة

it made them so happy and resigned
جعلتهم سعداء للغاية واستقالوا

and they felt neither fatigue nor inconvenience
ولم يشعروا بالتعب ولا الإزعاج

neither hunger, nor thirst, nor want of sleep
لا جوع ولا عطش ولا حاجة للنوم

soon the wagon had reached them
سرعان ما وصلت العربة إليهم

the little man turned straight to Candle-wick
تحول الرجل الصغير مباشرة إلى شمعدان الفتيل

he had a thousand smirks and grimaces
كان لديه ألف ابتسامة وتجهم

"Tell me, my fine boy;"
"قل لي يا ولدي الجميل؛"

"would you also like to go to the fortunate country?"
"هل ترغب أيضا في الذهاب إلى البلد المحظوظ؟"

"I certainly wish to go"
"بالتأكيد أتمنى أن أذهب"

"But I must warn you, my dear child"
"لكن يجب أن أحذرك يا طفلي العزيز"

"there is not a place left in the wagon"
"لم يتبق مكان في العربة"

"You can see for yourself that it is quite full"
"يمكنك أن ترى بنفسك أنها ممتلئة تماما"

"No matter," replied Candle-wick
"لا يهم "، أجاب كاندل ويك

"I do not need to sit in the wagon"
"لست بحاجة للجلوس في العربة"

"I will sit on the arch of the wheel"
"سأجلس على قوس العجلة"

And with a leap he sat above the wheel
ومع قفزة جلس فوق عجلة القيادة

"And you, my love!" said the little man
"وأنت يا حبي "إقال الرجل الصغير

and he turned in a flattering manner to Pinocchio
واستدار بطريقة جذابة إلى بينوكيو

"what do you intend to do?"
"ماذا تنوي أن تفعل؟"

"Are you coming with us?
"هل أنت قادم معنا؟

"or are you going to remain behind?"
"أم أنك ستبقى في الخلف؟"

"I will remain behind," answered Pinocchio
"سأبقى في الخلف "، أجاب بينوكيو

"I am going home," he answered proudly
"أنا ذاهب إلى المنزل "، أجاب بفخر

"I intend to study, as all well conducted boys do"
"أنوي الدراسة ، كما يفعل جميع الأولاد الذين يمارسون السلوك الجيد"

"Much good may it do you!"
"الكثير من الخير قد تفعل لك"!

"Pinocchio!" called out Candle-wick
"بينوكيو "إنادى شمعة الفتيل

"come with us and we shall have such fun"
"تعال معنا وسنستمتع بمثل هذا"

"No, no, and no again!" answered Pinocchio
"لا ، لا ، ولا مرة أخرى "!أجاب بينوكيو

a chorus of hundred voices shouted from the the coach
صاحت جوقة من مئات الأصوات من المدرب

"Come with us and we shall have so much fun"
"تعال معنا وسنستمتع كثيرا"

but the puppet was not at all sure
لكن الدمية لم تكن متأكدة على الإطلاق

"if I come with you, what will my good Fairy say?"
"إذا جئت معك ، فماذا ستقول جنيتي الطيبة؟"

and he was beginning to yield
وكان قد بدأ في الاستسلام

"Do not trouble your head with melancholy thoughts"
"لا تزعج رأسك بأفكار حزينة"
"consider only how delightful it will be"
"فكر فقط في مدى متعة ذلك"
"we are going to the Land of the Boobies"
"نحن ذاهبون إلى أرض المغفلين"
"all day we shall be at liberty to run riot"
"طوال اليوم سنكون أحرارا في القيام بأعمال شغب"
Pinocchio did not answer, but he sighed
لم يجب بينوكيو ، لكنه تنهد
he sighed again, and then sighed for the third time
تنهد مرة أخرى ، ثم تنهد للمرة الثالثة
finally Pinocchio made up his mind
أخيرا اتخذ بينوكيو قراره
"Make a little room for me"
"إفساح المجال قليلا لي"
"because I would like to come, too"
"لأنني أود أن آتي أيضا"
"The places are all full," replied the little man
"الأماكن كلها ممتلئة "، أجاب الرجل الصغير
"but, let me show you how welcome you are"
"لكن ، دعني أريكم مدى ترحيبك"
"I will let you have my seat on the box"
"سأسمح لك بالحصول على مقعدي على الصندوق"
"And where will you sit?"
"وأين ستجلس؟"
"Oh, I will go on foot"
"أوه ، سأذهب سيرا على الأقدام"
"No, indeed, I could not allow that"
"لا ، في الواقع ، لم أستطع السماح بذلك"
"I would rather mount one of these donkeys"
"أفضل ركوب أحد هذه الحمير"
so Pinocchio went up the the first donkey
لذلك صعد بينوكيو أول حمار

and he attempted to mount the animal
وحاول تركيب

but the little donkey turned on him
لكن الحمار الصغير انقلب عليه

and the donkey gave him a great blow in the stomach
وأعطاه الحمار ضربة كبيرة في المعدة

and it rolled him over with his legs in the air
ودحرجته وساقاه في الهواء

all the boys had been watching this
كان جميع الأولاد يشاهدون هذا

so you can imagine the laughter from the wagon
لذلك يمكنك أن تتخيل الضحك من العربة

But the little man did not laugh
لكن الرجل الصغير لم يضحك

He approached the rebellious donkey
اقترب من الحمار المتمرد

and at first he pretended to kiss him
وفي البداية تظاهر بتقبيله

but then he bit off half of his ear
ولكن بعد ذلك عض نصف أذنه

Pinocchio in the meantime had gotten up from the ground
بينوكيو في هذه الأثناء نهض من الأرض

he was still very cross with the animal
كان لا يزال متقاطعا جدا مع

but with a spring he jumped onto him
ولكن مع ربيع قفز عليه

and he seated himself on the poor animal's back
وجلس على ظهر المسكين

And he sprang so well that the boys stopped laughing
وانطلق بشكل جيد لدرجة أن الأولاد توقفوا عن الضحك

and they began to shout: "Hurrah, Pinocchio!"
وبدأوا في الصراخ: "يا هلا ، بينوكيو"!

and they clapped their hands and applauded him
وصفقوا بأيديهم وصفقوا له

soon the donkeys were galloping down the track
سرعان ما كانت الحمير تركض على المسار

and the wagon was rattling over the stones
وكانت العربة تهتز فوق الحجارة
but the puppet thought that he heard a low voice
لكن الدمية اعتقدت أنه سمع صوتًا منخفضًا
"Poor fool! you should have followed your own way"
"أحمق مسكين !كان يجب أن تتبع طريقتك الخاصة"
"but but you will repent having come!"
"ولكن سوف تتوب بعد أن جئت"!
Pinocchio was a little frightened by what he had heard
كان بينوكيو خائفا قليلا مما سمعه
he looked from side to side to see what it was
نظر من جانب إلى آخر ليرى ما كان عليه
he tried to see where these words could have come from
حاول أن يرى من أين يمكن أن تأتي هذه الكلمات
but regardless of of where he looked he saw nobody
ولكن بغض النظر عن المكان الذي نظر إليه لم ير أحدا
The donkeys galloped and the wagon rattled
ركضت الحمير وهزت العربة
and all the while the boys inside slept
وطوال الوقت كان الأولاد في الداخل ينامون
Candle-wick snored like a dormouse
شمعة الفتيل الشخير مثل الزغب
and the little man seated himself on the box
وجلس الرجل الصغير على الصندوق
and he sang songs between his teeth
وغنى الأغاني بين أسنانه
"During the night all sleep"
"خلال الليل كل النوم"
"But I sleep never"
"لكنني لا أنام أبدا"
soon they had gone another mile
سرعان ما ذهبوا ميلا آخر
Pinocchio heard the same little low voice again
سمع بينوكيو نفس الصوت المنخفض الصغير مرة أخرى
"Bear it in mind, simpleton!"
"ضع في اعتبارك ، بسيط"!

"there are boys who refuse to study"

"هناك أولاد يرفضون الدراسة"

"they turn their backs upon books"

"يديرون ظهورهم للكتب"

"they think they're too good to go to school

"يعتقدون أنهم جيدون جدا للذهاب إلى المدرسة

"and they don't obey their masters"

"وهم لا يطيعون أسيادهم"

"they pass their time in play and amusement"

"يقضون وقتهم في اللعب والتسلية"

"but sooner or later they come to a bad end"

"لكن عاجلا أم آجلا يصلون إلى نهاية سيئة"

"I know it from my experience"

"أنا أعرف ذلك من تجربتي"

"and I can tell you how it always ends"

"ويمكنني أن أخبرك كيف ينتهي دائما"

"A day will come when you will weep"

"سيأتي يوم تبكي فيه"

"you will weep just as I am weeping now"

"سوف تبكي كما أبكي الآن"

"but then it will be too late!"

"ولكن بعد ذلك سيكون الأوان قد فات"!

the words had been whispered very softly

كانت الكلمات تهمس بهدوء شديد

but Pinocchio could be sure of what he had heard

لكن بينوكيو كان متأكدا مما سمعه

the puppet was more frightened than ever

كانت الدمية خائفة أكثر من أي وقت مضى

he sprang down from the back of his donkey

نزل من ظهر حماره

and he went and took hold of the donkey's mouth

فذهب وأمسك بفم الحمار

you can imagine Pinocchio's surprise at what he saw

يمكنك أن تتخيل مفاجأة بينوكيو لما رآه

the donkey was crying just like a boy!

كان الحمار يبكي مثل الصبي!

"Eh! Sir Coachman," cried Pinocchio

"إيه !سيدي كوتشمان»، بكى بينوكيو

"here is an extraordinary thing!"

"هنا شيء غير عادي"!

"This donkey is crying"

"هذا الحمار يبكي"

"Let him cry," said the coachman

»دعه يبكي»، قال المدرب

"he will laugh when he is a bridegroom"

"سوف يضحك عندما يكون عريسا"

"But have you by chance taught him to talk?"

"لكن هل علمته بالصدفة أن يتكلم؟"

"No; but he spent three years with learned dogs"

"لا بلكنه أمضى ثلاث سنوات مع المتعلمة"

"and he learned to mutter a few words"

"وتعلم أن يتمتم ببضع كلمات"

"Poor beast!" added the coachman

"الوحش المسكين "!أضاف المدرب

"but don't you worry," said the little man

"لكن لا تقلق "، قال الرجل الصغير

"don't let us waste time in seeing a donkey cry"

"لا تدعنا نضيع الوقت في رؤية حمار يبكي"

"Mount him and let us go on"

"اركبه ودعنا نمضي"

"the night is cold and the road is long"

"الليل بارد والطريق طويل"

Pinocchio obeyed without another word

أطاع بينوكيو دون كلمة أخرى

In the morning about daybreak they arrived
في الصباح عند الفجر وصلوا

they were now safely in the Land of Boobie Birds
كانوا الآن بأمان في أرض الطيور المغفلة

It was a country unlike any other country in the world
لقد كانت دولة لا مثيل لها في أي دولة أخرى في العالم

The population was composed entirely of boys
كان السكان يتألفون بالكامل من الأولاد

The oldest of the boys were fourteen
كان أكبر الأولاد في الرابعة عشرة من عمرهم

and the youngest were scarcely eight years old
وكان أصغرهم بالكاد يبلغ من العمر ثماني سنوات

In the streets there was great merriment
في الشوارع كان هناك فرح كبير

the sight of it was enough to turn anybody's head
كان منظرها كافيا لتحويل رأس أي شخص

There were troops of boys everywhere
كانت هناك قوات من الأولاد في كل مكان

Some were playing with nuts they had found
كان البعض يلعبون بالمكسرات التي وجدوها

some were playing games with battledores
كان البعض يلعب ألعابا مع باتلدورس
lots of boys were playing football
كان الكثير من الأولاد يلعبون كرة القدم
Some rode velocipedes, others wooden horses
ركب البعض فيلوسيبيديس ، والبعض الآخر خيول خشبية
A party of boys were playing hide and seek
كانت مجموعة من الأولاد يلعبون الغميضة
a few boys were chasing each other
كان عدد قليل من الأولاد يطاردون بعضهم البعض
Some were reciting and singing songs
كان البعض يقرأ ويغني الأغاني
others were just leaping into the air
كان آخرون يقفزون في الهواء
Some amused themselves with walking on their hands
البعض يسلي أنفسهم بالمشي على أيديهم
others were trundling hoops along the road
كان آخرون يدحرجون الأطواق على طول الطريق
and some were strutting about dressed as generals
وكان البعض يتبختر حول ارتداء زي الجنرالات
they were wearing helmets made from leaves
كانوا يرتدون خوذات مصنوعة من أوراق الشجر
and they were commanding a squadron of cardboard soldiers
وكانوا يقودون سربا من جنود الورق المقوى
Some were laughing and some shouting
كان البعض يضحك والبعض الآخر يصرخ
and some were calling out silly things
وكان البعض ينادي بأشياء سخيفة
others clapped their hands, or whistled
صفق آخرون بأيديهم أو صفروا
some clucked like a hen who has just laid an egg
بعض قرقع مثل الدجاجة التي وضعت للتو بيضة
In every square, canvas theatres had been erected
في كل ساحة ، أقيمت مسارح قماشية
and they were crowded with boys all day long

وكانوا مزدحمين بالأولاد طوال اليوم

On the walls of the houses there were inscriptions

على جدران المنازل كانت هناك نقوش

"Long live the playthings"

"تحيا الألعاب"

"we will have no more schools"

"لن يكون لدينا المزيد من المدارس"

"down the toilet with arithmetic"

"أسفل المرحاض مع الحساب"

and similar other fine sentiments were written

ومشاعر رائعة أخرى مماثلة تمت كتابتها

of course all the slogans were in bad spelling

طبعا كل الشعارات كانت بتهجئة سيئة

Pinocchio, Candle-wick and the other boys went to the town

ذهب بينوكيو وكاندل ويك والأولاد الآخرون إلى المدينة

they were in the thick of the tumult

كانوا في خضم الاضطراب

and I need not tell you how fun it was

ولست بحاجة إلى إخبارك كم كان الأمر ممتعا

within minutes they acquainted themselves with everybody

في غضون دقائق تعرفوا على الجميع

Where could happier or more contented boys be found?

أين يمكن العثور على الأولاد الأكثر سعادة أو أكثر رضا؟

the hours, days and weeks passed like lightning

مرت الساعات والأيام والأسابيع مثل البرق

time flies when you're having fun

الوقت يمر بسرعة عندما تستمتع

"Oh, what a delightful life!" said Pinocchio

"أوه ، يا لها من حياة ممتعة "إقال بينوكيو

"See, then, was I not right?" replied Candle-wick

"انظر ، إذن ، ألم أكن على حق؟ "أجاب كاندل وتيل

"And to think that you did not want to come!"

"والتفكير في أنك لا تريد أن تأتي"!

"imagine you had returned home to your Fairy"

"تخيل أنك عدت إلى المنزل إلى جنيتك"

"you wanted to lose your time in studying!"

"أردت أن تضيع وقتك في الدراسة"!

"now you are free from the bother of books"

"الآن أنت حر من عناء الكتب"

"you must acknowledge that you owe it to me"

"يجب أن تقرّ بأنك مدين لي"

"only friends know how to render such great services"

"الأصدقاء فقط يعرفون كيفية تقديم مثل هذه الخدمات الرائعة"

"It is true, Candle-wick!" confirmed Pinocchio

"هذا صحيح ، شمعة الفتيل "!أكد بينوكيو

"If I am now a happy boy, it is all your doing"

"إذا كنت الآن فتى سعيدا ، فهذا كل ما تفعله"

"But do you know what the master used to say?"

"ولكن هل تعرف ما كان يقوله السيد؟"

"Do not associate with that rascal Candle-wick"

"لا ترتبط مع هذا الفتيل شمعة الوغد"

"because he is a bad companion for you"

"لأنه رفيق سيء لك"

"and he will only lead you into mischief!"

"وسوف يقودك فقط إلى الأذى"!

"Poor master!" replied the other, shaking his head

"سيد مسكين "!أجاب الآخر وهو يهز رأسه

"I know only too well that he disliked me"

"أعرف جيدا أنه يكرهني"

"and he amused himself by making my life hard"

"وكان يسلي نفسه بجعل حياتي صعبة"

"but I am generous, and I forgive him!"

"لكنني كريم ، وأنا أسامحه"!

"you are a noble soul!" said Pinocchio

"أنت روح نبيلة "!قال بينوكيو

and he embraced his friend affectionately

واحتضن صديقه بمودة

and he kissed him between the eyes

وقبله بين عينيه

This delightful life had gone on for five months
استمرت هذه الحياة المبهجة لمدة خمسة أشهر
The days had been entirely spent in play and amusement
لقد أمضيت الأيام بالكامل في اللعب والتسلية
not a thought was spent on books or school
لم يتم إنفاق فكرة على الكتب أو المدرسة
but one morning Pinocchio awoke to a most disagreeable surprise
ولكن في صباح أحد الأيام استيقظ بينوكيو على مفاجأة بغيضة للغاية
what he saw put him into a very bad humour
ما رآه وضعه في فكاهة سيئة للغاية

Pinocchio Turns into a Donkey
بينوكيو يتحول إلى حمار

when Pinocchio awoke he scratched his head
عندما استيقظ بينوكيو خدش رأسه
when scratching his head he discovered something...
عندما حك رأسه اكتشف شيئا...
his ears had grown more than a hand!
نمت أذناه أكثر من يد!
You can imagine his surprise
يمكنك أن تتخيل دهشته
because he had always had very small ears
لأنه كان لديه دائما آذان صغيرة جدا
He went at once in search of a mirror
ذهب في الحال بحثا عن مرآة
he had to have a better look at himself
كان عليه أن يلقي نظرة أفضل على نفسه
but he was not able to find any kind of mirror
لكنه لم يتمكن من العثور على أي نوع من المرآة
so he filled the basin with water
لذلك ملأ الحوض بالماء
and he saw a reflection he never wished to see
ورأى انعكاسا لم يرغب أبدا في رؤيته

a magnificent pair of donkey's ears embellished his head!

زوج رائع من آذان الحمار يزين رأسه!

think of poor Pinocchio's sorrow, shame and despair!

فكر في حزن بينوكيو المسكين وعاره ويأسه!

He began to cry and roar

بدأ يبكي ويزأر

and he beat his head against the wall

وضرب رأسه بالحائط

but the more he cried the longer his ears grew

ولكن كلما بكى كلما نمت أذنيه

and his ears grew, and grew, and grew

ونمت أذناه ونمت ونمت

and his ears became hairy towards the points

وأصبحت أذنيه مشعرتين نحو النقاط

a little Marmot heard Pinocchio's loud cries

سمع المرموط قليلا صرخات بينوكيو العالية

Seeing the puppet in such grief she asked earnestly:

عندما رأت الدمية في مثل هذا الحزن سألت بجدية:

"What has happened to you, my dear fellow-lodger?"

"ماذا حدث لك يا زميلي العزيز المقيم؟"

"I am ill, my dear little Marmot"

"أنا مريض يا عزيزي المرموط الصغير"

"very ill, and my illness frightens me"

"مريض جدا ، ومرضي يخيفني"

"Do you understand counting a pulse?"

"هل تفهم عد النبض؟"

"A little," sobbed Pinocchio

"قليلا "، بكى بينوكيو

"Then feel and see if by chance I have got fever"

"ثم أشعر ومعرفة ما إذا كنت قد أصبت بالحمى بالصدفة"

The little Marmot raised her right fore-paw

رفعت المرموط الصغيرة مخلبها الأمامي الأيمن

and the little Marmot felt Pinocchio's pulse

وشعر المرموط الصغير بنبض بينوكيو

and she said to him, sighing:

فقالت له وهي تتنهد:

"My friend, it grieves me very much"

"صديقي ، يحزنني كثيرا"

"but I am obliged to give you bad news!"

"لكنني مضطر لإعطائك أخبارا سيئة"!

"What is it?" asked Pinocchio

"ما هذا؟ "سأل بينوكيو

"You have got a very bad fever!"

"لقد أصبت بحمى سيئة للغاية"!

"What fever is it?"

"ما هي الحمى؟"

"you have a case of donkey fever"

"لديك حالة من حمى الحمار"

"That is a fever that I do not understand"

"هذه حمى لا أفهمها"

but he understood it only too well

لكنه فهمها جيدا

"Then I will explain it to you," said the Marmot

"ثم سأشرح لك ذلك "، قال المرموط

"soon you will no longer be a puppet"

"قريبا لن تكون دمية بعد الآن"

"it won't take longer than two or three hours"

"لن يستغرق الأمر أكثر من ساعتين أو ثلاث ساعات"

"nor will you be a boy either"

"ولن تكون صبيا أيضا"

"Then what shall I be?"

"ثم ماذا أكون؟"

"you will well and truly be a little donkey"

"سوف تكون جيدا وحقا حمار صغير"

"a donkey like those that draw the carts"

"حمار مثل أولئك الذين يرسمون العربات"

"a donkey that carries cabbages to market"

"حمار يحمل الملفوف إلى السوق"

"Oh, how unfortunate I am!" cried Pinocchio

"أوه ، كم أنا مؤسف "إصرخ بينوكيو
and he seized his two ears with his hands
وأمسك أذنيه بيديه
and he pulled and tore at his ears furiously
وسحب ومزق أذنيه بشراسة
he pulled as if they had been someone else's ears
سحب كما لو كانوا آذان شخص آخر
"My dear boy," said the Marmot
"ابني العزيز "، قال المرموط
and she did her best to console him
وبذلت قصارى جهدها لتعزيته
"you can do nothing about it"
"لا يمكنك فعل أي شيء حيال ذلك"
"It is your destiny to become a donkey"
"مصيرك أن تصبح حمار"
"It is written in the decrees of wisdom"
"مكتوب في مراسيم الحكمة"
"it happens to all boys who are lazy"
"يحدث ذلك لجميع الأولاد الكسالى"
"it happens to the boys that dislike books"
"يحدث للأولاد الذين يكرهون الكتب"
"it happens to the boys that don't go to schools"
"يحدث ذلك للأولاد الذين لا يذهبون إلى المدارس"
"and it happens to boys who disobey their masters"
"وهذا يحدث للأولاد الذين يعصون أسيادهم"
"all boys who pass their time in amusement"
"جميع الأولاد يقضون وقتهم في التسلية"
"all the boys who play games all day"
"جميع الأولاد الذين يلعبون الألعاب طوال اليوم"
"boys who distract themselves with diversions"
"الأولاد الذين يلهون أنفسهم بالتحويلات"
"the same fate awaits all those boys"
"نفس المصير ينتظر كل هؤلاء الأولاد"
"sooner or later they become little donkeys"

"عاجلا أم آجلا يصبحون حميرا صغيرة"

"But is it really so?" asked the puppet, sobbing

"ولكن هل هو كذلك حقا؟" سألت الدمية وهي تبكي

"It is indeed only too true!"

"هذا صحيح جدا في الواقع"!

"And tears are now useless"

"والدموع الآن عديمة الفائدة"

"You should have thought of it sooner!"

"كان يجب أن تفكر في الأمر عاجلا"!

"But it was not my fault; believe me, little Marmot"

"لكن هذا لم يكن خطأي. صدقني أيها المرموط الصغير"

"the fault was all Candle-wick's!"

"كان الخطأ كله شمعة الفتيل"!

"And who is this Candle-wick?"

"ومن هو فتيل الشمعة هذا؟"

"Candle-wick is one of my school-fellows"

"شمعة الفتيل هو أحد زملائي في المدرسة"

"I wanted to return home and be obedient"

"أردت العودة إلى المنزل وأن أكون مطيعا"

"I wished to study and be a good boy"

"تمنيت أن أدرس وأن أكون ولدا جيدا"

"but Candle-wick convinced me otherwise"

"لكن شمعة الفتيل أقنعني بخلاف ذلك"

'Why should you bother yourself by studying?'

"لماذا يجب أن تزعج نفسك بالدراسة؟"

'Why should you go to school?'

"لماذا يجب أن تذهب إلى المدرسة؟"

'Come with us instead to the Land of Boobies Birds'

"تعال معنا بدلا من ذلك إلى أرض الطيور المغفلهة"

'there we shall none of us have to learn'

"هناك لن يكون على أي منا أن يتعلم"

'we will amuse ourselves from morning to night'

"سنسلي أنفسنا من الصباح إلى الليل"

'and we shall always be merry'

"وسنكون دائما فرحين"
"that friend of yours was false"
"صديقك هذا كان كاذبا"
"why did you follow his advice?"
"لماذا اتبعت نصيحته؟"
"Because, my dear little Marmot, I am a puppet"
"لأنني ، يا عزيزي المرموط الصغير ، أنا دمية"
"I have no sense and no heart"
"ليس لدي أي إحساس ولا قلب"
"if I had had a heart I would never have left"
"لو كان لدي قلب لما غادرت أبدا"
"I left my good Fairy who loved me like a mamma"
"تركت جنيتي الطيبة التي أحبتني مثل ماما"
"the good Fairy who had done so much for me!"
"الجنية الجيدة التي فعلت الكثير من أجلي"!
"And I was going to be a puppet no longer"
"وكنت سأكون دمية بعد الآن"
"I would by this time have become a little boy"
"بحلول هذا الوقت كنت سأصبح صبيا صغيرا"
"and I would be like the other boys"
"وسأكون مثل الأولاد الآخرين"
"But if I meet Candle-wick, woe to him!"
"ولكن إذا قابلت فتيل الشموع ، ويل له"!
"He shall hear what I think of him!"
"سوف يسمع ما أفكر فيه"!
And he turned to go out
واستدار ليخرج
But then he remembered he had donkey's ears
ولكن بعد ذلك تذكر أن لديه آذان حمار
of course he was ashamed to show his ears in public
بالطبع كان يخجل من إظهار أذنيه في الأماكن العامة
so what do you think he did?
إذن ماذا تعتقد أنه فعل؟
He took a big cotton hat

أخذ قبعة قطنية كبيرة
and he put the cotton hat on his head
ووضع القبعة القطنية على رأسه
and he pulled the hat well down over his nose
وسحب القبعة جيدا على أنفه
He then set out in search of Candle-wick
ثم انطلق بحثا عن فتيل الشموع
He looked for him in the streets
بحث عنه في الشوارع
and he looked for him in the little theatres
وبحث عنه في المسارح الصغيرة
he looked in every possible place
نظر في كل مكان ممكن
but he could not find him wherever he looked
لكنه لم يجده أينما نظر
He inquired for him of everybody he met
استفسر عنه من كل من قابله
but no one seemed to have seen him
لكن يبدو أن أحدا لم يره
He then went to seek him at his house
ثم ذهب للبحث عنه في منزله
and, having reached the door, he knocked
وبعد أن وصل إلى الباب ، طرق
"Who is there?" asked Candle-wick from within
"من هناك؟" سأل كاندل ويك من الداخل
"It is I!" answered the puppet
"إنه أنا!" أجابت الدمية
"Wait a moment and I will let you in"
"انتظر لحظة وسأسمح لك بالدخول"
After half an hour the door was opened
بعد نصف ساعة تم فتح الباب
now you can imagine Pinocchio's feeling at what he saw
الآن يمكنك أن تتخيل شعور بينوكيو بما رآه
his friend also had a big cotton hat on his head
كان لدى صديقه أيضا قبعة قطنية كبيرة على رأسه
At the sight of the cap Pinocchio felt almost consoled

على مرأى من الغطاء شعر بينوكيو بالمواساة تقريبا

and Pinocchio thought to himself:

وفكر بينوكيو في نفسه:

"Has my friend got the same illness that I have?"

"هل أصيب صديقي بنفس المرض الذي أصبت به؟"

"Is he also suffering from donkey fever?"

"هل يعاني أيضا من حمى الحمير؟"

but at first Pinocchio pretended not to have noticed

لكن في البداية تظاهر بينوكيو بأنه لم يلاحظ

he just casually asked him a question, smiling:

لقد سأله سؤالا عرضا ، مبتسما:

"How are you, my dear Candle-wick?"

"كيف حالك يا عزيزي شمعدان ويك؟"

"as well as a mouse in a Parmesan cheese"

"وكذلك فأر في جبنة البارميزان"

"Are you saying that seriously?"

"هل تقول ذلك بجدية؟"

"Why should I tell you a lie?"

"لماذا يجب أن أقول لك كذبة؟"

"but why, then, do you wear a cotton hat?"

"ولكن لماذا ، إذن ، ترتدي قبعة قطنية؟"

"is covers up all of your ears"

"يغطي كل أذنيك"

"The doctor ordered me to wear it"

"أمرني الطبيب بارتدائه"

"because I have hurt this knee"

"لأنني أصبت في هذه الركبة"

"And you, dear puppet," asked Candle-wick

"وأنت ، عزيزي الدمية "، سأل كاندل ويك

"why have you pulled that cotton hat passed your nose?"

"لماذا سحبت تلك القبعة القطنية التي مرت أنفك؟"

"The doctor prescribed it because I have grazed my foot"

"وصفه الطبيب لأنني رعيت قدمي"

"Oh, poor Pinocchio!" - "Oh, poor Candle-wick!"

"أوه ، بينوكيو المسكين" - "أوه ، مسكين شمعة الفتيل"!

After these words a long silence followed

بعد هذه الكلمات تبع ذلك صمت طويل

the two friends did nothing but look mockingly at each other

لم يفعل الصديقان شيئا سوى النظر بسخرية إلى بعضهما البعض

At last the puppet said in a soft voice to his companion:

أخيرا قالت الدمية بصوت ناعم لرفيقه:

"Satisfy my curiosity, my dear Candle-wick"

"إرضاء فضولي ، عزيزي شمعة الفتيل"

"have you ever suffered from disease of the ears?"

"هل سبق لك أن عانيت من مرض في الأذنين؟"

"I have never suffered from disease of the ears!"

"لم أعاني أبدا من مرض الأذنين"!

"And you, Pinocchio?" asked Candle-wick

"وأنت ، بينوكيو؟" سأل كاندل ويك

"have you ever suffered from disease of the ears?"

"هل سبق لك أن عانيت من مرض في الأذنين؟"

"I have never suffered from that disease either"

"لم أعاني أبدا من هذا المرض أيضا"

"Only since this morning one of my ears aches"

"فقط منذ هذا الصباح واحدة من أذني تؤلمني"

"my ear is also paining me"

"أذني تؤلمني أيضا"

"And which of your ears hurts you?"

"وأي من أذنيك يؤلمك؟"

"Both of my ears happen to hurt"

"كلتا أذني تؤلمني"

"And what about you?"

"وماذا عنك؟"

"Both of my ears happen to hurt too"

"كلتا أذني تؤلمني أيضا"

Can we have got the same illness?

هل يمكن أن نكون قد أصبنا بنفس المرض؟"

"I fear we might have caught a fever"

"أخشى أننا قد أصبنا بالحمى"

"Will you do me a kindness, Candle-wick?"

"هل ستفعل لي اللطف ، شمعة الفتيل؟"

"Willingly! With all my heart"

"عن طيب خاطر! من كل قلبي"

"Will you let me see your ears?"

"هل ستسمح لي برؤية أذنيك؟"

"Why would I deny your request?"

"لماذا أرفض طلبك؟"

"But first, my dear Pinocchio, I should like to see yours"

"لكن أولا ، عزيزي بينوكيو ، أود أن أراك أنت"

"No: you must do so first"

"لا: يجب أن تفعل ذلك أولا"

"No, dear. First you and then I!"

"لا يا عزيزي. أولا أنت ثم أنا!"

"Well," said the puppet

"حسنا "، قالت الدمية

"let us come to an agreement like good friends"

"دعونا نتوصل إلى اتفاق مثل الأصدقاء الحميمين"

"Let me hear what this agreement is"

"دعني أسمع ما هو هذا الاتفاق"

"We will both take off our hats at the same moment"

"كلانا سيخلع قبعاتنا في نفس اللحظة"

"Do you agree to do it?"

"هل توافق على القيام بذلك؟"

"I agree, and you have my word"

"أوافق ، ولديك كلمتي"

And Pinocchio began to count in a loud voice:

وبدأ بينوكيو في العد بصوت عال:

"One, two, three!" he counted

"واحد ، اثنان ، ثلاثة "!أحصى

At "Three!" the two boys took off their hats

في" ثلاثة "!خلع الصبيان قبعتيهما

and they threw their hats into the air
وألقوا قبعاتهم في الهواء
and you should have seen the scene that followed
وكان يجب أن ترى المشهد الذي أعقب ذلك
it would seem incredible if it were not true
سيبدو الأمر لا يصدق إذا لم يكن صحيحا
they saw they were both struck by the same misfortune
رأوا أنهم أصيبوا بنفس المحنة
but they felt neither mortification nor grief
لكنهم لم يشعروا بالموت ولا الحزن
instead they began to prick their ungainly ears
بدلا من ذلك بدأوا في وخز آذانهم غير المرغوبة
and they began to make a thousand antics
وبدأوا في صنع ألف الغريبة
they ended by going into bursts of laughter
انتهوا بالدخول في رشقات نارية من الضحك
And they laughed, and laughed, and laughed
وضحكوا وضحكوا وضحكوا
until they had to hold themselves together
حتى اضطروا إلى تماسك أنفسهم

But in the midst of their merriment something happened
ولكن في خضم فرحهم حدث شيء ما

Candle-wick suddenly stopped laughing and joking
توقف فتيل الشموع فجأة عن الضحك والمزاح

he staggered around and changed colour
ترنح حولها وغير لونها

"Help, help, Pinocchio!" he cried
"إصرخ "مساعدة ، مساعدة ، بينوكيو

"What is the matter with you?"
"ما الأمر معك؟"

"Alas, I cannot any longer stand upright"
"للأسف ، لم يعد بإمكاني الوقوف منتصبا"

"Neither can I," exclaimed Pinocchio
"ولا أنا "، هتف بينوكيو

and he began to totter and cry
وبدأ يترنح ويبكي

And whilst they were talking, they both doubled up
وبينما كانا يتحدثان ، تضاعف كلاهما

and they began to run round the room on their hands and feet
وبدأوا في الركض حول الغرفة على أيديهم وأرجلهم

And as they ran, their hands became hoofs
وبينما كانوا يركضون ، أصبحت أيديهم حوافر

their faces lengthened into muzzles
تطول وجوههم إلى كمامات

and their backs became covered with a light gray hairs
وأصبحت ظهورهم مغطاة بشعر رمادي فاتح

and their hair was sprinkled with black
وتم رش شعرهم باللون الأسود

But do you know what was the worst moment?
لكن هل تعرف ما هي أسوأ لحظة؟

one moment was worse than all the others
لحظة واحدة كانت أسوأ من كل اللحظات الأخرى

both of the boys grew donkey tails
نما كل من الأولاد ذيول الحمير

the boys were vanquished by shame and sorrow

هزم الأولاد بالعار والحزن

and they wept and lamented their fate

وبكوا وندبوا مصيرهم

Oh, if they had but been wiser!

أوه ، إذا كانوا أكثر حكمة!

but they couldn't lament their fate

لكنهم لم يتمكنوا من رثاء مصيرهم

because they could only bray like asses

لأنهم لا يستطيعون سوى براي مثل الحمير

and they brayed loudly in chorus: "Hee-haw!"

ونهقوا بصوت عال في جوقة" :هي-هاو"!

Whilst this was going on someone knocked at the door

بينما كان هذا يحدث ، طرق شخص ما الباب

and there was a voice on the outside that said:

وكان هناك صوت في الخارج يقول:

"Open the door! I am the little man"

"افتح الباب !أنا الرجل الصغير"

"I am the coachman who brought you to this country"

"أنا المدرب الذي أتى بك إلى هذا البلد"

"Open at once, or it will be the worse for you!"

"افتح في الحال ، أو سيكون الأسوأ بالنسبة لك"!

Pinocchio gets Trained for the Circus
بينوكيو يتدرب على السيرك

the door wouldn't open at his command
لن يفتح الباب بأمره

so the little man gave the door a violent kick
لذلك أعطى الرجل الصغير الباب ركلة عنيفة

and the coachman burst into the room
واقتحم المدرب الغرفة

he spoke with his usual little laugh:
تحدث بضحكته الصغيرة المعتادة:

"Well done, boys! You brayed well"
"أحسنت يا أولاد !لقد نهقت جيدا"

"and I recognized you by your voices"
"وتعرفت عليكم من أصواتكم"

"That is why I am here"
"لهذا السبب أنا هنا"

the two little donkeys were quite stupefied
كان الحميران الصغيران في حالة ذهول تام

they stood with their heads down
وقفوا ورؤوسهم إلى أسفل

they had their ears lowered
خفضت آذانهم

and they had their tails between their legs
وكان لديهم ذيولهم بين أرجلهم

At first the little man stroked and caressed them
في البداية قام الرجل الصغير بمداعبتهم ومداعبتهم

then he took out a currycomb
ثم أخرج مشط الكاري

and he currycombed the donkeys well
وقام بتمشيط الحمير بالكاري جيدا

by this process he had polished them
من خلال هذه العملية قام بتلميعهم

and the two donkeys shone like two mirrors
وأشرق الحمارين مثل مرآتين

he put a halter around their necks

وضع رسنا حول أعناقهم

and he led them to the market-place

وقادهم إلى السوق

he was in hopes of selling them

كان يأمل في بيعها

he thought he could get a good profit

كان يعتقد أنه يمكن أن يحصل على ربح جيد

And indeed there were buyers for the donkeys

وبالفعل كان هناك مشترون للحمير

Candle-wick was bought by a peasant

تم شراء شمعة الفتيل من قبل فلاح

his donkey had died the previous day

كان حماره قد مات في اليوم السابق

Pinocchio was sold to the director of a company

تم بيع بينوكيو لمدير شركة

they were a company of buffoons and tight-rope dancers

كانوا شركة من المهرجين والراقصين على الحبال المشدودة

he bought him so that he might teach him to dance

اشتراه ليعلمه الرقص

he could dance with the other circus animals
يمكنه الرقص مع السيرك الأخرى
And now, my little readers, you understand
والآن ، أيها القراء الصغار ، أنت تفهم
the little man was just a businessman
كان الرجل الصغير مجرد رجل أعمال
and it was a profitable business that he led
وكان عملا مربحا قاده
The wicked little monster with a face of milk and honey
الوحش الصغير الشرير ذو وجه الحليب والعسل
he made frequent journeys round the world
قام برحلات متكررة حول العالم
he promised and flattered wherever he went
وعد وشعر بالإطراء أينما ذهب
and he collected all the idle boys
وجمع كل الأولاد العاطلين
and there were many idle boys to collect
وكان هناك العديد من الأولاد العاطلين عن العمل لجمعها
all the boys who had taken a dislike to books
جميع الأولاد الذين كرهوا الكتب
and all the boys who weren't fond of school
وجميع الأولاد الذين لم يكونوا مولعين بالمدرسة
each time his wagon filled up with these boys
في كل مرة تمتلئ عربته بهؤلاء الأولاد
and he took them all to the Land of Boobie Birds
وأخذهم جميعا إلى أرض الطيور المغفلة
here they passed their time playing games
هنا قضوا وقتهم في ممارسة الألعاب
and there was uproar and much amusement
وكان هناك ضجة والكثير من التسلية
but the same fate awaited all the deluded boys
لكن نفس المصير ينتظر كل الأولاد المخدوعين
too much play and no study turned them into donkeys
الكثير من اللعب وعدم وجود دراسة حولتهم إلى حمير
then he took possession of them with great delight
ثم استولى عليها بفرحة عظيمة

and he carried them off to the fairs and markets
وحملهم إلى المعارض والأسواق
And in this way he made heaps of money
وبهذه الطريقة صنع أكواما من المال
What became of Candle-wick I do not know
ما حدث من شمعة الفتيل لا أعرف
but I do know what happened to poor Pinocchio
لكنني أعرف ما حدث لبينوكيو المسكين
from the very first day he endured a very hard life
منذ اليوم الأول تحمل حياة صعبة للغاية
Pinocchio was put into his stall
تم وضع بينوكيو في كشكه
and his master filled the manger with straw
وملأ سيده المذود بالقش
but Pinocchio didn't like eating straw at all
لكن بينوكيو لم يحب أكل القش على الإطلاق
and the little donkey spat the straw out again
وبصق الحمار الصغير القشة مرة أخرى
Then his master, grumbling, filled the manger with hay
ثم سيده ، متذمرا ، ملأ المذود بالتبن
but hay did not please Pinocchio either
لكن القش لم يرضي بينوكيو أيضا
"Ah!" exclaimed his master in a passion
"آه !"هتف سيده في شغف
"Does not hay please you either?"
"ألا يرضيك التبن أيضا؟"
"Leave it to me, my fine donkey"
"اترك الأمر لي يا حماري الجميل"
"I see you are full of caprices"
"أرى أنك مليء بالنزوات"
"but worry not, I will find a way to cure you!"
"لكن لا تقلق ، سأجد طريقة لعلاجك"!
And he struck the donkey's legs with his whip
وضرب ساقي الحمار بسوطه
Pinocchio began to cry and bray with pain

بدأ بينوكيو في البكاء و bray من الألم

"Hee-haw! I cannot digest straw!"

"هيه هاو !إلا أستطيع هضم القش!"

"Then eat hay!" said his master

"ثم أكل القش "إقال سيده

he understood perfectly the asinine dialect

لقد فهم تماما لهجة الأسينين

"Hee-haw! hay gives me a pain in my stomach"

"هيه هاو !القش يعطيني ألما في معدتي"

"I see how it is little donkey"

"أرى كيف هو حمار صغير"

"you would like to be fed with capons in jelly"

"ترغب في أن تتغذى على كابونات في هلام"

and he got more and more angry

وغضب أكثر فأكثر

and he whipped poor Pinocchio again

وجلد بينوكيو المسكين مرة أخرى

the second time Pinocchio held his tongue

في المرة الثانية أمسك بينوكيو لسانه

and he learned to say nothing more

وتعلم أن يقول شيئا أكثر

The stable was then shut

ثم تم إغلاق الإسطبل

and Pinocchio was left alone

وترك بينوكيو وحده

He had not eaten for many hours

لم يأكل منذ ساعات طويلة

and he began to yawn from hunger

وبدأ يتثاءب من الجوع

his yawns seemed as wide as an oven

بدا تثاؤبه عريضا مثل الفرن

but he found nothing else to eat

لكنه لم يجد شيئا آخر يأكله

so he resigned himself to his fate

لذلك استسلم لمصيره

and he gave in and chewed a little hay
واستسلم ومضغ القليل من التبن
he chewed the hay well, because it was dry
مضغ القش جيدا ، لأنه كان جافا
and he shut his eyes and swallowed it
وأغمض عينيه وابتلعها
"This hay is not bad," he said to himself
"هذا التبن ليس سيئا "، قال لنفسه
"but better would have been if I had studied!"
"ولكن كان من الأفضل لو كنت قد درست"!
"Instead of hay I could now be eating bread"
"بدلا من التبن يمكنني الآن تناول الخبز"
"and perhaps I would have been eating fine sausages"
"وربما كنت سأتناول النقانق الجيدة"
"But I must have patience!"
"لكن يجب أن أتحلى بالصبر"!
The next morning he woke up again
في صباح اليوم التالي استيقظ مرة أخرى
he looked in the manger for a little more hay
نظر في المذود لمزيد من التبن
but there was no more hay to be found
ولكن لم يكن هناك المزيد من التبن الذي يمكن العثور عليه
for he had eaten all the hay during the night
لأنه أكل كل التبن أثناء الليل
Then he took a mouthful of chopped straw
ثم أخذ فم من القش المفروم
but he had to acknowledge the horrible taste
لكن كان عليه أن يعترف بالطعم الرهيب
it tasted not in the least like macaroni or pie
طعمها ليس على الأقل مثل المعكرونة أو الفطيرة
"I hope other naughty boys learn from my lesson"
"آمل أن يتعلم الأولاد المشاغبون الآخرون من درسي"
"But I must have patience!"
"لكن يجب أن أتحلى بالصبر"!
and the little donkey kept chewing the straw

وظل الحمار الصغير يمضغ القشة

"Patience indeed!" shouted his master

"الصبر حقا" إصاح سيده

he had come at that moment into the stable

لقد جاء في تلك اللحظة إلى الإسطبل

"but don't get too comfortable, my little donkey"

"لكن لا تشعر بالراحة يا حماري الصغير"

"I didn't buy you to give you food and drink"

"لم أشتريك لأعطيك الطعام والشراب"

"I bought you to make you work"

"لقد اشتريتك لأجعلك تعمل"

"I bought you so that you earn me money"

"لقد اشتريتك حتى تكسبني المال"

"Up you get, then, at once!"

"حتى تحصل ، إذن ، في وقت واحد"!

"you must come with me into the circus"

"يجب أن تأتي معي إلى السيرك"

"there I will teach you to jump through hoops"

"هناك سأعلمك القفز من خلال الأطواق"

"you will learn to stand upright on your hind legs"

"سوف تتعلم الوقوف منتصبا على رجلتيك الخلفيتين"

"and you will learn to dance waltzes and polkas"

"وسوف تتعلم الرقص الفالس والبولكا"

Poor Pinocchio had to learn all these fine things

كان على بينوكيو المسكين أن يتعلم كل هذه الأشياء الجميلة

and I can't say it was easy to learn

ولا أستطيع أن أقول أنه كان من السهل التعلم

it took him three months to learn the tricks

استغرق الأمر منه ثلاثة أشهر لتعلم الحيل

he got many a whipping that nearly took off his skin

حصل على العديد من الجلد الذي كاد أن يخلع جلده

At last his master made the announcement

أخيرا أعلن سيده

many coloured placards stuck on the street corners

العديد من اللافتات الملونة عالقة في زوايا الشوارع

"Great Full Dress Representation"

"عظيم تمثيل اللباس الكامل"

"TONIGHT will Take Place the Usual Feats and Surprises"

"الليلة ستحدث المآثر والمفاجآت المعتادة"

"Performances Executed by All the Artists and horses"

"العروض التي نفذها جميع الفنانين والخيول"

"and moreover; The Famous LITTLE DONKEY PINOCCHIO"

"وعلاوة على ذلك؛ الحمار الصغير الشهير بينوكيو"

"THE STAR OF THE DANCE"

"نجم الرقص"

"the theatre will be brilliantly illuminated"

"سيتم إضاءة المسرح ببراعة"

you can imagine how crammed the theatre was

يمكنك أن تتخيل كيف كان المسرح مكتظا

The circus was full of children of all ages

كان السيرك مليئا بالأطفال من جميع الأعمار

all came to see the famous little donkey Pinocchio dance

جاء الجميع لرؤية رقصة الحمار الصغير الشهير بينوكيو

the first part of the performance was over

انتهى الجزء الأول من الأداء

the director of the company presented himself to the public

قدم مدير الشركة نفسه للجمهور

he was dressed in a black coat and white breeches

كان يرتدي معطفا أسود ومؤخرات بيضاء

and big leather boots that came above his knees

والأحذية الجلدية الكبيرة التي جاءت فوق ركبتيه

he made a profound bow to the crowd

لقد انحنى بعمق للحشد

he began with much solemnity a ridiculous speech:

بدأ بكثير من الجدية خطابا سخيفا:

"Respectable public, ladies and gentlemen!"

"الجمهور المحترم ، سيداتي وسادتي"!

"it is with great honour and pleasure"

"إنه لشرف وسرور كبيرين"

"I stand here before this distinguished audience"
"أقف هنا أمام هذا الجمهور المميز"
"and I present to you the celebrated little donkey"
"وأقدم لكم الحمار الصغير الشهير"
"the little donkey who has already had the honour"
"الحمار الصغير الذي كان له الشرف بالفعل"
"the honour of dancing in the presence of His Majesty"
"شرف الرقص بحضور جلالة الملك"
"And, thanking you, I beg of you to help us"
"وأشكركم ، أتوسل إليكم لمساعدتنا"
"help us with your inspiring presence"
"ساعدنا بحضورك الملهم"
"and please, esteemed audience, be indulgent to us"
"ومن فضلكم، أيها الجمهور الكريم، كونوا متسامحين معنا"
This speech was received with much laughter and applause
وقد قوبل هذا الخطاب بالكثير من الضحك والتصفيق
but the applause soon was even louder than before
لكن التصفيق سرعان ما كان أعلى من ذي قبل.
the little donkey Pinocchio made his appearance
ظهر الحمار الصغير بينوكيو
and he stood in the middle of the circus
ووقف في منتصف السيرك
He was decked out for the occasion
تم تزيينه لهذه المناسبة
He had a new bridle of polished leather
كان لديه لجام جديد من الجلد المصقول
and he was wearing brass buckles and studs
وكان يرتدي أبازيم وأزرار نحاسية
and he had two white camellias in his ears
وكان لديه اثنين من الكاميليا البيضاء في أذنيه
His mane was divided and curled
كان بده منقسما وكرة لولبية
and each curl was tied with bows of coloured ribbon
وتم ربط كل حليقة بأقواس من الشريط الملون
He had a girth of gold and silver round his body

كان لديه محيط من الذهب والفضة حول جسده
his tail was plaited with amaranth and blue velvet ribbons
كان ذيله مضفرا بشرائط قطيفة ومخملية زرقاء
He was, in fact, a little donkey to fall in love with!
لقد كان ، في الواقع ، حمارا صغيرا يقع في حبه!
The director added these few words:
أضاف المخرج هذه الكلمات القليلة:
"My respectable auditors!"
"مراجعي الحسابات المحترمين"!
"I am not here to tell you falsehoods"
"أنا لست هنا لأخبرك بالأكاذيب"
"there were great difficulties I had to overcome"
"كانت هناك صعوبات كبيرة كان علي التغلب عليها"
"I understood and subjugated this mammifer"
"لقد فهمت وأخضعت هذا الثدي"
"he was grazing at liberty amongst the mountains"
"كان يرعى بحرية بين الجبال"
"he lived in the plains of the torrid zone"
"عاش في سهول المنطقة الحارة"
"I beg you will observe the wild rolling of his eyes"
"أتوسل إليك أن تلاحظ التدحرج البري لعينيه"
"Every means had been tried in vain to tame him"
"لقد جربت كل الوسائل عبثا لترويضه"
"I have accustomed him to the life of domestic quadrupeds"
"لقد اعتدت عليه على حياة أربعة أضعاف المحلية"
"and I spared him the convincing argument of the whip"
"وجنبته حجة السوط المقنعة"
"But all my goodness only increased his viciousness"
"لكن كل إلهي زاد من شراسته"
"However, I discovered in his cranium a bony cartilage"
"ومع ذلك ، اكتشفت في جمجمته غضروف عظمي"
"I had him inspected by the Faculty of Medicine of Paris"
"لقد قمت بتفتيشه من قبل كلية الطب في باريس"
"I spared no cost for my little donkey's treatment"

"لم أدخر أي تكلفة لعلاج حماري الصغير"

"in him the doctors found the regenerating cortex of dance"

"فيه وجد الأطباء قشرة الرقص المتجددة"

"For this reason I have not only taught him to dance"

"لهذا السبب لم أعلمه الرقص فقط"

"but I also taught him to jump through hoops"

"لكنني علمته أيضا القفز من خلال الأطواق"

"Admire him, and then pass your opinion on him!"

"معجب به ، ثم مرر رأيك فيه"!

"But before taking my leave of you, permit me this;"

"ولكن قبل أن أتركك ، اسمح لي بهذا؛"

"ladies and gentlemen, esteemed members of the crowd"

"السيدات والسادة، أعضاء الحشد الكرام"

"I invite you to tomorrow's daily performance"

"أدعوكم إلى الأداء اليومي غدا"

Here the director made another profound bow

هنا قدم المخرج انحناءة عميقة أخرى

and, then turning to Pinocchio, he said:

ثم التفت إلى بينوكيو ، وقال:

"Courage, Pinocchio! But before you begin:"

"الشجاعة ، بينوكيو !ولكن قبل أن تبدأ":

"bow to this distinguished audience"

"انحني لهذا الجمهور المميز"

Pinocchio obeyed his master's commands

أطاع بينوكيو أوامر سيده

and he bent both his knees till they touched the ground

وثني ركبتيه حتى لامسا الأرض

the director cracked his whip and shouted:

كسر المدير سوطه وصرخ:

"At a foot's pace, Pinocchio!"

"بوتيرة قدم ، بينوكيو"!

Then the little donkey raised himself on his four legs

ثم رفع الحمار الصغير نفسه على رجليه الأربعة.

and he began to walk round the theatre

وبدأ يمشي حول المسرح
and the whole time he kept at a foot's pace
وطوال الوقت حافظ على وتيرة القدم
After a little time the director shouted again:
بعد قليل صرخ المدير مرة أخرى:
"Trot!" and Pinocchio, obeyed the order
"الهرولة "!وبينوكيو ، أطاع الأمر
and he changed his pace to a trot
وغير وتيرته إلى الهرولة
"Gallop!" and Pinocchio broke into a gallop
"العدو "!واقتحم بينوكيو الفرس
"Full gallop!" and Pinocchio went full gallop
"الفرس الكامل "!وذهب بينوكيو بالفرس الكامل
he was running round the circus like a racehorse
كان يركض حول السيرك مثل حصان السباق
but then the director fired off a pistol
ولكن بعد ذلك أطلق المدير مسدسا
at full speed he fell to the floor
بأقصى سرعة سقط على الأرض
and the little donkey pretended to be wounded
وتظاهر الحمار الصغير بأنه مصاب
he got up from the ground amidst an outburst of applause
نهض من الأرض وسط موجة من التصفيق
there were shouts and clapping of hands
كانت هناك صيحات وتصفيق بالأيدي
and he naturally raised his head and looked up
ورفع رأسه بشكل طبيعي ونظر إلى الأعلى
and he saw in one of the boxes a beautiful lady
ورأى في أحد الصناديق سيدة جميلة
she wore round her neck a thick gold chain
ارتدت حول عنقها سلسلة ذهبية سميكة
and from the chain hung a medallion
ومن السلسلة علقت ميدالية
On the medallion was painted the portrait of a puppet
على الميدالية رسمت صورة دمية
"That is my portrait!" realized Pinocchio

"That lady is the Fairy!" said Pinocchio to himself

"تلك السيدة هي الجنية "!قال بينوكيو لنفسه

"هذه هي صورتي "!أدرك بينوكيو

Pinocchio had recognized her immediately

تعرف عليها بينوكيو على الفور

and, overcome with delight, he tried to call her

وتغلب عليها البهجة ، حاول الاتصال بها

"Oh, my little Fairy! Oh, my little Fairy!"

"أوه ، جنيتي الصغيرة !أوه ، جنيتي الصغيرة!"

But instead of these words a bray came from his throat

ولكن بدلا من هذه الكلمات جاء براي من حلقه

a bray so prolonged that all the spectators laughed

براي مطول لدرجة أن جميع المتفرجين ضحكوا

and all the children in the theatre especially laughed

وضحك جميع الأطفال في المسرح بشكل خاص

Then the director gave him a lesson

ثم أعطاه المخرج درسا

it is not good manners to bray before the public

ليس من حسن الخلق أن تبكي أمام الجمهور

with the handle of his whip he smacked the donkey's nose

بمقبض سوطه صفع أنف الحمار

The poor little donkey put his tongue out an inch

الحمار الصغير المسكين أخرج لسانه شبرا واحدا

and he licked his nose for at least five minutes

ولعق أنفه لمدة خمس دقائق على الأقل

he thought perhaps that it would ease the pain

اعتقد أنه ربما سيخفف الألم

But how he despaired when looking up a second time

ولكن كيف يأس عندما نظر مرة ثانية

he saw that the seat was empty

رأى أن المقعد فارغ

the good Fairy of his had disappeared!

اختفت الجنية الطيبة له!

He thought he was going to die

كان يعتقد أنه سيموت

his eyes filled with tears and he began to weep

امتلأت عيناه بالدموع وبدأ يبكي

Nobody, however, noticed his tears

ومع ذلك ، لم يلاحظ أحد دموعه

"Courage, Pinocchio!" shouted the director

"الشجاعة ، بينوكيو "إصاح المدير

"show the audience how gracefully you can jump through the hoops"

"أظهر للجمهور كيف يمكنك القفز بأمان من خلال الأطواق"

Pinocchio tried two or three times

حاول بينوكيو مرتين أو ثلاث مرات

but going through the hoop is not easy for a donkey

لكن المرور عبر الطوق ليس بالأمر السهل على الحمار

and he found it easier to go under the hoop

ووجد أنه من الأسهل الذهاب تحت الطوق

At last he made a leap and went through the hoop

أخيرا قام بقفزة وذهب من خلال الطوق

but his right leg unfortunately caught in the hoop

لكن ساقه اليمنى اشتعلت للأسف في الطوق

and that caused him to fall to the ground

وهذا تسبب في سقوطه على الأرض

he was doubled up in a heap on the other side

تم مضاعفته في كومة على الجانب الآخر

When he got up he was lame

عندما نهض كان أعرج

only with great difficulty did he return to the stable

فقط بصعوبة كبيرة عاد إلى الإسطبل

"Bring out Pinocchio!" shouted all the boys

"أخرج بينوكيو "إصاح جميع الأولاد

"We want the little donkey!" roared the theatre

"نريد الحمار الصغير "إزأر المسرح

they were touched and sorry for the sad accident

لقد تأثروا وآسفون على الحادث المحزن

But the little donkey was seen no more that evening

لكن الحمار الصغير لم يعد يرى في ذلك المساء

The following morning the veterinary paid him a visit

في صباح اليوم التالي قام الطبيب البيطري بزيارته

the vets are doctors to the animals

الأطباء البيطريون هم أطباء للحيوانات

and he declared that he would remain lame for life

وأعلن أنه سيبقى عرجاء مدى الحياة

The director then said to the stable-boy:

ثم قال المدير لصبي الإسطبل:

"What do you suppose I can do with a lame donkey?"

"ماذا تفترض أنني أستطيع أن أفعل بحمار أعرج؟"

"He will eat food without earning it"

"سوف يأكل الطعام دون أن يكسبه"

"Take him to the market and sell him"

"خذه إلى السوق وبعه"

When they reached the market a purchaser was found at once

عندما وصلوا إلى السوق تم العثور على مشتر في الحال

He asked the stable-boy:

سأل الصبي المستقر:

"How much do you want for that lame donkey?"

"كم تريد لهذا الحمار الأعرج؟"

"Twenty dollars and I'll sell him to you"

"عشرون دولارا وسأبيعه لك"

"I will give you two dollars"

"سأعطيك دولارين"

"but don't suppose that I will make use of him"

"لكن لا تفترض أنني سأستخدمه"

"I am buying him solely for his skin"

"أنا أشتريه فقط لبشرته"

"I see that his skin is very hard"

"أرى أن بشرته صلبة جدا"

"I intend to make a drum with him"

"أنوي صنع طبل معه"

he heard that he was destined to become a drum!

سمع أنه مقدر له أن يصبح طبلا!

you can imagine poor Pinocchio's feelings

يمكنك أن تتخيل مشاعر بينوكيو المسكينة
the two dollars were handed over
تم تسليم الدولارين
and the man was given his donkey
وأعطي الرجل حماره
he led the little donkey to the seashore
قاد الحمار الصغير إلى شاطئ البحر
he then put a stone round his neck
ثم وضع حجرا حول عنقه
and he gave him a sudden push into the water
وأعطاه دفعة مفاجئة في الماء
Pinocchio was weighted down by the stone
تم وزن بينوكيو بالحجر
and he went straight to the bottom of the sea
وذهب مباشرة إلى قاع البحر
his owner kept tight hold of the cord
أبقى صاحبه قبضة محكمة من الحبل
he sat down quietly on a piece of rock
جلس بهدوء على قطعة من الصخر
and he waited until the little donkey was drowned
وانتظر حتى غرق الحمار الصغير
and then he intended to skin him
ثم قصد أن يسلخه

Pinocchio gets Swallowed by the Dog-Fish
بينوكيو يبتلعه السمك

Pinocchio had been fifty minutes under the water
كان بينوكيو خمسين دقيقة تحت الماء

his purchaser said aloud to himself:
قال مشتريه بصوت عالٍ لنفسه:

"My little lame donkey must by now be quite drowned"
"يجب أن يكون حماري الصغير الأعرج قد غرق تماما الآن"

"I will therefore pull him out of the water"
"لذلك سأسحبه من الماء"

"and I will make a fine drum of his skin"
"وسأصنع طبلة دقيقة من جلده"

And he began to haul in the rope
وبدأ في سحب الحبل

the rope he had tied to the donkey's leg
الحبل الذي ربطه بساق الحمار

and he hauled, and hauled, and hauled
وسحب ، وسحب ، وسحب

he hauled until at last...
لقد سحب حتى أخيرا...

what do you think appeared above the water?
ما رأيك ظهر فوق الماء؟

he did not pull a dead donkey to land
لم يسحب حمارا ميتا إلى الأرض

instead he saw a living little puppet
بدلا من ذلك رأى دمية صغيرة حية

and this little puppet was wriggling like an eel!
وكانت هذه الدمية الصغيرة تتلوى مثل ثعبان البحر!
the poor man thought he was dreaming
ظن الرجل الفقير أنه كان يحلم
and he was struck dumb with astonishment
وأصيب بالبكم من الدهشة
he eventually recovered from his stupefaction
تعافى في النهاية من ذهوله
and he asked the puppet in a quavering voice:
وسأل الدمية بصوت مرتجف:
"where is the little donkey I threw into the sea?"
"أين الحمار الصغير الذي رميته في البحر؟"
"I am the little donkey!" said Pinocchio
"أنا الحمار الصغير "!قال بينوكيو
and Pinocchio laughed at being a puppet again
وضحك بينوكيو لكونه دمية مرة أخرى
"How can you be the little donkey??"
"كيف يمكنك أن تكون الحمار الصغير ؟؟"
"I was the little donkey," answered Pinocchio

"كنت الحمار الصغير"، أجاب بينوكيو

"and now I'm a little puppet again"

"والآن أنا دمية صغيرة مرة أخرى"

"Ah, a young scamp is what you are!!"

"آه، شاب شاب هو ما أنت عليه"!!

"Do you dare to make fun of me?"

"هل تجرؤ على السخرية مني؟"

"To make fun of you?" asked Pinocchio

"أن يسخر منك؟ "سأل بينوكيو

"Quite the contrary, my dear master?"

"على العكس تماما، سيدي العزيز؟"

"I am speaking seriously with you"

"أنا أتحدث معك بجدية"

"a short time ago you were a little donkey"

"منذ وقت قصير كنت حمارا صغيرا"

"how can you have become a wooden puppet?"

"كيف يمكن أن تصبح دمية خشبية؟"

"being left in the water does not do that to a donkey!"

"أن تترك في الماء لا تفعل ذلك لحمار"!

"It must have been the effect of sea water"

"يجب أن يكون تأثير مياه البحر"

"The sea causes extraordinary changes"

"البحر يسبب تغييرات غير عادية"

"Beware, puppet, I am not in the mood!"

"احذر، دمية، أنا لست في مزاج"!

"Don't imagine that you can amuse yourself at my expense"

"لا تتخيل أنه يمكنك تسلية نفسك على حسابي"

"Woe to you if I lose patience!"

"ويل لك إذا فقدت صبري"!

"Well, master, do you wish to know the true story?"

"حسنا، يا معلم، هل ترغب في معرفة القصة الحقيقية؟"

"If you set my leg free I will tell it you"

"إذا حررت ساقي سأخبرك بها"

The good man was curious to hear the true story

كان الرجل الطيب فضوليا لسماع القصة الحقيقية
and he immediately untied the knot
وقام على الفور بفك العقدة
Pinocchio was again as free as a bird in the air
كان بينوكيو مرة أخرى حرا مثل طائر في الهواء
and he commenced to tell his story
وبدأ يروي قصته
"You must know that I was once a puppet"
"يجب أن تعرف أنني كنت دمية ذات يوم"
"that is to say, I wasn't always a donkey"
"وهذا يعني أنني لم أكن دائما حمارا"
"I was on the point of becoming a boy"
"كنت على وشك أن أصبح صبيا"
"I would have been like the other boys in the world"
"كنت سأكون مثل الأولاد الآخرين في العالم"
"but like other boys, I wasn't fond of study"
"لكن مثل الأولاد الآخرين ، لم أكن مولعا بالدراسة"
"and I followed the advice of bad companions"
"واتبعت نصيحة الصحابة السيئين"
"and finally I ran away from home"
"وأخيرا هربت من المنزل"
"One fine day when I awoke I found myself changed"
"في أحد الأيام الجميلة عندما استيقظت وجدت قد تغيرت"
"I had become a donkey with long ears"
"لقد أصبحت حمارا بأذنين طويلتين"
"and I had grown a long tail too"
"وكنت قد نمت ذيلا طويلا أيضا"
"What a disgrace it was to me!"
"يا له من عار بالنسبة لي"!
"even your worst enemy would not inflict it upon you!"
"حتى أسوأ عدو لك لن يلحقها بك"!
"I was taken to the market to be sold"
"تم نقلي إلى السوق ليتم بيعي"
"and I was bought by an equestrian company"

"وتم شرائي من قبل شركة فروسية"

"they wanted to make a famous dancer of me"

"أرادوا أن يصنعوا راقصة مشهورة لي"

"But one night during a performance I had a bad fall"

"لكن في إحدى الليالي أثناء الأداء ، تعرضت لسقوط سيء"

"and I was left with two lame legs"

"وتركت بساقين عرجاء"

"I was of no use to the circus no more"

"لم أعد مفيدا للسيرك"

"and again I was taken to the market

"ومرة أخرى تم نقلي إلى السوق

"and at the market you were my purchaser!"

"وفي السوق كنت مشتري"!

"Only too true," remembered the man

"صحيح جدا "، تذكر الرجل

"And I paid two dollars for you"

"ودفعت دولارين من أجلك"

"And now, who will give me back my good money?"

"والآن ، من سيعيد لي أموالي الجيدة؟"

"And why did you buy me?"

"ولماذا اشتريتني؟"

"You bought me to make a drum of my skin!"

"لقد اشتريتني لأصنع طبلة من بشرتي"!

"Only too true!" said the man

"فقط صحيح جدا "إقال الرجل

"And now, where shall I find another skin?"

"والآن ، أين أجد جلدا آخر؟"

"Don't despair, master"

"لا تيأس يا سيد"

"There are many little donkeys in the world!"

"هناك العديد من الحمير الصغيرة في العالم"!

"Tell me, you impertinent rascal;"

"قل لي ، أيها الوغد الوقح ؛"

"does your story end here?"

"هل تنتهي قصتك هنا؟"

"No," answered the puppet

"لا "، أجابت الدمية

"I have another two words to say"

"لدي كلمتان أخريان لأقولهما"

"and then my story shall have finished"

"وبعد ذلك تنتهي قصتي"

"you brought me to this place to kill me"

"لقد أحضرتني إلى هذا المكان لتقتلني"

"but then you yielded to a feeling of compassion"

"ولكن بعد ذلك استسلمت لشعور بالتعاطف"

"and you preferred to tie a stone round my neck

"وفضلت ربط حجر حول رقبتي"

"and you threw me into the sea"

"ورميتني في البحر"

"This humane feeling does you great honour"

"هذا الشعور الإنساني يشرفك كثيرا"

"and I shall always be grateful to you"

"وسأكون دائما ممتنا لك"

"But, nevertheless, dear master, you forgot one thing"

"لكن ، مع ذلك ، سيدي العزيز ، لقد نسيت شيئا واحدا"

"you made your calculations without considering the Fairy!"

"لقد أجريت حساباتك دون النظر في الجنية"!

"And who is the Fairy?"

"ومن هي الجنية؟"

"She is my mamma," replied Pinocchio

"إنها أمي "، أجاب بينوكيو

"and she resembles all other good mammas"

"وهي تشبه جميع الأمهات الطيبات الأخريات"

"and all good mammas care for their children"

"وكل الأمهات الطيبات يهتمن بأطفالهن"

"mammas who never lose sight of their children""

"الأمهات اللواتي لا يغفلن أبدا عن أطفالهن"

"mammas who help their children lovingly"

"الأمهات اللواتي يساعدن أطفالهن بمحبة"

"and they love them even when they deserve to be abandoned"

"وهم يحبونهم حتى عندما يستحقون التخلي عنهم"

"my good mamma kept me in her sight"

"أمي الطيبة أبقتني في بصرها"

"and she saw that I was in danger of drowning"

"ورأت أنني كنت في خطر الغرق"

"so she immediately sent an immense shoal of fish"

"لذلك أرسلت على الفور مياه ضحلة هائلة من الأسماك"

"first they really thought I was a little dead donkey"

"في البداية اعتقدوا حقا أنني حمار ميت قليلا"

"and so they began to eat me in big mouthfuls"

"وهكذا بدأوا يأكلونني في أفواه كبيرة"

"I never knew fish were greedier than boys!"

"لم أكن أعرف أبدا أن الأسماك كانت أكثر جشعا من الأولاد"!

"Some ate my ears and my muzzle"

"أكل البعض أذني وكمامتي"

"and other fish my neck and mane"

"وغيرها من الأسماك رقبتي وبدة"

"some of them ate the skin of my legs"

"بعضهم أكل جلد ساقي"

"and others took to eating my fur"

"وأخذ آخرون يأكلون فروي"

"Amongst them there was an especially polite little fish"

"من بينهم كان هناك سمكة صغيرة مهذبة بشكل خاص"

"and he condescended to eat my tail"

"وتنازل ليأكل ذيلي"

the purchaser was horrified by what he heard

كان المشتري مرعوبا مما سمعه

"I swear that I will never touch fish again!"

"أقسم أنني لن ألمس السمك مرة أخرى"!

"imagine opening a mullet and finding a donkey's tail!"

"تخيل فتح البوري والعثور على ذيل حمار"!

"I agree with you," said the puppet, laughing
"أنا أتفق معك"، قالت الدمية وهي تضحك
"However, I must tell you what happened next"
"ومع ذلك ، يجب أن أخبرك بما حدث بعد ذلك"
"the fish had finished eating the donkey's hide"
"كانت السمكة قد انتهت من أكل جلود الحمار"
"the donkey's hide that had covered me"
"جلد الحمار الذي غطاني"
"then they naturally reached the bone"
"ثم وصلوا بشكل طبيعي إلى العظام"
"but it was not bone, but rather wood"
"لكنه لم يكن عظما ، بل خشبا"
"for, as you see, I am made of the hardest wood"
"لأني ، كما ترى ، مصنوع من أصعب الخشب"
"they tried to take a few more bites"
"حاولوا أخذ بضع لدغات أخرى"
"But they soon discovered I was not for eating"
"لكنهم سرعان ما اكتشفوا أنني لست لتناول الطعام"
"disgusted with such indigestible food, they swam off"
"بالاشمئزاز من مثل هذا الطعام غير القابل للهضم ، سبحوا"
"and they left without even saying thank you"
"وغادروا دون أن يقولوا شكرا"
"And now, at last, you have heard my story"
"والآن ، أخيرا ، سمعت قصتي"
"and that is why you didn't find a dead donkey"
"ولهذا السبب لم تجد حمارا ميتا"
"and instead you found a living puppet"
"وبدلا من ذلك وجدت دمية حية"
"I laugh at your story," cried the man in a rage
"أنا أضحك على قصتك"، صرخ الرجل في غضب
"I only know that I spent two dollars to buy you"
"أعرف فقط أنني أنفقت دولارين لشرائها"
"and I will have my money back"
"وسأسترد أموالي"

"Shall I tell you what I will do?"

"هل أخبرك بما سأفعله؟"

"I will take you back to the market"

"سأعيدك إلى السوق"

"and I will sell you by weight as seasoned wood"

"وسأبيعك بالوزن كخشب محنك"

and the purchaser can light fires with you"

"ويمكن للمشتري إشعال النيران معك"

Pinocchio was not too worried about this

لم يكن بينوكيو قلقا جدا بشأن هذا

"Sell me if you like; I am content"

"بعني إذا أردت. أنا راض"

and he plunged back into the water

وسقط مرة أخرى في الماء

he swam gaily away from the shore

سبح بفرح بعيدا عن الشاطئ

and he called to his poor owner

ودعا صاحبه المسكين

"Good-bye, master, don't forget me"

"وداعا يا سيد، لا تنساني"

"the wooden puppet you wanted for its skin"

"الدمية الخشبية التي تريدها لبشرتها"

"and I hope you get your drum one day"

"وآمل أن تحصل على طبلك يوما ما"

And he laughed and went on swimming

وضحك وذهب يسبح

and after a while he turned around again

وبعد فترة استدار مرة أخرى

"Good-bye, master," he shouted louder

"وداعا يا سيد"، صرخ بصوت أعلى

"and remember me when you need well seasoned wood"

"وتذكرني عندما تحتاج إلى خشب محنك جيدا"

"and think of me when you're lighting a fire"

"وفكر بي عندما تشعل النار"

soon Pinocchio had swam towards the horizon

سرعان ما سبح بينوكيو نحو الأفق
and now he was scarcely visible from the shore
والآن كان بالكاد مرئيا من الشاطئ
he was a little black speck on the surface of the sea
كان بقعة سوداء صغيرة على سطح البحر
from time to time he lifted out of the water
من وقت لآخر كان يرفع من الماء
and he leaped and capered like a happy dolphin
وقفز وتقلب مثل دولفين سعيد
Pinocchio was swimming and he knew not whither
كان بينوكيو يسبح ولم يكن يعرف إلى أين
he saw in the midst of the sea a rock
رأى في وسط البحر صخرة
the rock seemed to be made of white marble
يبدو أن الصخرة مصنوعة من الرخام الأبيض
and on the summit there stood a beautiful little goat
وعلى القمة وقفت عنزة صغيرة جميلة
the goat bleated lovingly to Pinocchio
نزف الماعز بمحبة إلى بينوكيو
and the goat made signs to him to approach
وقدم له الماعز إشارات للاقتراب
But the most singular thing was this:
لكن الشيء الأكثر تميزا كان هذا:
The little goat's hair was not white nor black
لم يكن شعر الماعز الصغير أبيض ولا أسود
nor was it a mixture of two colours
كما أنه لم يكن مزيجا من لونين
this is usual with other goats
هذا هو المعتاد مع الماعز الأخرى
but the goat's hair was a very vivid blue
لكن شعر الماعز كان أزرق زاهي للغاية
a vivid blue like the hair of the beautiful Child
أزرق زاهي مثل شعر الطفل الجميل
imagine how rapidly Pinocchio's heart began to beat
تخيل مدى سرعة نبض قلب بينوكيو
He swam with redoubled strength and energy

سبح بقوة وطاقة مضاعفة

and in no time at all he was halfway there

وفي أي وقت من الأوقات على الإطلاق كان في منتصف الطريق

but then he saw something came out the water

ولكن بعد ذلك رأى شيئا يخرج من الماء

the horrible head of a sea-monster!

الرأس الرهيب لوحش البحر!

His mouth was wide open and cavernous

كان فمه مفتوحا على مصراعيه وكهفيا

there were three rows of enormous teeth

كان هناك ثلاثة صفوف من الأسنان الضخمة

even a picture of if would terrify you

حتى صورة إذا كان من شأنه أن يرعبك

And do you know what this sea-monster was?

وهل تعرف ما هو وحش البحر هذا؟

it was none other than that gigantic Dog-Fish

لم يكن سوى ذلك السمكة العملاقة

the Dog-Fish mentioned many times in this story

ذكر والسمك عدة مرات في هذه القصة

I should tell you the name of this terrible fish

يجب أن أخبرك باسم هذه السمكة الرهيبة

Attila of Fish and Fishermen

أتيلا للأسماك والصيادين

on account of his slaughter and insatiable voracity

بسبب ذبحه وشره الذي لا يشبع

think of poor Pinocchio's terror at the sight

فكر في رعب بينوكيو المسكين في الأفق

a true sea monster was swimming at him

كان وحش البحر الحقيقي يسبح في وجهه

He tried to avoid the Dog-Fish

حاول تجنب السمك

he tried to swim in other directions

حاول السباحة في اتجاهات أخرى

he did everything he could to escape

فعل كل ما في وسعه للهروب

but that immense wide-open mouth was too big

لكن هذا الفم الهائل المفتوح على مصراعيه كان كبيرا جدا
and it was coming with the velocity of an arrow
وكان قادما بسرعة سهم
the beautiful little goat tried to bleat
حاول الماعز الصغير الجميل أن ينفخ
"Be quick, Pinocchio, for pity's sake!"
"كن سريعا ، بينوكيو ، من أجل الشفقة"!
And Pinocchio swam desperately with all he could
وسبح بينوكيو يائسا بكل ما في وسعه
his arms, his chest, his legs, and his feet
ذراعيه وصدره وساقيه وقدميه
"Quick, Pinocchio, the monster is close upon you!"
"سريع ، بينوكيو ، الوحش قريب منك"!
And Pinocchio swam quicker than ever
وسبح بينوكيو أسرع من أي وقت مضى
he flew on with the rapidity of a ball from a gun
طار بسرعة كرة من بندقية
He had nearly reached the rock
كان قد وصل تقريبا إلى الصخرة
and he had almost reached the little goat
وكان قد وصل تقريبا إلى الماعز الصغير
and the little goat leaned over towards the sea
وانحنى الماعز الصغير نحو البحر
she stretched out her fore-legs to help him
مدت ساقيها الأماميتين لمساعدته
perhaps she could get him out of the water
ربما يمكنها إخراجه من الماء
But all their efforts were too late!
لكن كل جهودهم كانت متأخرة جدا!
The monster had overtaken Pinocchio
كان الوحش قد تجاوز بينوكيو
he drew in a big breath of air and water
رسم نفسا كبيرا من الهواء والماء
and he sucked in the poor puppet
وامتص الدمية المسكينة
like he would have sucked a hen's egg

and the Dog-Fish swallowed him whole
كما لو كان قد امتص بيضة دجاجة
وابتلعته سمكة بالكامل

Pinocchio tumbled through his teeth
سقط بينوكيو من خلال أسنانه
and he tumbled down the Dog-Fish's throat
وسقط في حلق السمكة
and finally he landed heavily in his stomach
وأخيرا هبط بشدة في معدته
he remained unconscious for a quarter of an hour
بقي فاقدا للوعي لمدة ربع ساعة
but eventually he came to himself again
ولكن في النهاية جاء إلى نفسه مرة أخرى
he could not in the least imagine in what world he was
لم يستطع على الأقل أن يتخيل في أي عالم كان
All around him there was nothing but darkness
في كل مكان حوله لم يكن هناك شيء سوى الظلام
it was as if he had fallen into a pot of ink
كان الأمر كما لو أنه سقط في قدر من الحبر

He listened, but he could hear no noise
استمع ، لكنه لم يسمع أي ضجيج

occasionally great gusts of wind blew in his face
في بعض الأحيان هبت رياح كبيرة في وجهه

first he could not understand from where it came from
في البداية لم يستطع أن يفهم من أين أتى

but at last he discovered the source
ولكن في النهاية اكتشف المصدر

it came out of the monster's lungs
خرج من رئتي الوحش

there is one thing you must know about the Dog-Fish
سمكة الكلب عن تعرفه أن يجب واحد شيء هناك

the Dog-Fish suffered very much from asthma
عانى السمك كثيرا من الربو

when he breathed it was exactly like the north wind
عندما تنفس كان تماما مثل ريح الشمال

Pinocchio at first tried to keep up his courage
حاول بينوكيو في البداية الحفاظ على شجاعته

but the reality of the situation slowly dawned on him
لكن حقيقة الوضع بزغت عليه ببطء

he was really shut up in the body of this sea-monster
لقد كان مغلقا حقا في جسد وحش البحر هذا

and he began to cry and scream and sob
وبدأ يبكي ويصرخ وينتحب

"Help! help! Oh, how unfortunate I am!"
"مساعدة !تعليمات !أوه ، كم أنا مؤسف!"

"Will nobody come to save me?"
"ألن يأتي أحد لإنقاذي؟"

from the dark there came a voice
من الظلام جاء صوت

the voice sounded like a guitar out of tune
بدا الصوت وكأنه غيتار خارج اللحن

"Who do you think could save you, unhappy wretch?"
"من برأيك يمكن أن ينقذك أيها البائس التعيس؟"

Pinocchio froze with terror at the voice
تجمد بينوكيو من الرعب في الصوت

"Who is speaking?" asked Pinocchio, finally

"من يتكلم؟" "سأل بينوكيو ، أخيرا

"It is I! I am a poor Tunny Fish"

"إنه أنا !أنا سمكة توني فقيرة"

"I was swallowed by the Dog-Fish along with you"

"لقد ابتلعني السمك معك"

"And what fish are you?"

"وما هي سمكتك؟"

"I have nothing in common with fish"

"ليس لدي أي شيء مشترك مع الأسماك"

"I am a puppet," added Pinocchio

"أنا دمية "، أضاف بينوكيو

"Then why did you let yourself be swallowed?"

"إذن لماذا سمحت لنفسك بالابتلاع؟"

"I didn't let myself be swallowed"

"لم أسمح لنفسي بالابتلاع"

"it was the monster that swallowed me!"

"كان الوحش الذي ابتلعني"!

"And now, what are we to do here in the dark?"

"والآن ، ماذا نفعل هنا في الظلام؟"

"there's not much we can do but to resign ourselves"

"ليس هناك الكثير الذي يمكننا القيام به سوى الاستقالة"

"and now we wait until the Dog-Fish has digested us"

"والآن ننتظر حتى يهضمنا والسمكة"

"But I do not want to be digested!" howled Pinocchio

"لكنني لا أريد أن أهضم !"عوى بينوكيو

and he began to cry again

وبدأ في البكاء مرة أخرى

"Neither do I want to be digested," added the Tunny Fish

"ولا أريد أن يتم هضمي "، أضاف توني فيش

"but I am enough of a philosopher to console myself"

"لكنني فيلسوف بما فيه الكفاية لمواساة"

"when one is born a Tunny Fish life can be made sense of"

"عندما يولد المرء ، يمكن فهم حياة سمك التونة"

"it is more dignified to die in the water than in oil"
"الموت في الماء أكثر كرامة منه في النفط"
"That is all nonsense!" cried Pinocchio
"هذا كله هراء "إصرخ بينوكيو
"It is my opinion," replied the Tunny Fish
"هذا رأيي "، أجاب توني فيش
"and opinions ought to be respected"
"ويجب احترام الآراء"
"that is what the political Tunny Fish say"
"هذا ما يقوله السياسي توني فيش"
"To sum it all up, I want to get away from here"
"لتلخيص كل شيء ، أريد الابتعاد عن هنا"
"I do want to escape."
"أريد الهروب."
"Escape, if you are able!"
"الهروب ، إذا كنت قادرا"!
"Is this Dog-Fish who has swallowed us very big?"
"هل هذا السمكة الذي ابتلعنا كبيرا جدا؟"
"Big? My boy, you can only imagine"
"كبير؟ يا ولدي ، يمكنك فقط أن تتخيل"
"his body is two miles long without counting his tail"
"يبلغ طول جسده ميلين دون حساب ذيله"
they held this conversation in the dark for some time
عقدوا هذه المحادثة في الظلام لبعض الوقت
eventually Pinocchio's eyes adjusted to the darkness
في نهاية المطاف عيون بينوكيو تكيفت مع الظلام
Pinocchio thought that he saw a light a long way off
اعتقد بينوكيو أنه رأى ضوءا بعيدا
"What is that little light I see in the distance?"
"ما هو هذا الضوء الصغير الذي أراه من بعيد؟"
"It is most likely some companion in misfortune"
"من المرجح أن يكون رفيقا في مصيبة"
"he, like us, is waiting to be digested"
"هو ، مثلنا ، ينتظر أن يتم هضمه"

"I will go and find him"

"سأذهب وأجده"

"perhaps it is an old fish that knows his way around"

"ربما هي سمكة قديمة تعرف طريقها"

"I hope it may be so, with all my heart, dear puppet"

"آمل أن يكون الأمر كذلك ، من كل قلبي ، دمية عزيزة"

"Good-bye, Tunny Fish" - "Good-bye, puppet"

"وداعا ، توني فيش" - "وداعا ، دمية"

"and I wish a good fortune to you"

"وأتمنى لك حظا سعيدا"

"Where shall we meet again?"

"أين سنلتقي مرة أخرى؟"

"Who can see such things in the future?"

"من يستطيع رؤية مثل هذه الأشياء في المستقبل؟"

"It is better not even to think of it!"

"من الأفضل عدم التفكير في الأمر"!

A Happy Surprise for Pinocchio
مفاجأة سعيدة لبينوكيو

Pinocchio said farewell to his friend the Tunny Fish

قال بينوكيو وداعا لصديقه سمكة توني

and he began to grope his way through the Dog-Fish

وبدأ يتلمس طريقه عبر سمكة الكلب

he took small steps in the direction of the light

اتخذ خطوات صغيرة في اتجاه الضوء

the small light shining dimly at a great distance

الضوء الصغير يسطع بشكل خافت على مسافة كبيرة

the farther he advanced the brighter became the light

كلما تقدم أكثر أصبح الضوء أكثر إشراقا

and he walked and walked until at last he reached it

ومشى ومشى حتى وصل إليه أخيرا

and when he reached the light, what did he find?

وعندما وصل إلى النور ، ماذا وجده؟

I will let you have a thousand and one guesses
سأسمح لك بالحصول على ألف تخمين وواحد

what he found was a little table all prepared
ما وجده كان طاولة صغيرة معدة بالكامل

on the table was a lighted candle in a green bottle
على الطاولة كانت شمعة مضاءة في زجاجة خضراء

and seated at the table was a little old man
وكان يجلس على الطاولة رجل عجوز قليلا

the little old man was eating some live fish
كان الرجل العجوز الصغير يأكل بعض الأسماك الحية

and the little live fish were very much alive
وكانت الأسماك الحية الصغيرة على قيد الحياة

some of the little fish even jumped out of his mouth
حتى أن بعض الأسماك الصغيرة قفزت من فمه

at this sight Pinocchio was filled with happiness
في هذا المنظر كان بينوكيو مليئا بالسعادة

he became almost delirious with unexpected joy
أصبح يهذي تقريبا بفرح غير متوقع

He wanted to laugh and cry at the same time
أراد أن يضحك ويبكي في نفس الوقت

he wanted to say a thousand things at once
أراد أن يقول ألف شيء دفعة واحدة

but all he managed were a few confused words
لكن كل ما تمكن منه كان بضع كلمات مشوشة

At last he succeeded in uttering a cry of joy
في النهاية نجح في إطلاق صرخة فرح

and he threw his arm around the little old man
وألقى ذراعه حول الرجل العجوز الصغير

"Oh, my dear papa!" he shouted with joy
"أوه ، يا بابا العزيز" إصرخ بفرح

"I have found you at last!" cried Pinocchio
"لقد وجدتك أخيرا" إصرخ بينوكيو

"I will never never never never leave you again"
"لن أتركك أبدا أبدا مرة أخرى"

the little old man couldn't believe it either
لم يستطع الرجل العجوز الصغير تصديق ذلك أيضا

"are my eyes telling the truth?" he said

"هل عيناي تقولان الحقيقة؟ "قال

and he rubbed his eyes to make sure

وفرك عينيه للتأكد

"then you are really my dear Pinocchio?"

"إذن أنت حقا عزيزي بينوكيو؟"

"Yes, yes, I am Pinocchio, I really am!"

"نعم ، نعم ، أنا بينوكيو ، أنا حقا"!

"And you have forgiven me, have you not?"

"وقد غفرت لي ، أليس كذلك؟"

"Oh, my dear papa, how good you are!"

"أوه ، يا بابا العزيز ، كم أنت جيد"!

"And to think how bad I've been to you"

"والتفكير في مدى سوء ما كنت عليه بالنسبة لك"

"but if you only knew what I've gone through"

"ولكن إذا كنت تعرف فقط ما مررت به"

"all the misfortunes I've had poured on me"

"كل المصائب التي سكبتها علي"

"and all the other things that have befallen me!"

"وكل الأشياء الأخرى التي حلت بي"!

"oh think back to the day you sold your jacket"

"أوه فكر في اليوم الذي بعت فيه سترتك"

"oh you must have been terribly cold"

"أوه ، لا بد أنك كنت باردا بشكل رهيب"

"but you did it to buy me a spelling book"

"لكنك فعلت ذلك لتشتري لي كتابا إملائيا"

"so that I could study like the other boys"

"حتى أتمكن من الدراسة مثل الأولاد الآخرين"

"but instead I escaped to see the puppet show"

"ولكن بدلا من ذلك هربت لرؤية عرض الدمى"

"and the showman wanted to put me on the fire"

"وأراد رجل الاستعراض أن يضعني على النار"

"so that I could roast his mutton for him"

"حتى أتمكن من تحميص لحم الضأن له"

"but then the same showman gave me five gold pieces"
"ولكن بعد ذلك أعطاني رجل الاستعراض نفسه خمس قطع ذهبية"
"he wanted me to give you the gold"
"أراد مني أن أعطيك الذهب"
"but then I met the Fox and the Cat"
"ولكن بعد ذلك قابلت الثعلب والقط"
"and they took me to the inn of The Red Craw-Fish"
"وأخذوني إلى نزل "The Red Craw-Fish
"and at the inn they ate like hungry wolves"
"وفي النزل أكلوا مثل الذئاب الجائعة"
"and I left by myself in the middle of the night"
"وغادرت وحدي في منتصف الليل"
"and I encountered assassins who ran after me"
"وواجهت قتلة ركضوا ورائي"
"and I ran away from the assassins"
"وهربت من القتلة"
"but the assassins followed me just as fast"
"لكن القتلة تبعوني بنفس السرعة"
"and I ran away from them as fast as I could"
"وهربت منهم بأسرع ما يمكن"
"but they always followed me however fast I ran"
"لكنهم كانوا يتبعونني دائما مهما ركضت بسرعة"
"and I kept running to get away from them"
"وظللت أركض للابتعاد عنهم"
"but eventually they caught me after all"
"لكن في النهاية أمسكوا بي بعد كل شيء"
"and they hung me to a branch of a Big Oak"
"وعلقوني إلى فرع بلوط كبير"
"but then there was the beautiful Child with blue hair"
"ولكن بعد ذلك كان هناك الطفل الجميل ذو الشعر الأزرق"
"she sent a little carriage to fetch me"
"أرسلت عربة صغيرة لإحضاري"
"and the doctors all had a good look at me"
"والأطباء جميعا ألقوا نظرة فاحصة علي"

"and they immediately made the same diagnosis"
"وقاموا على الفور بنفس التشخيص"
"If he is not dead, it is a proof that he is still alive"
"إذا لم يكن ميتا ، فهذا دليل على أنه لا يزال على قيد الحياة"
"and then by chance I told a lie"
"ثم بالصدفة قلت كذبة"
"and my nose began to grow and grow and grow"
"وبدأ أنفي ينمو وينمو وينمو"
"and soon I could no longer get through the door"
"وسرعان ما لم يعد بإمكاني الدخول من الباب"
"so I went again with the Fox and the Cat"
"لذلك ذهبت مرة أخرى مع الثعلب والقط"
"and together we buried the four gold pieces"
"ومعا دفنا القطع الذهبية الأربعة"
"because one piece of gold I had spent at the inn"
"لأن قطعة واحدة من الذهب كنت قد قضيت في النزل"
"and the Parrot began to laugh at me"
"وبدأ الببغاء يضحك علي"
"and there were not two thousand pieces of gold"
"ولم يكن هناك ألفي قطعة من الذهب"
"there were no pieces of gold at all anymore"
"لم تعد هناك قطع من الذهب على الإطلاق"
"so I went to the judge of the town to tell him"
"فذهبت إلى قاضي البلدة لأخبره"
"he said I had been robbed, and put me in prison"
"قال إنني تعرضت للسرقة، ووضعني في السجن"
"while escaping I saw a beautiful bunch of grapes"
"أثناء الهروب رأيت عنقود عنب جميل"
"but in the field I was caught in a trap"
"لكن في الميدان وقعت في فخ"
"and the peasant had every right to catch me"
"وكان للفلاح كل الحق في الإمساك بي"
"he put a dog-collar round my neck"
"وضع طوق حول رقبتي"

"and he made me the guard dog of the poultry-yard"
"وجعلني حراسة ساحة الدواجن"
"but he acknowledged my innocence and let me go"
"لكنه اعترف ببراءتي وتركني أذهب"
"and the Serpent with the smoking tail began to laugh"
"وبدأ الثعبان ذو الذيل المدخن يضحك"
"but the Serpent laughed until he broke a blood-vessel"
"لكن الثعبان ضحك حتى كسر وعاء دموي"
"and so I returned to the house of the beautiful Child"
"وهكذا عدت إلى بيت الطفل الجميل"
"but then the beautiful Child was dead"
"ولكن بعد ذلك مات الطفل الجميل"
"and the Pigeon could see that I was crying"
"وكان الحمام يرى أنني كنت أبكي"
"and the Pigeon said, 'I have seen your father'"
"فقالت الحمامة: لقد رأيت أباك"
'he was building a little boat to search of you'
"كان يبني قاربا صغيرا للبحث عنك"
"and I said to him, 'Oh! if I also had wings,'"
"وقلت له: أوه! إذا كان لدي أيضا أجنحة."
"and he said to me, 'Do you want to see your father?'"
"فقال لي: هل تريد أن ترى أباك؟"
"and I said, 'Without doubt I would like to see him!'"
"فقلت: بلا شك أود أن أراه!"
"'but who will take me to him?' I asked"
"ولكن من سيأخذني إليه؟ سألت"
"and he said to me, 'I will take you,'"
"فقال لي: آخذك،"
"and I said to him, 'How will you take me?'"
"فقلت له: كيف تأخذني؟"
"and he said to me, 'Get on my back,'"
"فقال لي: اركب على ظهري."
"and so we flew through all that night"
"وهكذا طرنا طوال تلك الليلة"

"and then in the morning there were all the fishermen"
"ثم في الصباح كان هناك جميع الصيادين"

"and the fishermen were looking out to sea"
"وكان الصيادون ينظرون إلى البحر"

"and one said to me, 'There is a poor man in a boat'"
"فقال لي أحدهم: هناك رجل فقير في قارب"

"he is on the point of being drowned"
"إنه على وشك الغرق"

"and I recognized you at once, even at that distance
"وتعرفت عليك في الحال ، حتى على تلك المسافة

"because my heart told me that it was you"
"لأن قلبي أخبرني أنه أنت"

"and I made signs so that you would return to land"
"وصنعت آيات حتى تعود إلى الأرض"

"I also recognized you," said Geppetto
"لقد تعرفت عليك أيضا "، قال جيبيتو

"and I would willingly have returned to the shore"
"وكنت سأعود عن طيب خاطر إلى الشاطئ"

"but what was I to do so far out at sea?"
"ولكن ماذا كنت سأفعل حتى الآن في البحر؟"

"The sea was tremendously angry that day"
"كان البحر غاضبا للغاية في ذلك اليوم"

"and a great wave came over and upset my boat"
"وجاءت موجة عظيمة وأزعجت قاربي"

"Then I saw the horrible Dog-Fish"
"ثم رأيت سمكة الرهيبة"

"and the horrible Dog-Fish saw me too"
"ورآني السمكة الرهيب أيضا"

"and so the horrible Dog-Fish came to me"
"وهكذا جاء لي السمكة الرهيبة"

"and he put out his tongue and swallowed me"
"وأخرج لسانه وابتلعني"

"as if I had been a little apple tart"
"كما لو كنت لاذع التفاح قليلا"

"And how long have you been shut up here?"
"ومنذ متى وأنت صامت هنا؟"
"that day must have been nearly two years ago"
"لا بد أن ذلك اليوم كان منذ ما يقرب من عامين"
"two years, my dear Pinocchio," he said
"قال: سنتان يا عزيزي بينوكيو"
"those two years seemed like two centuries!"
"بدا هذان العامان وكأنهما قرنان"!
"And how have you managed to live?"
"وكيف تمكنت من العيش؟"
"And where did you get the candle?"
"ومن أين حصلت على الشمعة؟"
"And from where are the matches for the candle?
»ومن أين مباريات الشمعة؟
"Stop, and I will tell you everything"
"توقف ، وسأخبرك بكل شيء"
"I was not the only one at sea that day"
"لم أكن الوحيد في البحر في ذلك اليوم"
"the storm had also upset a merchant vessel"
"العاصفة أزعجت أيضا سفينة تجارية"
"the sailors of the vessel were all saved"
"تم إنقاذ جميع بحارة السفينة"
"but the cargo of the vessel sunk to the bottom"
"لكن شحنة السفينة غرقت في القاع"
"the Dog-Fish had an excellent appetite that day"
"كان لدى سمكة الكلب شهية ممتازة في ذلك اليوم"
"after swallowing me he swallowed the vessel"
"بعد أن ابتلعني ابتلع الوعاء"
"How did he swallow the entire vessel?"
"كيف ابتلع السفينة بأكملها؟"
"He swallowed the whole boat in one mouthful"
"ابتلع القارب كله في فم واحد"
"the only thing that he spat out was the mast"
"الشيء الوحيد الذي بصق به هو الصاري"

"it had stuck between his teeth like a fish-bone"
"لقد علقت بين أسنانه مثل عظم السمكة"
"Fortunately for me, the vessel was fully laden"
"لحسن الحظ بالنسبة لي ، كانت السفينة محملة بالكامل"
"there were preserved meats in tins, biscuit"
"كانت هناك لحوم محفوظة في علب وبسكويت"
"and there were bottles of wine and dried raisins"
"وكانت هناك زجاجات من النبيذ والزبيب المجفف"
"and I had cheese and coffee and sugar"
"وكان لي الجبن والقهوة والسكر"
"and with the candles were boxes of matches"
"ومع الشموع كانت صناديق أعواد الثقاب"
"With this I have been able to live for two years"
"مع هذا تمكنت من العيش لمدة عامين"
"But I have arrived at the end of my resources"
"لكنني وصلت إلى نهاية مواردي"
"there is nothing left in the larder"
"لم يتبق شيء في الخزانة"
"and this candle is the last that remains"
"وهذه الشمعة هي آخر ما تبقى"
"And after that what will we do?"
"وبعد ذلك ماذا سنفعل؟"
"oh my dear boy, Pinocchio," he cried
"يا ولدي العزيز ، بينوكيو "، بكى
"After that we shall both remain in the dark"
"بعد ذلك سنبقى كلانا في الظلام"
"Then, dear little papa there is no time to lose"
"إذن ، عزيزي بابا الصغير ، ليس هناك وقت نضيعه"
"We must think of a way of escaping"
"يجب أن نفكر في طريقة للهروب"
"what way of escaping can we think of?"
"ما هي طريقة الهروب التي يمكننا التفكير فيها؟"
"We must escape through the mouth of the Dog-Fish"
"يجب أن نهرب من خلال فم سمكة"

"we must throw ourselves into the sea and swim away"
"يجب أن نلقي بأنفسنا في البحر ونسبح بعيدا"
"You talk well, my dear Pinocchio"
"أنت تتحدث جيدا يا عزيزي بينوكيو"
"but I don't know how to swim"
"لكنني لا أعرف كيف أسبح"
"What does that matter?" replied Pinocchio
"ما أهمية ذلك؟ "أجاب بينوكيو
"I am a good swimmer," he suggested
"أنا سباح جيد "، اقترح
"you can get on my shoulders"
"يمكنك الحصول على كتفي"
"and I will carry you safely to shore"
"وسأحملك بأمان إلى الشاطئ"
"All illusions, my boy!" replied Geppetto
"كل الأوهام يا ولدي !"أجاب جيبيتو
and he shook his head with a melancholy smile
وهز رأسه بابتسامة حزينة
"my dear Pinocchio, you are scarcely a yard high"
"عزيزي بينوكيو ، أنت بالكاد على ارتفاع ياردة"
"how could you swim with me on your shoulders?"
"كيف يمكنك السباحة معي على كتفيك؟"
"Try it and you will see!" replied Pinocchio
"جربه وسوف ترى "!أجاب بينوكيو
Without another word Pinocchio took the candle
بدون كلمة أخرى أخذ بينوكيو الشمعة
"Follow me, and don't be afraid"
"اتبعني، ولا تخافوا"
and they walked for some time through the Dog-Fish
وساروا لبعض الوقت من خلال السمك
they walked all the way through the stomach
ساروا على طول الطريق من خلال المعدة
and they were where the Dog-Fish's throat began
وكانوا حيث بدأ حلق السمكة

and here they thought they should better stop
وهنا اعتقدوا أنه من الأفضل أن يتوقفوا

and they thought about the best moment for escaping
وفكروا في أفضل لحظة للهروب

Now, I must tell you that the Dog-Fish was very old
الآن ، يجب أن أخبرك أن سمكة الكلب كان قديما جدا

and he suffered from asthma and heart palpitations
وعانى من الربو وخفقان القلب

so he was obliged to sleep with his mouth open
لذلك اضطر إلى النوم وفمه مفتوح

and through his mouth they could see the starry sky
ومن خلال فمه يمكنهم رؤية السماء المرصعة بالنجوم

and the sea was lit up by beautiful moonlight
وأضاء البحر بضوء القمر الجميل

Pinocchio carefully and quietly turned to his father
التفت بينوكيو بعناية وهدوء إلى والده

"This is the moment to escape," he whispered to him
"هذه هي لحظة الهروب "، همس له

"the Dog-Fish is sleeping like a dormouse"
"السمك ينام مثل المهجع"

"the sea is calm, and it is as light as day"
"البحر هادئ ، وهو خفيف مثل النهار"

"follow me, dear papa," he told him
"اتبعني، يا بابا العزيز"، قال له

"and in a short time we shall be in safety"
"وفي وقت قصير سنكون في أمان"

they climbed up the throat of the sea-monster
صعدوا حلق وحش البحر

and soon they reached his immense mouth
وسرعان ما وصلوا إلى فمه الهائل

so they began to walk on tiptoe down his tongue
لذلك بدأوا في المشي على رؤوس أصابعهم أسفل لسانه

they were about to make the final leap
كانوا على وشك القيام بالقفزة النهائية

the puppet turned around to his father
استدار الدمية إلى والده

"Get on my shoulders, dear Papa," he whispered
"اجلس على كتفي يا بابا العزيز "، همس
"and put your arms tightly around my neck"
"وضع ذراعيك بإحكام حول رقبتي"
"I will take care of the rest," he promised
"سأعتني بالباقي "، وعد
soon Geppetto was firmly settled on his son's shoulders
سرعان ما استقر جيبيتو بحزم على أكتاف ابنه
Pinocchio took a moment to build up courage
استغرق بينوكيو لحظة لبناء الشجاعة
and then he threw himself into the water
ثم ألقى بنفسه في الماء
and began to swim away from the Dog-Fish
وبدأت تسبح بعيدا عن السمك
The sea was as smooth as oil
كان البحر سلسا مثل النفط
the moon shone brilliantly in the sky
أشرق القمر ببراعة في السماء
and the Dog-Fish was in deep sleep
وكان السمكة في نوم عميق
even cannons wouldn't have awoken him
حتى المدافع لم تكن لتوقظه

Pinocchio at last Ceases to be a Puppet and Becomes a Boy
بينوكيو أخيرا يتوقف عن أن يكون دمية ويصبح صبيا

Pinocchio was swimming quickly towards the shore
كان بينوكيو يسبح بسرعة نحو الشاطئ
Geppetto had his legs on his son's shoulders
كان جيبيتو ساقيه على كتفي ابنه
but Pinocchio discovered his father was trembling
لكن بينوكيو اكتشف أن والده كان يرتجف
he was shivering from cold as if in a fever
كان يرتجف من البرد كما لو كان في حمى

but cold was not the only cause of his trembling
لكن البرد لم يكن السبب الوحيد لارتعاشه

Pinocchio thought the cause of the trembling was fear
اعتقد بينوكيو أن سبب الارتعاش هو الخوف

and the Puppet tried to comfort his father
وحاول الدمية مواساة والده

"Courage, papa! See how well I can swim?"
"الشجاعة يا بابا !انظر إلى أي مدى يمكنني السباحة؟"

"In a few minutes we shall be safely on shore"
"في غضون دقائق قليلة سنكون بأمان على الشاطئ"

but his father had a higher vantage point
لكن والده كان لديه وجهة نظر أعلى

"But where is this blessed shore?"
"ولكن أين هذا الشاطئ المبارك؟"

and he became even more frightened
وأصبح أكثر خوفا

and he screwed up his eyes like a tailor
وأفسد عينيه مثل الخياط

when they thread string through a needle
عندما يخيطون الخيط من خلال إبرة

"I have been looking in every direction"
"لقد كنت أبحث في كل اتجاه"

"and I see nothing but the sky and the sea"
"ولا أرى سوى السماء والبحر"

"But I see the shore as well," said the puppet
"لكنني أرى الشاطئ أيضا"، قالت الدمية

"You must know that I am like a cat"
"يجب أن تعرف أنني مثل القطة"

"I see better by night than by day"
"أرى أفضل في الليل من النهار"

Poor Pinocchio was making a pretence
كان بينوكيو المسكين يتظاهر

he was trying to show optimism
كان يحاول إظهار التفاؤل

but in reality he was beginning to feel discouraged

his strength was failing him rapidly

لكن في الواقع بدأ يشعر بالإحباط

and he was gasping and panting for breath

كانت قوته تخذله بسرعة

He could not swim much further anymore

وكان يلهث ويلهث من أجل التنفس

and the shore was still far off

لم يعد بإمكانه السباحة أكثر من ذلك بكثير

He swam until he had no breath left

وكان الشاطئ لا يزال بعيدا

and then he turned his head to Geppetto

سبح حتى لم يبق له نفس

"Papa, help me, I am dying!" he said

ثم أدار رأسه إلى جيبيتو

The father and son were on the point of drowning

"بابا ، ساعدني ، أنا أموت "إقال

but they heard a voice like an out of tune guitar

كان الأب والابن على وشك الغرق

"Who is it that is dying?" said the voice

لكنهم سمعوا صوتا مثل غيتار خارج اللحن

"It is I, and my poor father!"

"من هو الذي يحتضر؟ "قال الصوت

"I know that voice! You are Pinocchio!"

"أنا وأبي المسكين"!

"Precisely; and you?" asked Pinocchio

"أنا أعرف هذا الصوت !أنت بينوكيو"!

"I am the Tunny Fish," said his prison companion

"على وجه التحديد. وأنت؟ "سأل بينوكيو

"we met in the body of the Dog-Fish"

"أنا سمكة توني "، قال رفيقه في السجن

"And how did you manage to escape?"

"التقينا في جسد السمكة"

"I followed your example"

"وكيف تمكنت من الفرار؟"

"لقد اتبعت مثالك"

"You showed me the road"

"لقد أرتني الطريق"

"and I escaped after you"

"وهربت بعدك"

"Tunny Fish, you have arrived at the right moment!"

"توني فيش ، لقد وصلت في اللحظة المناسبة"!

"I implore you to help us or we are dead"

"أتوسل إليكم أن تساعدونا وإلا سنموت"

"I will help you willingly with all my heart"

"سوف أساعدك عن طيب خاطر من كل قلبي"

"You must, both of you, take hold of my tail"

"يجب عليك ، كلاكما ، أن تمسك بذيلي"

"leave it to me to guide you

"اترك الأمر لي لأرشدك

"I will take you both on shore in four minutes"

"سآخذكما إلى الشاطئ في أربع دقائق"

I don't need to tell you how happy they were

لست بحاجة إلى إخبارك بمدى سعادتهم

Geppetto and Pinocchio accepted the offer at once

قبل جيبيتو وبينوكيو العرض على الفور

but grabbing the tail was not the most comfortable

لكن الاستيلاء على الذيل لم يكن الأكثر راحة

so they got on the Tunny Fish's back

لذلك حصلوا على ظهر توني فيش

The Tunny Fish did indeed take only four minutes
استغرق سمك توني بالفعل أربع دقائق فقط
Pinocchio was the first to jump onto the land
كان بينوكيو أول من قفز على الأرض
that way he could help his father off the fish
بهذه الطريقة يمكنه مساعدة والده على التخلص من الأسماك
He then turned to his friend the Tunny Fish
ثم التفت إلى صديقه توني فيش
"My friend, you have saved my papa's life"
"صديقي ، لقد أنقذت حياة أبي"
Pinocchio's voice was full of deep emotions
كان صوت بينوكيو مليئًا بالعواطف العميقة
"I can find no words with which to thank you properly"
"لا أجد كلمات أشكرك بها بشكل صحيح"
"Permit me at least to give you a kiss"
"اسمح لي على الأقل أن أعطيك قبلة"
"it is a sign of my eternal gratitude!"
"إنها علامة على امتناني الأبدي"!

The Tunny put his head out of the water
وضع توني رأسه من الماء
and Pinocchio knelt on the edge of the shore
وركع بينوكيو على حافة الشاطئ
and he kissed him tenderly on the mouth
وقبله بحنان على فمه
The Tunny Fish was not used to such warm affection
لم تكن سمكة توني معتادة على مثل هذه المودة الدافئة
he felt both very touched, but also ashamed
شعر بتأثر شديد ، لكنه خجل أيضا
because he had started crying like a small child
لأنه بدأ يبكي مثل طفل صغير
and he plunged back into the water and disappeared
وسقط مرة أخرى في الماء واختفى
By this time the day had dawned
بحلول هذا الوقت كان اليوم قد بزغ
Geppetto had scarcely breath to stand
كان لدى جيبيتو بالكاد يتنفس للوقوف
"Lean on my arm, dear papa, and let us go"
"اتكئ على ذراعي ، بابا العزيز ، ودعنا نذهب"
"We will walk very slowly, like the ants"
"سنمشي ببطء شديد ، مثل النمل"
"and when we are tired we can rest by the wayside"
"وعندما نكون متعبين يمكننا أن نرتاح على جانب الطريق"
"And where shall we go?" asked Geppetto
"وإلى أين نذهب؟" سأل جيبيتو
"let us search for some house or cottage"
"دعونا نبحث عن بعض المنازل أو الكوخ"
"there they will give us some charity"
"هناك سيعطوننا بعض الصدقة"
"perhaps we will receive a mouthful of bread"
"ربما سنحصل على فم من الخبز"
"and a little straw to serve as a bed"
"وقش صغير ليكون بمثابة سرير"
Pinocchio and his father hadn't walked very far

بينوكيو ووالده لم يمشيا بعيدا
they had seen two villainous-looking individuals
لقد رأوا شخصين خسيسين المظهر
the Cat and the Fox were at the road begging
كان القط والثعلب على الطريق يتسولان

but they were scarcely recognizable
لكن بالكاد كان من الممكن التعرف عليها
the Cat had feigned blindness all her life
كانت القطة قد تظاهرت بالعمى طوال حياتها
and now she became blind in reality
والآن أصبحت عمياء في الواقع
and a similar fate must have met the Fox
ومصير مماثل يجب أن يكون قد التقى الثعلب
his fur had gotten old and mangy
كان فروه قد أصبح قديما ومانجي
one of his sides was paralyzed
أصيب أحد جانبيه بالشلل
and he had not even his tail left
ولم يترك حتى ذيله

he had fallen in the most squalid of misery
لقد سقط في بؤس البؤس
and one fine day he was obliged to sell his tail
وفي أحد الأيام الجميلة اضطر إلى بيع ذيله
a travelling peddler bought his beautiful tail
اشترى بائع متجول ذيله الجميل
and now his tail was used for chasing away flies
والآن تم استخدام ذيله لمطاردة الذباب
"Oh, Pinocchio!" cried the Fox
"أوه ، بينوكيو "إصرخ الثعلب
"give a little in charity to two poor, infirm people"
"أعط القليل من الصدقة لشخصين فقيرين وعاجزين"
"Infirm people," repeated the Cat
"الناس العجزة "، كرر القط
"Be gone, impostors!" answered the puppet
"ارحلوا أيها المحتالون "أجابت الدمية
"You fooled me once with your tricks"
"لقد خدعتني مرة واحدة بحيلك"
"but you will never catch me again"
"لكنك لن تمسك بي مرة أخرى"
"this time you must believe us, Pinocchio"
"هذه المرة يجب أن تصدقنا ، بينوكيو"
"we are now poor and unfortunate indeed!"
"نحن الآن فقراء ومؤسفون حقا"!
"If you are poor, you deserve it"
"إذا كنت فقيرا ، فأنت تستحق ذلك"
and Pinocchio asked them to recollect a proverb
وطلب منهم بينوكيو أن يتذكروا مثلا
"Stolen money never fructifies"
"الأموال المسروقة لا تفسد أبدا"
"Be gone, impostors!" he told them
"ارحلوا أيها المحتالون "إقال لهم
And Pinocchio and Geppetto went their way in peace
وذهب بينوكيو وجيبيتو في طريقهما بسلام
soon they had gone another hundred yards

سرعان ما ذهبوا مائة ياردة أخرى

they saw a path going into a field

رأوا طريقا إلى حقل

and in the field they saw a nice little hut

وفي الميدان رأوا كوخا صغيرا لطيفا

the hut was made from tiles and straw and bricks

الكوخ مصنوع من البلاط والقش والطوب

"That hut must be inhabited by someone"

"يجب أن يسكن هذا الكوخ شخص ما"

"Let us go and knock at the door"

"دعونا نذهب ونطرق الباب"

so they went and knocked at the door

فذهبوا وطرقوا الباب

from in the hut came a little voice

من في الكوخ جاء صوت صغير

"who is there?" asked the little voice

"من هناك؟" سأل الصوت الصغير

Pinocchio answered to the little voice

أجاب بينوكيو على الصوت الصغير

"We are a poor father and son"

"نحن أب وابن فقير"

"we are without bread and without a roof"

"نحن بلا خبز وبلا سقف"

the same little voice spoke again:

تحدث نفس الصوت الصغير مرة أخرى:

"Turn the key and the door will open"

"أدر المفتاح وسيفتح الباب"

Pinocchio turned the key and the door opened

أدار بينوكيو المفتاح وفتح الباب

They went in and looked around

دخلوا ونظروا حولهم

they looked here, there, and everywhere

نظروا هنا وهناك وفي كل مكان

but they could see no one in the hut

لكنهم لم يتمكنوا من رؤية أحد في الكوخ

Pinocchio was much surprised the hut was empty
فوجئ بينوكيو كثيرا بأن الكوخ كان فارغا

"Oh! where is the master of the house?"
"أوه ! أين سيد البيت؟"

"Here I am, up here!" said the little voice
"ها أنا ذا ، هنا "!قال الصوت الصغير

The father and son looked up to the ceiling
نظر الأب والابن إلى السقف

and on a beam they saw the talking little Cricket
وعلى شعاع رأوا الكريكيت الصغير الحديث

"Oh, my dear little Cricket!" said Pinocchio
"أوه ، عزيزي الكريكيت الصغير "!قال بينوكيو

and Pinocchio bowed politely to the little Cricket
وانحنى بينوكيو بأدب للكريكيت الصغير

"Ah! now you call me your dear little Cricket"
"آه ! الآن أنت تدعوني عزيزي الكريكيت الصغير"

"But do you remember when we first met?"
"لكن هل تتذكر عندما التقينا لأول مرة؟"

"you wanted me gone from your house"
"كنت تريدني أن أذهب من منزلك"

"and you threw the handle of a hammer at me"
"ورميت مقبض مطرقة علي"

"You are right, little Cricket! Chase me away also!"
"أنت على حق ، الكريكيت الصغير !طاردني بعيدا أيضا!"

"Throw the handle of a hammer at me"
"ارم مقبض المطرقة في وجهي"

"but please, have pity on my poor papa"
"لكن من فضلك ، أشفق على بابا المسكين"

"I will have pity on both father and son"
"سأشفق على كل من الأب والابن"

"but I wish to remind you of my ill treatment"
"لكنني أود أن أذكركم بسوء معاملتي"

"the ill treatment I received from you"
"المعاملة السيئة التي تلقيتها منك"

"but there's a lesson I want you to learn"
"ولكن هناك درس أريدك أن تتعلمه"
"life in this world is not always easy"
"الحياة في هذا العالم ليست سهلة دائما"
"when possible, we must be courteous to everyone"
"عندما يكون ذلك ممكنا ، يجب أن نكون مهذبين مع الجميع"
"only so can we expect to receive courtesy"
"فقط هكذا يمكننا أن نتوقع الحصول على المجاملة"
"because we never know when we might be in need"
"لأننا لا نعرف أبدا متى قد نكون في حاجة"
"You are right, little Cricket, you are right"
"أنت على حق ، الكريكيت الصغير ، أنت على حق"
"and I will bear in mind the lesson you have taught me"
"وسأضع في اعتباري الدرس الذي علمتني إياه"
"But tell me how you managed to buy this beautiful hut"
"لكن أخبرني كيف تمكنت من شراء هذا الكوخ الجميل"
"This hut was given to me yesterday"
"أعطيت لي هذا الكوخ أمس"
"the owner of the hut was a goat"
"صاحب الكوخ كان عنزة"
"and she had wool of a beautiful blue colour"
"وكان لديها صوف من اللون الأزرق الجميل"
Pinocchio grew lively and curious at this news
أصبح بينوكيو مفعما بالحيوية والفضول في هذه الأخبار
"And where has the goat gone?" asked Pinocchio
"وأين ذهب الماعز؟ "سأل بينوكيو
"I do not know where she has gone"
"لا أعرف أين ذهبت"
"And when will the goat come back?" asked Pinocchio
"ومتى ستعود الماعز؟ "سأل بينوكيو
"oh she will never come back, I'm afraid"
"أوه لن تعود أبدا ، أخشى"
"she went away yesterday in great grief"
"ذهبت بالأمس في حزن شديد"

"her bleating seemed to want to say something"

"يبدو أن نزيفها يريد أن يقول شيئا"

"Poor Pinocchio! I shall never see him again"

"مسكين بينوكيو !لن أراه مرة أخرى"

"by now the Dog-Fish must have devoured him!"

"الآن يجب أن يكون سمكة قد التهمه"!

"Did the goat really say that?"

"هل قال الماعز ذلك حقا؟"

"Then it was she, the blue goat"

"ثم كانت هي ، الماعز الأزرق"

"It was my dear little Fairy," exclaimed Pinocchio

"لقد كانت جنيتي الصغيرة العزيزة "، هتف بينوكيو

and he cried and sobbed bitter tears

وبكى وبكى دموعا مريرة

When he had cried for some time he dried his eyes

عندما بكى لبعض الوقت جفف عينيه

and he prepared a comfortable bed of straw for Geppetto

وأعد سريرا مريحا من القش لGeppetto

Then he asked the Cricket for more help

ثم طلب من الكريكيت المزيد من المساعدة

"Tell me, little Cricket, please"

"قل لي ، الكريكيت الصغير ، من فضلك"

"where can I find a tumbler of milk"

"أين يمكنني العثور على كوب من الحليب"

"my poor papa has not eaten all day"

"بابا المسكين لم يأكل طوال اليوم"

"Three fields from here there lives a gardener"

"ثلاثة حقول من هنا يعيش بستاني"

"the gardener is called Giangio"

"البستاني يسمى جيانجيو"

"and in his garden he also has cows"

"وفي حديقته لديه أيضا أبقار"

"he will let you have the milk you want"

"سوف يسمح لك بالحصول على الحليب الذي تريده"

Pinocchio ran all the way to Giangio's house
ركض بينوكيو على طول الطريق إلى منزل جيانجيو
and the gardener asked him:
فسأله البستاني:
"How much milk do you want?"
"ما مقدار الحليب الذي تريده؟"
"I want a tumblerful," answered Pinocchio
"أريد بهلوان "، أجاب بينوكيو
"A tumbler of milk costs five cents"
"بهلوان الحليب يكلف خمسة سنتات"
"Begin by giving me the five cents"
"ابدأ بإعطائي الخمسة سنتات"
"I have not even one cent," replied Pinocchio
"ليس لدي حتى سنت واحد "، أجاب بينوكيو
and he was grieved from being so penniless
وكان حزينا من كونه مفلسا جدا
"That is bad, puppet," answered the gardener
"هذا سيء ، دمية "، أجاب البستاني
"If you have not one cent, I have not a drop of milk"
"إذا لم يكن لديك سنت واحد ، فليس لدي قطرة حليب"
"I must have patience!" said Pinocchio
"يجب أن أتحلى بالصبر "!قال بينوكيو
and he turned to go again
واستدار للذهاب مرة أخرى
"Wait a little," said Giangio
"انتظر قليلا "، قال جيانجيو
"We can come to an arrangement together"
"يمكننا التوصل إلى ترتيب معا"
"Will you undertake to turn the pumping machine?"
"هل ستتعهد بتشغيل آلة الضخ؟"
"What is the pumping machine?"
"ما هي آلة الضخ؟"
"It is a kind of wooden screw"
"إنه نوع من المسمار الخشبي"

"it serves to draw up the water from the cistern"
"إنه يعمل على سحب المياه من الخزان"

"and then it waters the vegetables"
"ثم يسقي الخضروات"

"I can try to turn the pumping machine"
"يمكنني محاولة تشغيل آلة الضخ"

"great, I need a hundred buckets of water"
"عظيم ، أحتاج إلى مائة دلو من الماء"

"and for the work you'll get a tumbler of milk"
"وللعمل ستحصل على كوب من الحليب"

"we have an agreement," confirmed Pinocchio
»لدينا اتفاق«، أكد بينوكيو

Giangio then led Pinocchio to the kitchen garden
ثم قاد جيانجيو بينوكيو إلى حديقة المطبخ

and he taught him how to turn the pumping machine
وعلمه كيفية تدوير آلة الضخ

Pinocchio immediately began to work
بدأ بينوكيو على الفور في العمل

but a hundred buckets of water was a lot of work
لكن مائة دلو من الماء كان الكثير من العمل

the perspiration was pouring from his head
كان العرق يتصبب من رأسه

Never before had he undergone such fatigue
لم يسبق له أن تعرض لمثل هذا التعب

the gardener came to see Pinocchio's progress
جاء البستاني لرؤية تقدم بينوكيو

"my little donkey used to do this work"
"كان حماري الصغير يقوم بهذا العمل"

"but the poor animal is dying"
"لكن المسكين يموت"

"Will you take me to see him?" said Pinocchio
"هل ستأخذني لرؤيته؟ "قال بينوكيو

"sure, please come to see my little donkey"
"بالتأكيد ، من فضلك تعال لرؤية حماري الصغير"

Pinocchio went into the stable

ذهب بينوكيو إلى الإسطبل

and he saw a beautiful little donkey

ورأى حمارا صغيرا جميلا

but the donkey was stretched out on the straw

لكن الحمار كان ممدودا على القش

he was worn out from hunger and overwork

كان منهكا من الجوع والإرهاق

Pinocchio was much troubled by what he saw

كان بينوكيو منزعجا كثيرا مما رآه

"I am sure I know this little donkey!"

"أنا متأكد من أنني أعرف هذا الحمار الصغير"!

"His face is not new to me"

"وجهه ليس جديدا بالنسبة لي"

and Pinocchio came closer to the little Donkey

واقترب بينوكيو من الحمار الصغير

and he spoke to him in asinine language:

وتحدث إليه بلغة أسينية:

"Who are you?" asked Pinocchio

"من أنت؟ "سأل بينوكيو

the little donkey opened his dying eyes

فتح الحمار الصغير عينيه المحتضرتين

and he answered in broken words in the same language:

وأجاب بكلمات متقطعة بنفس اللغة:

"I... am... Candle-wick"

"أنا ... أنا ... شمعة الفتيل"

And, having again closed his eyes, he died

وبعد أن أغمض عينيه مرة أخرى ، مات

"Oh, poor Candle-wick!" said Pinocchio

"أوه ، مسكين شمعة الفتيل "إقال بينوكيو

and he took a handful of straw

وأخذ حفنة من القش

and he dried a tear rolling down his face

وجف دمعة تتدحرج على وجهه

the gardener had seen Pinocchio cry

رأى البستاني بينوكيو يبكي

"Do you grieve for a dead donkey?"

"هل تحزن على حمار ميت؟"

"it was not even your donkey"

"لم يكن حتى حمارك"

"imagine how I must feel"

"تخيل كيف يجب أن أشعر"

Pinocchio tried to explain his grief

حاول بينوكيو شرح حزنه

"I must tell you, he was my friend!"

"يجب أن أخبرك ، لقد كان صديقي"!

"Your friend?" wondered the gardener

"صديقك؟ "تساءل البستاني

"yes, one of my school-fellows!"

"نعم ، أحد زملائي في المدرسة"!

"How?" shouted Giangio, laughing loudly

"كيف؟ "صاح جيانجيو وهو يضحك بصوت عال

"Did you have donkeys for school-fellows?"

"هل كان لديك حمير لزملاء المدرسة؟"

"I can imagine the wonderful school you went to!"

"أستطيع أن أتخيل المدرسة الرائعة التي ذهبت إليها"!

The puppet felt mortified at these words

شعرت الدمية بالخزي من هذه الكلمات

but Pinocchio did not answer the gardener

لكن بينوكيو لم يرد على البستاني

he took his warm tumbler of milk

أخذ بهلوانه الدافئ من الحليب

and he returned back to the hut

وعاد إلى الكوخ

for more than five months he got up at daybreak

لأكثر من خمسة أشهر استيقظ عند الفجر

every morning he turned the pumping machine

كل صباح كان يدير آلة الضخ

and each day he earned a tumbler of milk

وكل يوم كان يكسب بهلوان من الحليب

the milk was of great benefit to his father

كان الحليب ذا فائدة كبيرة لوالده

because his father was in a bad state of health

لأن والده كان في حالة صحية سيئة

but Pinocchio was now satisfied with working

لكن بينوكيو كان راضيا الآن عن العمل

during the daytime he still had time

خلال النهار كان لا يزال لديه الوقت

so he learned to make baskets of rushes

لذلك تعلم صنع سلال من الاندفاع

and he sold the baskets in the market

وباع السلال في السوق

and the money covered all their expenses

وغطت الأموال جميع نفقاتهم

he also constructed an elegant little wheel-chair

كما قام ببناء كرسي متحرك صغير أنيق

and he took his father out in the wheel-chair

وأخرج والده على كرسي متحرك

and his father got to breathe fresh air

وحصل والده على تنفس الهواء النقي

Pinocchio was a hard working boy

كان بينوكيو فتى مجتهدا

and he was ingenious at finding work

وكان بارعا في العثور على عمل

he not only succeeded in helping his father

لم ينجح فقط في مساعدة والده

but he also managed to save five dollars

لكنه تمكن أيضا من توفير خمسة دولارات

One morning he said to his father:

ذات صباح قال لوالده:

"I am going to the neighbouring market"

"أنا ذاهب إلى السوق المجاورة"

"I will buy myself a new jacket"

"سأشتري لنفسي سترة جديدة"

"and I will buy a cap and pair of shoes"

"وسأشتري قبعة وزوجا من الأحذية"

and Pinocchio was in jolly spirits

وكان بينوكيو في حالة معنوية مرحة
"when I return you'll think I'm a gentleman"
"عندما أعود ستعتقد أنني رجل نبيل"
And he began to run merrily and happily along
وبدأ يركض بمرح وسعادة
All at once he heard himself called by name
في كل مرة سمع نفسه ينادى بالاسم
he turned around and what did he see?
استدار وماذا رأى؟
he saw a Snail crawling out from the hedge
رأى حلزونا يزحف من السياج
"Do you not know me?" asked the Snail
"ألا تعرفني؟ "سأل الحلزون
"I'm sure I know you," thought Pinocchio
"أنا متأكد من أنني أعرفك "، فكر بينوكيو
"and yet I don't know from where I know you"
"ومع ذلك لا أعرف من أين أعرفك"
"Do you not remember the Snail?"
"ألا تتذكر الحلزون؟"
"the Snail who was a lady's-maid"
"الحلزون الذي كان خادمة سيدة"
"a maid to the Fairy with blue hair"
"خادمة للجنية ذات الشعر الأزرق"
"Do you not remember when you knocked on the door?"
"ألا تتذكر عندما طرقت الباب؟"
"and I came downstairs to let you in"
"ونزلت إلى الطابق السفلي للسماح لك بالدخول"
"and you had your foot caught in the door"
"وعلقت قدمك في الباب"
"I remember it all," shouted Pinocchio
"أتذكر كل شيء "، صرخ بينوكيو
"Tell me quickly, my beautiful little Snail"
"قل لي بسرعة ، يا حلزون صغير جميل"
"where have you left my good Fairy?"

"أين تركت جنيتي الطيبة؟"

"What is she doing?"

"ماذا تفعل؟"

"Has she forgiven me?"

"هل غفرت لي؟"

"Does she still remember me?"

"هل ما زالت تتذكرني؟"

"Does she still wish me well?"

"هل ما زالت تتمنى لي التوفيق؟"

"Is she far from here?"

"هل هي بعيدة عن هنا؟"

"Can I go and see her?"

"هل يمكنني الذهاب ورؤيتها؟"

these were a lot of questions for a snail

كانت هذه الكثير من الأسئلة للحلزون

but she replied in her usual phlegmatic manner

لكنها أجابت بطريقتها البلغمية المعتادة

"My dear Pinocchio," said the snail

"عزيزي بينوكيو "، قال الحلزون

"the poor Fairy is lying in bed at the hospital!"

"الجنية المسكينة ترقد في السرير في المستشفى"!

"At the hospital?" cried Pinocchio

"في المستشفى؟ "صرخ بينوكيو

"It is only too true," confirmed the snail

"هذا صحيح جدا "، أكد الحلزون

"she has been overtaken by a thousand misfortunes"

"لقد تجاوزتها ألف مصيبة"

"she has fallen seriously ill"

"لقد أصيبت بمرض خطير"

"she has not even enough to buy herself a mouthful of bread"

"ليس لديها حتى ما يكفي لشراء فم من الخبز "

"Is it really so?" worried Pinocchio

"هل هو كذلك حقا؟ "قلق بينوكيو

"Oh, what sorrow you have given me!"

"أوه ، ما الحزن الذي أعطيتني إياه"!

"Oh, poor Fairy! Poor Fairy! Poor Fairy!"

"أوه ، جنية مسكينة إجنية مسكينة إجنية مسكينة"!

"If I had a million I would run and carry it to her"

"لو كان لدي مليون لركضت وأحملها إليها"

"but I have only five dollars"

"لكن لدي خمسة دولارات فقط"

"I was going to buy a new jacket"

"كنت سأشتري سترة جديدة"

"Take my coins, beautiful Snail"

"خذ عملاتي المعدنية ، الحلزون الجميل"

"and carry the coins at once to my good Fairy"

"وحمل العملات المعدنية في وقت واحد إلى جنيتي الطيبة"

"And your new jacket?" asked the snail

"وسترتك الجديدة؟ "سأل الحلزون

"What matters my new jacket?"

"ما الذي يهم سترتي الجديدة؟"

"I would sell even these rags to help her"

"سأبيع حتى هذه الخرق لمساعدتها"

"Go, Snail, and be quick"

"اذهب ، الحلزون ، وكن سريعا"

"return to this place, in two days"

"العودة إلى هذا المكان ، في غضون يومين"

"I hope I can then give you some more money"

"آمل أن أتمكن بعد ذلك من إعطائك المزيد من المال"

"Up to now I worked to help my papa"

"حتى الآن عملت لمساعدة أبي"

"from today I will work five hours more"

"من اليوم سأعمل خمس ساعات أخرى"

"so that I can also help my good mamma"

"حتى أتمكن أيضا من مساعدة أمي الطيبة"

"Good-bye, Snail," he said

"وداعا يا الحلزون "، قال

"I shall expect you in two days"
"سأتوقعك في غضون يومين"
at this point the snail did something unusual
في هذه المرحلة ، فعل الحلزون شيئا غير عادي
she didn't move at her usual pace
لم تتحرك بوتيرتها المعتادة
she ran like a lizard across hot stones
ركضت مثل سحلية عبر الحجارة الساخنة
That evening Pinocchio sat up till midnight
في ذلك المساء جلس بينوكيو حتى منتصف الليل
and he made not eight baskets of rushes
ولم يصنع ثماني سلال من الاندفاع
but be made sixteen baskets of rushes that night
ولكن كن مصنوعا ستة عشر سلة من الاندفاع في تلك الليلة
Then he went to bed and fell asleep
ثم ذهب إلى الفراش ونام
And whilst he slept he thought of the Fairy
وبينما كان نائما فكر في الجنية
he saw the Fairy, smiling and beautiful
رأى الجنية مبتسمة وجميلة
and he dreamt she gave him a kiss
وحلم أنها أعطته قبلة
"Well done, Pinocchio!" said the fairy
"أحسنت يا بينوكيو "إقالت الجنية
"I will forgive you for all that is past"
"سأسامحك على كل ما مضى"
"To reward you for your good heart"
"لمكافأة لك على قلبك الطيب"
"there are boys who minister tenderly to their parents"
"هناك أولاد يخدمون والديهم بحنان"
"they assist them in their misery and infirmities"
"يساعدونهم في بؤسهم وعجزهم"
"such boys are deserving of great praise and affection"
"هؤلاء الأولاد يستحقون الثناء والمودة العظيمين"
"even if they cannot be cited as examples of obedience"

"حتى لو لم يكن من الممكن الاستشهاد بها كأمثلة على الطاعة"
"even if their good behaviour is not always obvious"
"حتى لو لم يكن سلوكهم الجيد واضحا دائما"
"Try and do better in the future and you will be happy"
"حاول أن تفعل ما هو أفضل في المستقبل وستكون سعيدا"
At this moment his dream ended
في هذه اللحظة انتهى حلمه
and Pinocchio opened his eyes and awoke
وفتح بينوكيو عينيه واستيقظ
you should have been there for what happened next
كان يجب أن تكون هناك لما حدث بعد ذلك
Pinocchio discovered that he was no longer a wooden puppet
اكتشف بينوكيو أنه لم يعد دمية خشبية
but he had become a real boy instead
لكنه أصبح صبيا حقيقيا بدلا من ذلك
a real boy just like all other boys
فتى حقيقي تماما مثل جميع الأولاد الآخرين
Pinocchio glanced around the room
نظر بينوكيو في جميع أنحاء الغرفة
but the straw walls of the hut had disappeared
لكن جدران الكوخ المصنوعة من القش اختفت
now he was in a pretty little room
الآن كان في غرفة صغيرة جدا
Pinocchio jumped out of bed
قفز بينوكيو من السرير
in the wardrobe he found a new suit of clothes
في خزانة الملابس وجد بدلة جديدة من الملابس
and there was a new cap and pair of boots
وكان هناك غطاء جديد وزوج من الأحذية
and his new clothes fitted him beautifully
وملابسه الجديدة تناسبه بشكل جميل
he naturally put his hands in his pocket
وضع يديه بشكل طبيعي في جيبه
and he pulled out a little ivory purse
وأخرج محفظة عاجية صغيرة

on on the purse were written these words:

على المحفظة كتبت هذه الكلمات:

"From the Fairy with blue hair"

"من الجنية ذات الشعر الأزرق"

"I return the five dollars to my dear Pinocchio"

"أعيد الخمسة دولارات إلى عزيزي بينوكيو"

"and I thank him for his good heart"

"وأشكره على قلبه الطيب"

He opened the purse to look inside

فتح المحفظة لينظر إلى الداخل

but there were not five dollars in the purse

ولكن لم يكن هناك خمسة دولارات في المحفظة

instead there were fifty shining pieces of gold

بدلا من ذلك كان هناك خمسون قطعة لامعة من الذهب

the coins had come fresh from the minting press

كانت العملات المعدنية قد جاءت طازجة من مكبس سك العملة

he then went and looked at himself in the mirror

ثم ذهب ونظر إلى نفسه في المرآة

and he thought he was someone else

وظن أنه شخص آخر

because he no longer saw his usual reflection

لأنه لم يعد يرى انعكاسه المعتاد

he no longer saw a wooden puppet in the mirror

لم يعد يرى دمية خشبية في المرآة

he was greeted instead by a different image

تم استقباله بدلا من ذلك بصورة مختلفة

the image of a bright, intelligent boy

صورة صبي مشرق وذكي

he had chestnut hair and blue eyes

كان لديه شعر كستنائي وعيون زرقاء

and he looked as happy as can be

وبدا سعيدا قدر الإمكان

as if it were the Easter holidays

كما لو كانت عطلة عيد الفصح

Pinocchio felt quite bewildered by it all

شعر بينوكيو بالحيرة من كل ذلك

he could not tell if he was really awake

لم يستطع معرفة ما إذا كان مستيقظا حقا

maybe he was dreaming with his eyes open

ربما كان يحلم وعيناه مفتوحتان

"Where can my papa be?" he exclaimed suddenly

"أين يمكن أن يكون أبي؟" صرخ فجأة

and he went into the next room

وذهب إلى الغرفة المجاورة

there he found old Geppetto quite well

وهناك وجد جيبيتو العجوز في حالة جيدة جدًا

he was lively, and in good humour

كان مفعما بالحيوية ، وفي روح الدعابة

just as he had been formerly

تماما كما كان سابقا

He had already resumed his trade of wood-carving

كان قد استأنف بالفعل تجارته في نحت الخشب

and he was designing a beautiful picture frame

وكان يصمم إطار صورة جميل

there were leaves flowers and the heads of animals

كانت هناك أوراق الشجر والزهور ورؤوس

"Satisfy my curiosity, dear papa," said Pinocchio

"أشبع فضولي يا بابا العزيز "، قال بينوكيو

and he threw his arms around his neck

وألقى ذراعيه حول رقبته

and he covered him with kisses

وغطاه بالقبلات

"how can this sudden change be accounted for?"

"كيف يمكن تفسير هذا التغيير المفاجئ؟"

"it comes from all your good doing," answered Geppetto

أجاب جيبيتو: "إنه يأتي من كل أعمالك الصالحة."

"how could it come from my good doing?"

"كيف يمكن أن يأتي من عملي الصالح؟"

"something happens when naughty boys turn over a new leaf"

"يحدث شيء ما عندما يقلب الأولاد المشاغبون صفحة جديدة"

"they bring contentment and happiness to their families"

"إنهم يجلبون الرضا والسعادة لعائلاتهم"

"And where has the old wooden Pinocchio hidden himself?"

"وأين اختبأ بينوكيو الخشبي القديم نفسه؟"

"There he is," answered Geppetto

"ها هو "، أجاب جيبيتو

and he pointed to a big puppet leaning against a chair

وأشار إلى دمية كبيرة تتكئ على كرسي

the Puppet had its head on one side

كان رأس الدمية على جانب واحد

its arms were dangling at its sides

كانت أذرعه تتدلى على جانبيه

and its legs were crossed and bent

وكانت ساقيها متقاطعة ومثنية

it was really a miracle that it remained standing

لقد كانت حقا معجزة أنها ظلت قائمة

Pinocchio turned and looked at it

استدار بينوكيو ونظر إليه

and he proclaimed with great complacency:

وأعلن برضا كبير:

"How ridiculous I was when I was a puppet!"

"كم كنت سخيفة عندما كنت دمية"!

"And how glad I am that I have become a well-behaved little boy!"

"وكم أنا سعيد لأنني أصبحت صبيا صغيرا حسن التصرف"!

www.ingramcontent.com/pod-product-compliance
Lightning Source LLC
Chambersburg PA
CBHW012000090526
44590CB00026B/3808